Shostakovich's Ballets and the Search for Soviet Dance

Shostakovich's Ballets and the Search for Soviet Dance

LAURA E. KENNEDY

OXFORD
UNIVERSITY PRESS

Oxford University Press is a department of the University of Oxford.
It furthers the University's objective of excellence in research, scholarship,
and education by publishing worldwide. Oxford is a registered trade mark of
Oxford University Press in the UK and in certain other countries.

Published in the United States of America by Oxford University Press
198 Madison Avenue, New York, NY 10016, United States of America.

© Oxford University Press 2025

All rights reserved. No part of this publication may be reproduced, stored in a retrieval system, transmitted, used for text and data mining, or used for training artificial intelligence, in any form or by any means, without the prior permission in writing of Oxford University Press, or as expressly permitted by law, by license or under terms agreed with the appropriate reprographics rights organization. Inquiries concerning reproduction outside the scope of the above should be sent to the Rights Department, Oxford University Press, at the address above.

You must not circulate this work in any other form and
you must impose this same condition on any acquirer

CIP data is on file at the Library of Congress

ISBN 9780197698051 (pbk.)
ISBN 9780197698044 (hbk.)

DOI: 10.1093/9780197698082.001.0001

In memory of Olga Dombrovskaya

Contents

Preface ix
Acknowledgments xi
Note on Names and Transliteration xiii
List of Archives xv

Introduction 1
   Soviet Ballet in the 1920s 2
   Shostakovich and Ballet 4
   Reception and Reassessment 8
   Archival Collections and Sources 11
   Shostakovich's Ballets and the Search for Soviet Dance 13

1. "Art without movement does not move me": Shostakovich and the Path to Ballet 16
   Shostakovich's Early Career 16
   The Ballet Theatre 22
      The Institution 22
      The Repertoire 24
      The Debates 29
   Shostakovich and Dance 30
      "Balletic Impressions" 30
      The Ballets 32

2. Petipa's Legacy: *The Golden Age* and Classical Ballet 36
   The Production of 1930 38
   Soviet "Classical" Ballet 43
      Act I: Ballet Classicism 47
      Act II: Sports 51
      Act III: The Modern Age 57
   New Directions 62

3. Amateur Dramatics: *The Bolt* and Modern Ballet 64
   The Milieu 66
   "High Art" versus "Popular Art" 68
      "High Art" 68
      "Popular Art" 70

    Soviet "Modern" Ballet   74
        ACT I: The Factory   74
        ACT II: The Village   78
        ACT III: The Club   79

4. Soviet Sylphs: *The Limpid Stream* and Romantic Ballet   99
    Soviet "Romantic" Ballet   101
        Act I: National Dance, Shakespearean Shores   103
        Act II: Soviet Sylphs, the Marxist Forest   107
        Act III: Classical veils   112
    The Artistic and Professional Milieu   115
        The State of Ballet   115
        Professional Collaborations   119
    The Limpid Stream in the National Enterprise   123

5. Shostakovich and Ballet: Lives and Afterlives   129
    "Symphonic Ballets"   130
        Massine's *Rouge et noir*   130
        Belsky's *Leningrad Symphony*   133
    The Revival of Shostakovich's Ballets   138
        Grigorovich's *The Golden Age*   138
        Ratmansky's *The Bright Stream* and *The Bolt*   142
    Epilogue   146

Appendix A   149
Appendix B: Librettos   151
Notes   163
Select Bibliography   177
Index   189

Preface

This book is about the ballets of Dmitri Shostakovich—*The Golden Age*, *The Bolt*, and *The Limpid Stream*. Produced in the early 1930s in Leningrad, these works occupied a unique moment in Soviet cultural history and in Shostakovich's oeuvre. But in 1936, eight days after the condemnation of Shostakovich's opera *Lady Macbeth of Mtsensk District*, *The Limpid Stream* was denounced in the Soviet press and immediately withdrawn from the stage. Shostakovich never composed another ballet and distanced himself from the three he had written, often suggesting, however, that weaknesses lay in components other than his music. Yet he declined to revive his ballets in his lifetime, and subsequent scholarship has long regarded these works as secondary in his creative output.

This book tells a new, and more nuanced, story about Shostakovich and ballet. It examines his relationship to the genre and draws on the remarkable range of archival materials and critical commentary that survive from this early period. Collections in St. Petersburg and Moscow—preserving orchestral scores, *répétiteurs*, photographs, libretti, costumes, sketches, set designs, theatre and administrative documents, and annals of performances—document the creative history of Shostakovich's ballets and invite a fresh assessment of his interaction with the balletic tradition. This book takes up the source record to illuminate how Shostakovich, together with his artistic collaborators, sought to reimagine the legacy of Russian ballet as Soviet modernism. Its purpose is to tell a story that has not been told about Shostakovich's ballets—their depth of engagement with the heritage of ballet in Russia, their role in the development of a "Soviet" approach to the genre, their importance in the composer's creative legacy, and their impact on the reception of Shostakovich's music in dance.

This book is for scholars, but it is also for dancers, musicians, designers, and other readers who wish to know more about Shostakovich, ballet, and Russia. The book's sources—many of them previously unexamined or even unknown—invite the reader on a journey through archives, libraries, theatres, museums, interviews, and private apartments in Moscow and St. Petersburg. They allow readers to "hear" Shostakovich's pianos, to visit the rooms where he hosted the afterparty for the premiere of *The Bolt*, to see his writing desk—and the photograph of Mussorgsky that he kept there, under glass, as a kind of creative conscience about what had merit in his music—to visit the sewing workshops of the Bolshoi Theatre, to follow in dancers' footsteps along the halls of the Vaganova Ballet Academy, and to enter the temple of St. Petersburg's musical history, the Music Library of the Mariinsky Theatre. The story begins on a broad canvas, characterizing Shostakovich's path to ballet in the heady artistic milieu of the 1920s. Its central narrative is devoted to Shostakovich's three ballets and the models they invoke from the Russian and Western traditions, and its conclusion examines how Shostakovich's music in dance has lived on, emblematizing the dramatic potential of the composer's work. The lives and afterlives of Shostakovich's ballets expand our understanding of the composer's contributions to dance in Russia. Most significantly, they invite us to engage Shostakovich as ballet composer, an identity that has long been suppressed or denied, but which shaped both his artistic career and the developments of the genre in the twentieth century.

Acknowledgments

This book is based on research undertaken in Russia in 2019–20 with the support of a Fulbright US Scholar grant. My heartfelt thanks go to the Fulbright Program and to the Fulbright Office in Moscow.

Among the many colleagues who supported this project, I particularly wish to thank Olga Digonskaya and the late Olga Dombrovskaya, chief archivists of the Dmitri Shostakovich Archive, whose tireless assistance, guidance, and friendship have been a mainstay of my research for years; Natalya Metelitsa, director of the St. Petersburg State Museum of Theatrical and Musical Art, and the archivist Sergei Laletin for whom no research request was too much; Natalya Serdyuk, who provided expert guidance to the collections of the Mikhailovsky Theatre Archives; Lidya Kharina, director of the Bolshoi Theatre Museum, for access to the Museum's archives, as well as Yekaterina Churakova, chief curator, for an unforgettable afternoon at the Bolshoi's costume warehouse; Maria Shcherbakova, director of the Central Music Library of the State Academic Mariinsky Theatre, for opening the storied collection; and Larisa Abyzova and Natalya Zozulina for sharing records from the Vaganova Ballet Academy. The Bakhrushin State Central Theatre Museum, the Russian State Archives of Literature and Art in both St. Petersburg and Moscow, and the Russian National Library and the State Theatre Library in St. Petersburg offered every possible assistance. The British Library, the Archives of the Royal Opera House, and the Jerome Robbins Dance Division of the New York Public Library provided research support through the COVID-19 pandemic. The staff in all these institutions assisted with unfailing courtesy and goodwill.

I am grateful to Lorca Massine, Tatiana Massine Weinbaum, and Theodor Massine and to the Henri Matisse Estate for permission to access materials relating to the Massine-Matisse collaboration on the ballet *Rouge et noir* to Shostakovich's music.

Many scholars helped me locate sources and refine my assessment of materials. I am enormously grateful to the late Elizabeth Souritz for her generous hospitality, sharp insights, and assistance in facilitating contacts and access to personal collections. Olga Manulkina offered advice on sources in

St. Petersburg and Moscow. Anna Fortunova and Elizabeth Stern gave personal copies of their dissertations. Natalya Voskrensenskaya shared materials on Lopukhov's *Dance Symphony*. Boris Mukosei offered vital assistance on sources in Moscow. Marina Harss shared a pre-print copy of her biography on Alexei Ratmansky. I also owe a debt of gratitude to Maureen Carr for her encouragement of this project from its inception, for her scholarly instincts and practical help as the work took shape, and for the many personal introductions she facilitated through all stages of research and publication.

This book would not have been possible without the generous support of Furman University. Dean Jeremy Cass awarded research funds and gave a leave of absence for creative work. John Beckford championed every stage of the project. My colleagues in the Music Department took on additional duties during my time away from campus. The Furman Libraries, especially the Music Library, offered unflagging research support, assistance, and insight. The Interlibrary Loan office facilitated my requests, often amid significant challenges due to the rarity of sources as well as temporary closures of institutions. Above all, my colleague Patricia Sasser, director of the Music Library, tirelessly read drafts of chapters, located resources that no one else could find, navigated multiple languages and alphabets, and championed the project with scholarly insight, stalwart friendship, and moral support.

I am hugely grateful to my editor, Norm Hirschy, for his encouragement and guidance in preparing this book. I thank Mark Sutcliffe for his expert translations of the ballet librettos and for the nuance he brought to the etymology of rare (and sometimes invented) Russian words.

My sincere thanks go to the Dom Druzhby in St. Petersburg for their friendship over two decades, especially Margarita Mudrak and Frida Zaitseva. I am indebted to Svetlana Bukreyeva, whose interest in this project led to many happy hours of discussion and whose patience in probing the nuances of the research (in Russian) did much to refine my linguistic command and scholarly expression. My family provided constant encouragement, especially my late father and my mother, who inspired my interest in Russia, and my husband, whose patience and good humor have carried me through the many stages of this book.

Note on Names and Transliteration

Names of places and institutions changed frequently in the early Soviet period. Petrograd became Leningrad in 1924 (and had been St. Petersburg until 1914). The Imperial Mariinsky Theatre was renamed the Leningrad State Academic Theatre for Opera and Ballet (GATOB) in 1920 and then the Kirov Theatre in 1935. The city's second stage, the Mikhailovsky Theatre, became the Leningrad State Academic Maly Opera Theatre (MALEGOT). The Imperial Ballet School became the Leningrad Choreographic Institute, as well as the Choreographic Tekhnikum for a few years and later the Vaganova Ballet Academy. For the sake of clarity, I mostly use a single designation for each entity—the name by which a place or institution was primarily known in the period under discussion, although this approach occasionally results in anachronism. Hence I refer to the city as Leningrad (even before 1924), to the stages as the Leningrad State Academic Theatre (with some exceptions) and the Maly Opera Theatre, and to the ballet academy as the Choreographic Institute. Some variations occur. Where "Mariinsky" or "Imperial Theatre" appears in the text, the designation connotes the pre-Revolutionary period or the Imperial legacy. Shostakovich and his contemporaries used the Theatre's pre-Revolutionary name in this way. In Chapter 5, I use the designation "Kirov Theatre" since by the 1960s the Theatre had carried the name "Kirov" for almost three decades.

I use the title *The Limpid Stream* for Shostakovich's third ballet in line with the *New Collected Works* edition of the score (vols. 64–65), the *Shostakovich Catalogue*, and Laurel Fay's biography of the composer. In contemporary staged productions, the work is called *The Bright Stream*, and I use that designation solely for Ratmansky's revival of the ballet in 2003.

In transliterating from Russian to English, I have adopted a modified version of standard practices. For the various forms of the Cyrillic *i*, и, and й are rendered as *i*, and ы as *y*. The soft vowels ю, я, and ё are represented with *yu* and *ya*, and *yo*, respectively, while е is rendered as *e*, but at the beginning of a word or after a soft sign or vowel, as *ye*. In the text, I have omitted transliterating the Cyrillic soft sign ь but have retained it (') in citations. Where names are commonly used in English, I have adopted standard designations in the text but have followed transliteration practices in footnotes and bibliography. For example, "Sollertinsky" and "Asafyev" appear thus in the text but are rendered as "Sollertinskii" and "Asaf'yev" in citations of their published writings. For readability, "Maly" is used over "Malyi." These modifications are made in the hope of facilitating ease of reading while ensuring accuracy of reference.

List of Archives

DSA—Arkhiv D. D. Shostakovicha [Archive of D. D. Shostakovich, also known as the Dmitri Shostakovich Archive]

GTsTM—Gosudarstvennyi tsentral'nyi teatral'nyi muzei imeni A. A. Bakhrushina [Bakhrushin State Central Theatre Museum (Moscow)]

GABT—Gosudarstvennyi akademicheskii Bol'shoi teatr [State Academic Bolshoi Theatre (Moscow)]

GAMT—Gosudarstvennyi akademicheskii Mariinskii teatr [State Academic Mariinsky Theatre]

GMTMI (SPb)—Sankt-Peterburgskii gosudarstvennyi muzei teatral'nogo i muzykal'nogo iskusstva [St. Petersburg State Museum of Theatrical and Musical Art]

MT—Mikhailovskii teatr [Mikhailovsky Theatre]

RGALI—Rossiiskii gosudarstvennyi arkhiv literatury i iskusstva [Russian State Archive of Literature and Art (Moscow)]

RNB (SPb)—Rossiiskaya natsional'naya biblioteka (Sankt Peterburg) [Russian National Library (St Petersburg)]

SPbGTB—Sankt-Peterburgskaya gosudarstvennaya teatral'naya biblioteka [St Petersburg State Theatre Library]

TsGALI—Tsentral'nyi gosudarstvennyi arkhiv literatury i iskusstva [Central State Archive of Literature and Art (St Petersburg)]

TsMB (GAMT)—Tsentral'naya muzykal'naya biblioteka gosudarstvennogo akademicheskogo Mariinskogo teatra [Central Music Library of the State Academic Mariinsky Theatre]

Introduction

On December 21, 1935, the Bolshoi Theatre prepared to celebrate one of the most important events in the Soviet calendar: Stalin's birthday. This special occasion demanded equally significant works, and the Bolshoi chose Shostakovich's new ballet *The Limpid Stream*. The ballet had premiered in Leningrad six months earlier to enormous acclaim. Performances were sold out, reviews were exuberant, and the choreographer Fyodor Lopukhov was quickly invited to mount the ballet in Moscow and become the Bolshoi's artistic director. Lopukhov brought two of his dancers from Leningrad, both of whom were intended for the ranks of the Bolshoi's artists; and Shostakovich also traveled to Moscow, staying in housing arranged by the theatre as he collaborated on the production. On December 3, Stalin attended a performance of the ballet. That same night the Bolshoi hosted a delegation of visiting Cossacks from collective farms along the Don River—the location, roughly, in which the ballet was set. By the time the Bolshoi chose *The Limpid Stream* for a slate of birthday repertoire later that month, the ballet had won widespread praise. Its presentation on Stalin's birthday marked a historic and cultural achievement in Soviet dance.

Shostakovich composed his three ballets—*The Golden Age* (1930), *The Bolt* (1931), and *The Limpid Stream* (1935)—during his early professional career in Leningrad in the same period in which he wrote extensively for other dramatic genres, most famously his two operas as well as his music for early Soviet film and stage plays. His ballets document his interaction with the genre and provide insight into the development of early Soviet dance. They also illuminate his creative collaborations, notably with the choreographer Lopukhov, whose involvement Shostakovich demanded on *The Golden Age* and who choreographed *The Bolt* and *The Limpid Stream*. Shostakovich's ballets did not survive on the Soviet stage. *The Golden Age* had some initial popularity but fell out of the repertoire in its first season. *The Bolt* was panned at its premiere. *The Limpid Stream* was by far the most successful of the three works for a time; but in 1936, the ballet was condemned in *Pravda*, just a week after the newspaper's denunciation of the composer's opera *Lady Macbeth of Mtsensk District*, and it was withdrawn from the theatre.[1] Shostakovich's ballet scores were not published in his lifetime, and his manuscripts did not remain in his possession. The impact of Shostakovich's ballets in the Soviet period was truncated due to their brief time on the stage, their exploration of paths not taken in the genre's development, limited access to the music, loss of the choreography, and the legacy of denunciation and repression.

Before their lapse into obscurity, however, Shostakovich's ballets contributed to the genre at a critical period of its development in Soviet Russia. They explored different models of dance and revealed the depth and variety of the composer's interest in the balletic tradition. At the same time, they shaped the search for a "Soviet" approach to ballet and illuminated the pressures and concerns that vied for dominance in the experimental environment of the late 1920s and early 1930s. Archival materials in St. Petersburg and Moscow preserve the creative record of Shostakovich's ballets in scores, *répétiteurs*, photographs, libretti, costume sketches, set designs, theatre documents, and annals of performance. These sources offer new discoveries about the ballets and their place both in Shostakovich's output and in the history of Soviet dance.

Drawing on the source record, this book charts the complex histories of Shostakovich's ballets, their contributions to dance in Russia, and their impact on the composer's artistic career and the genre of ballet in the twentieth century. Shostakovich's ballets document the composer's engagement with one of the era's chief creative enterprises and illuminate how he navigated the artistic and political forces, historical precedents, and ideological demands of ballet in the early Soviet period. Materials of creation and reception, moreover, record decisions that he and other artists made about music, dance, and design in the ballets and contextualize how such components were understood by contemporary audiences. Shostakovich's ballets responded to the demands of a genre whose heritage extended deep into the Imperial period, and beyond, yet whose essentials had been fundamentally challenged by developments at home and abroad.

Soviet Ballet in the 1920s

Soviet ballet had been through a tumultuous period of redefinition after the Revolution. Beset by internal and external stresses, it was caught between the innovations of Russian ballet abroad and economic, political, cultural, and artistic pressures at home. Awareness of (and anxiety over) innovations in the West was a long-standing thread of Russian artistic discourse, and as this thread emerged afresh in the early Soviet period, the innovations of Sergei Diaghilev in the West created unique pressures on Soviet dance. Diaghilev had founded the Ballets Russes in St. Petersburg and taken his company to Paris in 1909, where its ballets advanced the most avant-garde ideas about dance. The Ballets Russes was noted in Europe for its exoticism and its "Russian-ness" (an identity that was redefined several times over the impresario's twenty-year tenure), but it grew increasingly detached from its Russian roots. This was especially true after 1917, when Diaghilev no longer had access to Russian dancers, choreographers, musicians, artists, or Imperial patronage. The Soviets were acutely aware of Diaghilev's achievements and more than once anticipated his return to his homeland to participate in the making of Soviet ballet. Diaghilev never went back, however, though he often contemplated doing so; and as "Soviet" and "Russian" traditions confronted each other—an encounter symbolized in a meeting between Diaghilev and Anatoly Lunacharsky in 1927—the two traditions were, to recall Tim Scholl's description, "drifting steadily away from one another."[2] Soviet artists in the post-Revolutionary period would remain attuned to Western innovations, but the struggle to define a new creative path in Soviet ballet would encompass artistic concerns in tension with political ones.

By the early 1920s, Soviet ballet was in crisis. Appalling economic conditions threatened ballet theatres and schools. An exodus of talent had stripped their ranks. Ideological questions were raised about ballet's right to exist in a proletarian society. Moreover, debates about the future of ballet became entwined with financial ones about how the State should spend its money—on old tsarist institutions or new Soviet initiatives, on ideologically weak theatres or robust proletarian enterprises. In Christina Ezrahi's words, a central question of the early Soviet cultural project was "if, and how, Russia's prerevolutionary cultural heritage could, and should, be adapted to the new cultural needs of Soviet Russia."[3] As this applied to ballet, questions turned on the genre's relevance, its bourgeois heritage, its continuity with the past, and its ability (and willingness) to seek new content and forms reflecting ideologies of the present.

The Bolshoi and the Mariinsky Theatres were called upon to adapt to these "new cultural needs" but were frequently berated for their slowness in doing so. Meanwhile, other venues and studios popped up, aiming to explore alternative approaches to dance or, as some hoped, to generate "a new choreographic art" that might replace ballet altogether.[4] Much of this experimentation took place in Moscow studios, where influential ideas focused on liberation of the body (Isadora Duncan, Inna Chernetskaya, Vera Maya), eurhythmics (Émile Jacques-Dalcroze's methods), biomechanics (Vsevolod Meyerhold's theatre), gymnastics and acrobatics (from several sources including the *fizkultura* movement and the circus), "eccentric" dances (Kasyan Goleizovsky), and "machine dances" and circus acrobatics (Nikolai Foregger)—to name a few. None of these directions articulated a clear course for the development of Soviet ballet, but some ideas filtered into the work of certain choreographers and repertoire. For example, Foregger's machine dances, Meyerhold's biomechanics, and the *fizkultura* movement provided precedents that were explored by Lopukhov in *The Bolt*, a ballet that seemed (albeit briefly) to offer a corrective to stylized fantasies about Soviet modernism. But *The Bolt* failed as a model for Soviet dance, as did most of the balletic experiments that preceded it. Indeed, the diversity and fragmentation of choreographic approaches through the 1920s underscored a crisis of identity in Soviet ballet, a crisis marked by resistance to and confusion over change within the ballet theatres and by complex internal and external pressures.

In addition to conflicting aesthetic demands, practical challenges affected work in the ballet theatre, and the uncertain situation had an acute impact on Soviet ballet composers. Music's position—and particularly the way in which composer and choreographer worked together—was not yet fixed for Soviet ballet. Composers were sometimes commissioned long before choreographers were confirmed (as happened to Shostakovich with *The Golden Age*). Ideology drove decisions about "collective choreography" (involving multiple choreographers in a production) and directors from opera and dramatic theatres (who could, theoretically, enhance dramaturgy in ballet through a cross-pollination of ideas). These approaches greatly complicated a composer's experience of working with a choreographer or even a director who understood dance and also affected the creation of ballet scores and how ballet music might be used in a production.

Shostakovich and Ballet

Shostakovich's path to ballet ran through these complexities of the 1920s and through tensions between institutional conservatism and avant-garde experimentation in dance. As a young man, Shostakovich frequented the ballet theatre as spectator and critic (not to mention ardent admirer of the ballerinas). His compositional interest in ballet began as a teenager, when he engaged both story ballet (an unrealized project on *The Little Mermaid*) and modern choreography of his music (Mariya Ponna's performance to his *Three Fantastic Dances*). He recorded his love of Tchaikovsky's ballets, admiration for Marius Petipa's creations, reserve over Pavel Petrov's ideas, interest in Goleizovsky's methods, and encounters with Lopukhov's choreographies. The 1920s was also the time when Shostakovich achieved success in other dramatic genres—his opera *The Nose* (1928), his collaboration with Meyerhold on *The Bedbug* (1929), and his first film scores. By the time Shostakovich wrote *The Golden Age* at the end of the decade, he had imbibed theatrical principles across different stages and he served on the Artistic Council of the Leningrad State Academic Theatre, where his thoughts and opinions about ballet were logged in transcripts of the council's meetings and in letters he wrote to the Theatre's directorate. The types of ballet projects that Shostakovich contemplated, and those he completed, revealed his tastes and opportunities, as well as the period's many demands of the genre.

Shostakovich's three completed ballets—*The Golden Age*, *The Bolt*, and *The Limpid Stream*—showed a conscious wrestling with the past, a tension between demands for new "Soviet" works alongside the reinvention of old classical ones and the pressures of modern models. In suggesting what "Soviet" ballet could be, Shostakovich's works adopted various models that both invoked the legacies of Russian ballet and offered new cultural markers for a socialist society. They took up new questions about the genre, prompted by evolving Soviet ideology, but they also returned to the genre's perennial questions of realism and narrative, now emerging in a new form but remaining unresolved. Each of the ballets was dressed up in a "proletarian skin" (to borrow Lynn Garafola's evocative phrase) of topical stories, but inside that skin, the works reimagined Russia's legacy of dance.[5]

Shostakovich's ballets explored, respectively, the classical, the modern, and the Romantic traditions of dance and illuminated how those traditions might be relevant to the development of Soviet ballet. *The Golden Age* invoked Petipa's legacy while giving the nod to contemporaneous topics. *The Bolt* responded to contemporary and modernist models at home and abroad. *The Limpid Stream* reimagined Romantic ballet in the improbable setting of a collective farm. No single model, tradition, or synthesis emerged from these experiments, and this is part of the reason these ballets have resisted analysis for so long. But when we grasp the interaction of balletic models in the collaborations, we understand how these ballets came to be and the place they held in Shostakovich's creative legacy and in the development of Soviet dance.

Beyond the creative context of Shostakovich's ballets, what can be said of their *music*? It is insufficient to explain Shostakovich's ballet music by invoking either his operas (as better) or his film music (as comparable). By the time Shostakovich composed his ballets, ballet music in Russia had developed a robust set of conventions, but the relationship between music and dance had also shifted dramatically. As Roland John Wiley and Lynn Garafola have explained, two primary models of music existed for Russian ballet—the "specialist" tradition of the nineteenth century, in which music was "written to order" in response to the choreographer's needs, and the "modernist" tradition, in which new choreography drew on new music, both modern ballet scores and "absolute" music from the concert repertoire.[6] The "symphonic" ballet scores epitomized by works like *Sleeping Beauty* in the late nineteenth century had shifted the "specialist" tradition toward musical cohesion, internal unity, and the communication of poetic or ineffable meanings, yet this music remained linked to the choreography it served. Diaghilev's modernist innovations arose in conjunction with his rejection of the "specialist" tradition. While he and the *mir iskusstniki* admired the coherence and quality of ballet scores by Léo Delibes, Pyotr Tchaikovsky, and Aleksandr Glazunov, they also recognized that new choreography necessitated new music. Diaghilev commissioned new scores from modernist composers like Igor Stravinsky and Sergei Prokofiev and also dipped into the canon of "absolute music," as Mikhail Fokine had already done at the Imperial Theatre. The "specialist" and the "modernist" traditions of ballet music thus offered two widely different precedents for Soviet dance.

Soviet ballet criticism sought some kind of middle ground between the two approaches as it celebrated "symphonic" scores, or *symphonism*, but it applied the term not only to "old" scores like *Sleeping Beauty* but also to modern scores like *Firebird*, and even at times to emerging examples of film music. (At the same time, *symphonism* was used to describe ballet itself, or what it should aim to be, in phrases like *dance symphonism* or *symphonic ballet*.[7] In these constructions, *symphonism* or *symphonic* sometimes emphasized the dance and sometimes the music. Definitions not infrequently ended up in tautologies. For Sollertinsky, *symphonism* expressed an equality between music and dance, a type of *Gesamtkunstwerk* that synthesized ballet's art forms.[8] For the musicologist Boris Asafyev, it implied musical value and significance, as in his explanation of "symphonic music to express choreographic concepts."[9] For Lopukhov, in *Dance Symphony: Magnificence of the Universe*, dance aimed to express the preexisting structures of the music.[10]) *Symphonism* in relation to ballet music remained ill-defined by Soviet critics, despite a robust body of writings that popularized the term across ballet, film, and concert music through the 1920s and 1930s. More recently, scholars have suggested that *symphonism* was linked to Soviet concepts of "intelligibility" and "musical narration" and, in relation to ballet specifically, to the presentation of large-scale forms, of complex or at least not "simple" music, and of scores that went beyond *dansante*.[11] In other words, as Scholl writes, it meant "the lack of 'bad' ballet music."[12] Yet early Soviet ballet failed to clarify what new relationships, if any, would be sought between music and dance or to examine how such relationships would affect the essential one between composer and choreographer. These ambiguities had an enormous impact on Shostakovich's work as a ballet composer and on the different approaches to ballet music that he explored in his three ballets.

Shostakovich's ballet scores did not fully fit into either the "specialist" or the "modernist" approach, and only the first, *The Golden Age*, was described by contemporaries as "symphonic." *The Golden Age* was his most independently written score. He composed most, if not all, of it before choreographers were confirmed, and he complained that his music never enjoyed a coherent choreographic vision even when the ballet was finally performed. Yet *The Golden Age* was, arguably, Shostakovich's most cohesive ballet score in terms of musical unity and artistic quality. Sollertinsky ranked it "among Shostakovich's best works" and hailed the composer as the balletic heir to Tchaikovsky and Stravinsky.[13] By contrast, *The Limpid Stream* was the ballet in which Shostakovich worked most closely with a choreographer, submitting individual dances to Lopukhov; writing numbers in response to instructions about mood, character, and movement; and even recasting some of his own pre-existing music. The result was a series of musical "sketches" (as the libretto termed them) without overall musical unity, yet it was also Shostakovich's most coherent ballet in the way that music, dance, design, and narrative worked together consistently through the work. The collaborative conditions for *The Limpid Stream* resembled, at least in some ways, the "specialist" tradition in which danceable music reflected the composer's grasp of choreographic requirements and stage conditions. This assessment in no way diminishes the ballet's musical charms—which are many. But it highlights a range of relationships between music and dance in Shostakovich's ballets, and this range helps to situate the ballet music both within the composer's output and within the larger discourse of early Soviet dance.

Shostakovich's ballet music also illuminated the balletic models with which he worked or of which he was at least conscious as he wrote. Allusions to Tchaikovsky, Delibes, and other ballet composers appear at critical dramatic moments in ways that document both Shostakovich's literacy in the ballet repertoire and the music and stage situations that were meaningful to the creation of his scores. At the same time, the ways in which he navigated both particular emotional suggestion and more general atmospheric conditions for the stage demonstrated his command of narrative and poetic possibility in his ballet music. Shostakovich's ballets witnessed to the composer's interest, or at least his willingness, in composing for the genre, his knowledge of the ballet music of his predecessors, his grasp of classical and modern models of ballets, and his awareness of complex questions about the genre's place in Soviet culture.

Reception and Reassessment

Shostakovich's ballets are important for the insight they offer into the young composer's creative collaborations and his interaction with one of the chief genres of Soviet cultural production, but they have been overshadowed in the scholarly reception of his music. Through the Soviet period, a lack of sources about the ballets made any assessment of them provisional, a fact that Soviet scholars were quick to acknowledge. In the years after Shostakovich's death, scholarship on his oeuvre flourished in Russia and abroad, with studies charting his life and works and his output in major genres, but the ballets were not typically a subject of these investigations. Among Shostakovich's dramatic works written before 1936, *Lady Macbeth* was the most significant and mature endeavor; its denunciation emblematized artistic repression and unleashed a campaign in which other works, including *The Limpid Stream*, were casualties. The fate of *Lady Macbeth* has tended to eclipse that of *The Limpid Stream* in the scholarly record, as it did in the composer's own estimation too. Shostakovich did not value his ballets as he did his operas—in fact, he expressed negative opinions about his ballets in ways that he never did about his operas, symphonies, or string quartets—and he did not revive his ballets in his lifetime, whereas he defended the quality of his operas and revived *Lady Macbeth* (as *Katerina Izmailova*) when the political climate allowed in the 1960s. Subsequent scholarship has supported this hierarchy of artistic merit and elaborated the composer's most innovative and profound dramatic achievements in his operas and, post-condemnation, in his symphonies. His ballets have been regarded as secondary in his creative output, as works written "for money" (the implication being that such works are inferior) comparable to his film and incidental music.

After Shostakovich's death, a reassessment of his ballets began among practitioners of dance. The Bolshoi's choreographer Yuri Grigorovich revived *The Golden Age* in 1982, albeit with an entirely new scenario and with only some music drawn from the original ballet score and some compiled from other works by Shostakovich. In effect, Grigorovich's *Golden Age* was a different ballet, which used the title of Shostakovich's first ballet but explored a range of the composer's dance and concert music in an altered narrative. In the early 2000s, Alexei Ratmansky led revivals of *The Bright Stream* (the title used for his production) and *The Bolt*. *The Bright Stream* was the more successful of the two ballets, as it had been in the 1930s, and it was regularly programmed by the Bolshoi and Western dance companies.[14] Ratmansky's revivals brought these ballets to international audiences and placed Shostakovich's music within the modern dance repertoire.

The changing attitudes that underpinned reengagement with Shostakovich's ballets also aligned with new questions about the early Soviet stage and ballet as a genre. Scholarship on early Soviet dance has charted the experimentalism of the 1920s through the codification of *drambalet* ("dramatic ballet") in the 1930s. The seminal text on the Soviet avant-garde in ballet was Elizabeth Souritz's *Soviet Choreographers in the 1920s*, published in Russian in 1970 and translated into English twenty years later. Building on Souritz's work, dance scholars have elaborated the disruptive ideas of early Soviet choreographers, the theory and politics of early Soviet ballet, the demands and agendas of ballet institutions in the early Soviet years, the development of the genre of *drambalet*, the role of Soviet ballet in cultural-political exchange, and the legacies of Russian ballet in the West.[15] Although Shostakovich's ballets are not a primary focus of this dance scholarship, insights into the composer's ballets appear in several texts. Christina Ezrahi, for example, examines the condemnation of *The Limpid Stream* in relation to the highly fluid artistic-political milieu of the mid-1930s. Simon Morrison offers a provisional reading of *The Bolt* as ideological satire, and Elizabeth Stern documents theatrical intrigues and debates surrounding the production of *The Golden Age*. Meanwhile, contextual studies and institutional histories of Soviet ballet offer important insights into the period, as in Scholl's discussion of the critical framework for production and reception of early Soviet ballet and Morrison's history of the Bolshoi Theatre.

Shostakovich was the most celebrated young composer in early Soviet Russia, and assessments of his legacy place him among the principal composers of his time. The work of Olga Digonskaya and Lyudmila Kovnatskaya in Russia, and Laurel Fay, Pauline Fairclough, and Elizabeth Wilson in Anglo-American scholarship, along with the endeavors of many other scholars, has defined the field of Shostakovich studies and continues to shape its activities. This scholarship documents Shostakovich's creative work and situates his music within contextual and hermeneutical frameworks. Broad studies also examine the increasingly tense relationship between art and politics in the 1920s as well as Shostakovich's place within an often experimental artistic milieu.[16] Meanwhile, the Dmitri Shostakovich Archive with its DSCH publishing wing brings to light archival treasures that continue to enrich our understanding of the composer's output. Among the works written "for money," Shostakovich's film music has enjoyed excellent treatment by Joan Titus, who—undeterred by the perception of this music as secondary—has explored Shostakovich's role as a composer for an emerging enterprise pressed by artistic, political, and technological forces. The rich scholarship on Shostakovich includes monographs on his string quartets, symphonies, film music, and other genres. While Shostakovich's ballets have garnered less attention than his other works, foundations for research have been laid in the Russian scholarship that chronicles instances of the composer's early interest in ballet and sets in order facts of creation and reception for his three balletic efforts.[17] Given how much we know about Shostakovich, it is important now to offer a scholarly assessment of his ballets, including their place in the composer's early development and their contributions to the Soviet cultural enterprise as well as to one of the foremost genres of Russian cultural production. Such an assessment allows us to examine more fully the scope of Shostakovich's early work, beyond his moments of full maturity (like *Lady Macbeth*). In this treatment, Shostakovich emerges as more richly complex, more contradictory, and more interesting, allowing us to better acknowledge the paradoxical and even incongruous nature of his art.

Archival Collections and Sources

Archival collections in St. Petersburg and Moscow hold musical scores and drafts for Shostakovich's ballets as well as *répétiteurs*, sketches for costumes and sets, surviving costumes, set models, photographs, personal documents, theatre protocols, and administrative papers. These sources chart artistic and practical decisions around the creation of Shostakovich's ballets and clarify the synthesis of elements that formed these works. Moreover, an extensive body of ballet criticism from the 1920s and 1930s chronicles contemporary discussions of Soviet ballet and helps to illuminate the cultural importance of Shostakovich's ballets within broader balletic discourse. Notable articles on Shostakovich's ballets were penned, for example, by Ivan Sollertinsky, who (along with other critics) did much to define Soviet ballet's critical framework in this period.

The archives of the St. Petersburg State Museum of Theatre and Music hold materials on *The Golden Age* and *The Bolt* as well as contemporaneous ballets that shed light on the artistic practices of early Soviet dance in Leningrad. Other important collections are housed by the Mariinsky, Mikhailovsky (former Maly), and Bolshoi Theatres. The Music Library of the Mariinsky Theatre holds a partial *répétiteur* and an orchestral score for *The Golden Age* as well as orchestral parts for *The Bolt*. The archives of the Mikhailovsky Theatre preserve materials for the Leningrad production of *The Limpid Stream*, including a *répétiteur*, an orchestral score, costume sketches, photographs, and a three-dimensional set model. In Moscow, the creative decisions surrounding the Bolshoi's production of *The Limpid Stream* can be traced in materials at the Bolshoi Theatre Archives, the Theatre's costume warehouses, and the Bakhrushin Museum. Large documentary collections from the running of the ballet theatres (including discussions of repertoire, logs of expenses, contracts for productions) are held at the Central State Archive of Literature and Arts in St. Petersburg (TsGALI) and at the Russian State Archive of Literature and Arts (RGALI) in Moscow. Finally, the Dmitri Shostakovich Archive, in conjunction with RGALI, holds autograph scores of Shostakovich's ballet music. These contain annotations, corrections, notes made during rehearsals (often in multiple hands), and—in a few exceptional cases—some choreographic notation.

A vital forum for describing a ballet's artistic and political credentials was the program booklet, published by the theatre and sold at the performances. These publications are preserved in theatre archive collections alongside materials from the ballet's original performance. The booklets contain not only the libretto of a ballet (explaining its story) but also articles by various contributors (explaining how to "read" the work). Such discussions were designed to educate an audience that was still largely ignorant about ballet, but they were also important for explaining and defending artistic decisions—especially about a non-verbal art form—in ideologically correct language. Like many such publications in the 1930s, the booklets accompanying the performances of Shostakovich's ballets aimed to shape contemporary reception. Shostakovich contributed articles to the program booklets for two of his ballets (*The Golden Age* and *The Limpid Stream*), as did the choreographers for these works (a collective of choreographers for the former ballet, and Lopukhov for the latter). Additional articles featured important figures in the emerging field of Soviet ballet criticism, like Sollertinsky (who wrote for *The Golden Age* and *The Bolt*) and Yuri Slonimsky (for *The Limpid Stream*).

Any source study of ballet presents challenges, and Shostakovich's ballets are no exception. The parts of the source record are not equally deep. Many sources are ephemeral. Some are fragile, like costumes, which are sensitive to light and deteriorate with exposure. Others are incomplete, like photographs, which show fascinating moments in the studio and on the stage but capture a mere snapshot of what took place. Many sources are also collected in different archives (and cities) with some institutions holding materials related to a single production and others preserving the components of an individual artist's oeuvre (of which materials related to a single ballet comprise only a part). Moreover, most of the choreography for Shostakovich's ballets is lost, and while annotated scores, drawings, and photographs offer tantalizing glimpses of choreographic moments, there is no solid evidence of movements and steps on the stage.

Of course, these are familiar problems in ballet research. But as Wiley and Marian Smith have convincingly demonstrated for this field, one of the most significant and coherent sources for understanding ballet is the musical score. It not only contextualizes and illuminates other, often partial records, but also witnesses to the actions, moods, and movements of characters and in doing so opens up the "sonic world" of the ballet. Complete scores exist for Shostakovich's ballets, thanks to the efforts of the Dmitri Shostakovich Archive, which has published the first authoritative scores in the *New Collected Works* edition. The publication project began in the early 2000s and spanned more than a decade with the final volume of the ballets appearing just seven years ago (2018). These scores make it feasible to see and study Shostakovich's ballets in ways that were formerly impossible. While any ballet score "fixes" an ephemeral art form in ways that belie its mutability on the stage, Shostakovich's scores attest to the musical conception of his works, if not always to the way his music was used for the stage.

It is important to note that in manuscript form, Shostakovich's ballet scores are not unified manuscripts. Their constituent parts must often be put together from multiple sources (many of which are not in Shostakovich's hand) and may also be housed in different archives, a situation that obscures their relationships. Moreover, *répétiteurs* and conductors' scores can show notable differences in numbering, placement, and inclusion of dances, suggesting just how malleable these scores were. Dances were ordered and reordered throughout the production process, and sometimes afterward too. The order in which dances appear in archival documents, or even in the published scores, does not necessarily document the order in which those dances appeared on the stage. When a ballet was produced twice—and differently, as *The Limpid Stream* was—differences among the musical manuscripts multiply. As a result, a "complete score" of any one of the ballets is an interpretation of the work. At the same time, each "complete score" illuminates unique elements at a distinct moment of creation. For example, rehearsal scores (*répétiteurs*) and performance scores can tell us much about the production of a ballet and help to clarify what was gained or lost in specific creative decisions. Despite barriers to understanding Shostakovich's (and many) ballets, the narrative that emerges from the source record allows us to grasp the artistic goals and accomplishments of Shostakovich's balletic efforts and to understand how those goals intersected with the creative impulses of the period.

Shostakovich's Ballets and the Search for Soviet Dance

Chapter 1 of this book sets out Shostakovich's early interest in ballet and explains the aesthetic and political debates about the genre that shaped the theatre scene as well as the composer's experiences within it. Although Shostakovich abandoned his first balletic attempt (and presumably destroyed his sketches), his experiences through the 1920s continued to connect him to Leningrad's theatrical circles and to the close-knit world of Leningrad ballet. He saw George Balanchine (then Georgii Balanchivadze) dance before

Balanchine left Russia. He collaborated with the avant-garde dancer Mariya Ponna. He met and eventually worked with the choreographer Lopukhov. He became close friends with the musicologist and critic Sollertinsky in the period in which Sollertinsky vociferously expressed his ideas on ballet and published a history of the genre. Together with Sollertinsky, Shostakovich served on the Artistic Council of the Leningrad State Academic Theatre, where the pressing issues of Soviet ballet were debated. The overriding questions asked what Soviet ballet would be. What topics would it take up? What choreography would it explore? What music would support the aesthetic and political goals of its new forms and content? Shostakovich's foray into ballet composition intersected with these debates about the future of Soviet dance and reflected the composer's varied experiences of ballet in Leningrad through a decade of experimentation and reassessment.

Chapters 2, 3, and 4 take up, respectively, the creative histories of *The Golden Age*, *The Bolt*, and *The Limpid Stream*. These were full-length narrative ballets on contemporary topics, and each aimed at a "Soviet" version of the genre. Despite their shared identity as "story ballets," however, the works were very different from one another, as each drew on a different balletic model and fused that model with Soviet concerns. *The Golden Age* examined the classical legacy of the Petipa repertoire while transforming the "old" ballet with sounds and movements drawn from popular and sporting cultures. *The Bolt* advanced Soviet modernist ballet through elements derived from the Soviet and the Western avant-garde movements and from Soviet amateur forms. *The Limpid Stream* created Soviet Romantic ballet, a synthesis in which the hallmarks of the Romantic genre were viewed through the prism of Soviet realism. In their references to the classical, the modernist, and the Romantic traditions of ballet, Shostakovich's works suggested new approaches for Soviet dance and also witnessed to the literacy and inventiveness with which the composer and his colleagues in the ballet theatre approached these works. Shostakovich's ballets were not simply three attempts at the genre—though they were that too—but they responded directly to the heritage of ballet as it had developed in Russia to that point.

Chapter 5 examines the ongoing legacy of Shostakovich's music in dance. Amid many possible examples, it takes up four case studies from four choreographers working in different times and contexts. After the suppression and abandonment of his ballets, Shostakovich's concert music quickly gained the interest of choreographers. Léonide Massine in the West (in the 1930s) and Igor Belsky in Russia (in the 1960s) created "symphonic" ballets based on music from the composer's symphonies. Although the choreographies had different aesthetic goals, they both emphasized the concert scores as a platform for choreographic innovation and artistic synthesis. After Shostakovich's death, Grigorovich and Ratmansky separately initiated revivals that returned Shostakovich's ballets to the ballet stage. The choreographers approached their revivals very differently, however, particularly in their treatment of Shostakovich's ballet music and of the ballets' Soviet topics. These "afterlives" of Shostakovich's ballets demonstrated the many ways in which the idea of Shostakovich as ballet composer lived on.

While Shostakovich's most profound utterances as a composer were made in other genres, his ballets were important culturally for the way they reflected the conflicting impulses of the early Soviet period, and creatively for the way they both prompted and constrained the composer's engagement with one of the foremost genres of Russian music. Shostakovich's balletic efforts documented his creative approaches to the genre early in his career, as well as the artistic resources available to him, and they witnessed to the pioneering endeavors yet increasing constraints in Leningrad's theatrical life. His three ballets appeared during a time of transition in Soviet dance between the experimentalism of the 1920s and the codification of *drambalet* in the 1930s. While the ballets did not participate fully in either of these approaches, they reflected elements of both the Soviet avant-garde and the conservatism that would ultimately underpin the development of an official Soviet genre. Moreover, the creation and reception of Shostakovich's ballets were forged in a rapidly changing political environment as cultural production shifted toward greater ideological militancy in the late 1920s and the doctrine of socialist realism emerged in the early 1930s, however inchoately, as an official mandate for the Soviet arts. In their complex relationships to aesthetic, ideological, creative, and practical questions, Shostakovich's ballets witnessed to the composer's interaction with the balletic tradition in Russia and illuminated the artistic and political evolution of early Soviet dance. The "afterlives" of these works, moreover, sealed the importance of Shostakovich's music in ballet and heralded the dramatic and choreographic possibilities of his oeuvre.

1
"Art without movement does not move me": Shostakovich and the Path to Ballet

In 1923, a seventeen-year-old Shostakovich wrote to his girlfriend, Tatiana Glivenko, that he was working hard on his first ballet.[1] The libretto, prepared by Yuri Slonimsky, was based on Hans Christian Anderson's fairytale *The Little Mermaid*, one of the composer's favorite stories, and the dances were to be choreographed by Vladimir Ponomarev for the graduation exercises of the Leningrad Choreographic Institute.[2] Early in 1924, Shostakovich abandoned his youthful ballet (and his sketches have never been found), but he continued to cultivate a taste for the genre. Attending performances and recording his impressions, he was an enthusiastic spectator as well as an increasingly astute judge of ballet's technical and aesthetic demands. "Art without movement does not move me," he confessed to Glivenko, as his tastes and experiences as well as his personal friendships and professional collaborations drew him toward Leningrad's balletic milieu.[3] In 1929, Shostakovich accepted the commission for *The Golden Age*, a ballet that offered the young composer his first opportunity to write for Leningrad's premiere ballet stage and whose topics, like those of his next ballets too, intersected with debates about artistic and political reform in Soviet dance. Shostakovich's path to ballet through the 1920s reflected his creative interest in the genre and illuminated the aesthetic and ideological pressures that shaped ballet's evolution in the early Soviet period.

Shostakovich's Early Career

Shostakovich composed his ballets in his early career in a period in which he wrote prolifically for dramatic genres. His "intensive, pioneering activity" as a composer for stage and screen (to quote his preeminent biographer Laurel

Fay) included contributions to Soviet opera, ballet, dramatic theatre, and the emerging industry of Soviet film.[4] Between 1928 and 1935, Shostakovich completed both of his operas, his three ballets, eight of his thirty-six film scores, a variety show, and incidental music for six stage plays (out of the eight plays for which he wrote during his lifetime). These endeavors contributed to the flowering of his professional career and built on the success he had enjoyed during his student days at the Leningrad Conservatory. By the time Shostakovich accepted the commission for *The Golden Age* in 1929, he had finished his first opera (*The Nose*), enjoyed his first collaboration for dramatic theatre (*The Bedbug*), and begun writing his first film music (*The New Babylon*). Music for dramatic genres was central to Shostakovich's professional endeavors at the outset of his career.

In this period, Shostakovich was living on Marat Street with his mother and sisters in the apartment where he had spent much of his youth.[5] Before the Revolution, the Shostakovich family had enjoyed relatively comfortable circumstances. Their brightly lit, seven-room apartment in the center of Leningrad was located a stone's throw from Nevsky Prospekt, the city's most elegant street, and minutes from the Moscow Railway Station, from which trains ran south to the (soon-to-be) capital. The location was ideal for access into the heart of Leningrad—with its theatres, palaces, public library, and institutions of learning and culture—and for a gateway out of the city toward the rest of Russia. After the Revolution, which the Shostakovich family largely welcomed, Shostakovich's parents anticipated changes to their circumstances. Foreseeing a reduction to their living space, they communalized their apartment themselves, inviting friends-of-friends to move in with them before the State assigned anyone else. Shostakovich's family occupied the three front rooms of the apartment overlooking Marat Street—a central, spacious living room with comfortable quarters on each side—while their new communal partners occupied the remaining rooms giving onto the building's inner courtyard.

The piano lay at the heart of family life, occupying a vital place not only in Shostakovich's musical development but also in the family's social activities and later its financial concerns. Shostakovich's parents were both musical. His father, a tenor, sang well, and his mother had studied piano at the Conservatory. Their artistic tastes and relative affluence before the Revolution allowed them to cultivate friendships among Leningrad's cultural elite and to host friends, musicians, artists, and intellectuals in their home as well as enjoy social invitations in return. It was in the soirées on Marat

Street that Shostakovich had some of his earliest musical encounters and met important members of Leningrad's artistic circles. Later, as his career blossomed, he too hosted events at the family apartment. The after-party for *The Bolt* was one of many celebrations that took place there. A now-familiar photograph, taken that evening, shows the composer surrounded by family members, artists, intellectuals, dancers, and friends. Shostakovich sits on the floor in the center of the picture; in his arms is his favorite ballerina.

After the Revolution, the Shostakovich family, like millions of other Russians, faced financial hardship. As hyper-inflation wiped out the value of the ruble, the economic situation deteriorated rapidly. The purchasing power of incomes was decimated, and the price of goods rose 10 million times in the first six years of the new regime (1917–23).[6] Starvation and unrest were widespread, public services faltered, industry collapsed. In the winter of 1922, at the height of the financial crisis, Shostakovich's father died. His salary, little as it could buy at that point, had been the family's only source of income, and they became destitute. Shostakovich's mother was forced to seek work for the first time but found only poorly paid positions in unskilled labor. She and Shostakovich's oldest sister supplemented the family's meager existence by teaching piano lessons.

In 1919, at the age of thirteen, Shostakovich enrolled at the Leningrad Conservatory, where his talent excited the highest expectations. Aleksandr Glazunov, the institution's director, assessed the young candidate as having "a gift comparable to that of Mozart."[7] Through hardship and privation, Shostakovich pursued his studies diligently. Due to the wider collapse of public services and infrastructure, he frequently had to walk from his home on Marat Street to the Conservatory, a distance of approximately two and a half miles. The most direct route lay across the Fontanka Canal with its magnificent palace facades, through the historic marketplace of Sennaya Ploshchad, and along Canal Griboyedova. His destination was Theatre Square, where the Conservatory had been built on the former site of the Bolshoi Kammeny Theatre in the late nineteenth century. Across the road from the institution where Shostakovich was educated as a musician stood the Mariinsky Theatre. Shostakovich's world as a student would run adjacent to the city's most storied stage for opera and ballet.

Shostakovich spent a decade at the Leningrad Conservatory, pursuing degrees in piano and composition. In these years, it was his concert music that first established him as Soviet Russia's most brilliant and promising young composer. Initially connected to coursework at the Conservatory, some of this music quickly became significant concert repertory. The foremost example was the *First Symphony* of 1926, written as a graduation piece for the Conservatory's undergraduate course in composition. Upon its premiere, the work was hailed as a major new contribution to the symphonic repertoire. In 1927, Bruno Walter heard it in Leningrad and took it back to Berlin to conduct its Western premiere with the Berlin Philharmonic. The success of the First Symphony catalyzed the first phase of Shostakovich's career and brought him international acclaim. Riding the triumph, he enjoyed fame, connections, and invitations for performances. A busy travel schedule saw him crossing western Russia and Ukraine—invited as both composer and concert pianist—and he started making plans to visit Paris. He was also chosen for the first Soviet delegation to the Chopin Competition in Warsaw, a selection that sealed his place among Soviet Russia's chief performers.[8]

After the success of the *First Symphony*, Shostakovich enrolled in the Conservatory's graduate program in composition (1926–29), where his creative efforts spanned avant-garde language and contemporary and popular forms. His *Third Symphony* ("First of May") in 1929 drew on these resources. Although Shostakovich disliked the poor quality of the text he had to set in this work, he wrote imaginatively, the quality of the source in no way undermining the quality of his music, and he submitted the symphony as part of his graduation portfolio. It was while working on the Third Symphony that he also started composing his ballet *The Golden Age*. Meanwhile, Shostakovich's compositional and performing careers intertwined as he expanded his concert repertoire with works of his Russian contemporaries abroad (like Prokofiev's *First Piano Concerto* and Stravinsky's *Les noces*) and with his own pieces that fully displayed his pianistic and compositional virtuosity (like the *First Piano Sonata* and later the *First Piano Concerto*). His repertoire as composer and pianist established his credibility, skill, and gravitas as a creator and interpreter of serious art music.

In 1928, while still a student at the Conservatory, Shostakovich embarked on a period of intensive composing for both art music like opera and ballet and popular forms like film and incidental music. His works drew fully on art and popular styles and demonstrated his fluency in the many musical approaches current in Leningrad's music scene. In just the three-year period in which he composed *The Golden Age* and *The Bolt* (1929–31), Shostakovich wrote in every dramatic genre involving music, and ideas from his stage works cross-pollinated his output (and occasionally reappeared in some recycled music across the dramatic works in these years). His opera *The Nose*, completed in

1928 and premiered in 1930, was influenced by Meyerhold's interpretations of Gogol. While composing the opera, Shostakovich had briefly worked as a rehearsal pianist in Meyerhold's Theatre and boarded with the Meyerhold family. In 1929, he wrote the incidental music for Meyerhold's production of *The Bedbug*. The work's use of popular dance forms, particularly the foxtrot, to satirize the excesses of bourgeois life engaged a topic and a satirical mode that would resonate in music for *The Golden Age* later that year. Shostakovich's experiences in the Meyerhold Theatre also allowed him to observe the director's most contemporary ideas, which in this period emphasized biomechanics, machine-like movements, cinematic devices, Constructivist elements, and codes for satire—elements later taken up in *The Bolt*.[9] Between 1929 and 1931, Shostakovich completed scores for three films (*The New Babylon, Alone,* and *Golden Mountains*), in which he worked out modes of "musical narration" and established a professional relationship with the Soviet film industry that continued throughout his life.[10] He also wrote music for three dramatic productions at the amateur "collective" Theatre of Working-Class Youth (TRAM).[11] These musical offerings for proletarian causes bolstered his political credentials while sustaining his appetite for amateur dramatics (in which he sometimes participated) and for debates about the future of "proletarian musical culture."[12]

Shostakovich's music for stage and screen generated a majority of his income early in his career, building his financial stability and contributing to his professional success.[13] He composed at speed, his productivity astonishing colleagues and collaborators, and he often fatigued himself with work, to the point that friends remarked on his haggard appearance.[14] Financial concerns partly impelled the unremitting pace. From the mid-1920s, Shostakovich had begun contributing to the family finances, and by 1927, five years after his father's death, he was fully supporting his mother and sisters. Some jobs were exhausting and held little appeal, like his work as a pianist in Leningrad cinemas where he improvised for silent films. Others were more stimulating but constrained his creative urges—like his work with Meyerhold in Moscow, an inspiring experience for the composer but one that bore richest fruit in *The Nose* rather than in direct collaborations with Meyerhold himself. Shostakovich also supported his family by taking commissions, concertizing, shepherding works to premiere, and serving on committees, juries, and other organizational bodies. Commissions for dramatic genres paid well. His first commission, for example—for the *Second Symphony* in 1927—brought him 500 rubles, whereas the commission for

The New Babylon two years later stood at four times that amount, or 2,000 rubles.[15] Shostakovich's three ballets were commissioned, the first two by the Leningrad State Academic Theatre and the third by the Maly Opera Theatre. The financial opportunities offered by these contracts were undoubtedly a factor in Shostakovich's acceptance of them.

Shostakovich soon grew frustrated with theatrical commissions, however. They resulted in a loss of creative agency for a composer, he argued, and music was treated dismissively in the theatre, never being permitted a primary or even equal role.[16] In an impassioned statement in 1931, published as "Declaration of a Composer's Duties," he suddenly denounced all his prior music for stage and screen (apart from *The Nose*), forswore theatrical commissions for five years, and called on composers to sever ties with the theatre because of the artistic compromise of collaborative productions. Despite his plea for artistic integrity and creative control, Shostakovich's plan was hardly practical or genuine. Not only did his income depend on music for dramatic genres, but he was at that time writing his second opera *Lady Macbeth of Mtsensk District*, which drew fully on his dramatic experiences and his mastery of art music and popular forms. He would also soon contemplate and commit to additional ballet projects.

Shostakovich's connections to the Soviet theatre shaped his early career, expanding his professional network, cultivating commissions, and exposing him to pressing artistic questions. As he wrote music for the stage, he honed his compositional craft and developed relationships across Leningrad's and Moscow's institutions of opera, theatre, and dance. His contributions to dramatic genres also intersected with contemporary discussions about what those genres would be and how they could be "Sovietized"—that is, how their innovations would reflect the artistic and ideological values of a new era. *The Nose* offered an example of Soviet opera. *The Golden Age* aimed to create Soviet ballet. The film music helped to nurture Soviet cinema. And the collaborations with Meyerhold and proletarian theatres offered opportunities to extend musically the ideas of Russia's most innovative thespians. At the same time, Shostakovich's success outside the theatre contributed to the prestige and value of his work within it and also distinguished him from composers who remained firmly within the popular milieu. His standing as a composer of art music made him attractive as a composer for Leningrad's stages too. His achievements emblematized the role that Russia's institutions—embodied by the Leningrad Conservatory and State Academic Theatre—would play in Soviet cultural life and suggested that these entities would make formative contributions of quality, significance, and import for years to come.

The Ballet Theatre

The Institution

Among those eminent institutions, the former Imperial Mariinsky Theatre housed the premiere stage for ballet in Leningrad. In the early Soviet period, the Mariinsky was renamed the Leningrad State Academic Theatre (1920) and would later be renamed again as the Kirov Theatre (1935). It underwent enormous transitions in leadership, audiences, administration, and modes of production, and in the complex network of relationships among composers, balletmasters, and the Theatre's varied constituents. In 1922, Lopukhov was appointed artistic director, a position in which he served until 1931. One of the leading choreographers of the period, Lopukhov aimed to preserve the legacy of Russian classical ballet while renewing the repertory for a modern age. This impulse toward reinventing the past—making, in Elizabeth Souritz's words, the "classical lexicon ... the language of modern art"—marked Lopukhov's brand of modern classicism.[17] His approach emphasized situating Soviet ballet vis-à-vis the nineteenth-century classics (the repertory and style of Marius Petipa and his colleagues, in which Italian technique was joined to French lyricism and elegance) while updating the topics and movements that Soviet ballet explored.[18]

The audience for this evolving ballet was entirely new. Whereas the balletomanes of the Imperial period had come from the aristocracy and the bourgeoisie, the spectators of the Soviet period came from the masses. They had never seen a ballet before or even the inside of a theatre; and they arrived from factories, trade unions, army barracks, and similar venues, where they had often received free or heavily subsidized tickets sponsored by a state eager to acculturate its workers.[19] Lopukhov recalled the uncertainty of performing for this new crowd, who knew nothing of the art form and who dressed and behaved in uncompromising ways. "Everyone's heart began to beat anxiously," he wrote, "[w]hen the auditorium, which had been intended for the 'cream' of the capital's society, filled with workers and peasants in grey greatcoats, in leather jackets, in shawls—in work and war clothes, now and then even with rifles in their hands ... The new audience made its appearance silently, concentrated, gloomily, as gloomy as were its clothes."[20]

Despite their forbidding demeanor, the workers proved enthusiastic about ballet. Commentators noted that they were "sensitive, responsive, and perceptive" although boisterous in their behavior, "applauding and howling with such violence" that even "the old theatre rats scurried off in horror."[21] These viewers were nothing like the balletomanes of old who shaped public taste. They were a new order of spectator who had never experienced high art but who would, the State planned, be shaped by encounters with it.

The Leningrad State Academic Theatre was not simply the city's "first stage" for ballet and opera, but also a complex organization with many divisions and an elaborate hierarchy of administrative bodies overseeing contributions to Soviet culture. The entity responsible for the Theatre itself, as well as theatrical life across the city, was the Directorate of State Academic Theatres, which influenced and sometimes dictated decisions about opera and ballet. At times members of the Theatre complained of interference, arguing that more decisions should be left up to them, rather than imposed from above. But others welcomed or at least sought to leverage authority from the top. In 1928, Zakhar Lyubinsky was appointed director of State Theatres in Leningrad. He was the authority with whom Shostakovich communicated frequently, bluntly, and earnestly about the fortunes (and misfortunes) of his theatrical enterprises in the late 1920s.

Within the Leningrad State Academic Theatre, newly formed or reorganized administrative entities played critical roles. The population of these groups was disparate, however, and their decisions unpredictable. As the historian Katerina Clark records, hundreds of workers were assigned to the boards of Leningrad's cultural institutions after the Revolution, but these individuals desperately needed training in "cultural competence."[22] They held power but were ignorant, and the results were often chaotic. In the ballet theatre, productions witnessed to a proliferating power structure, but it was often unclear who was in charge or who held ultimate authority. The balletmaster certainly did not. At every stage of development, a ballet was scrutinized for ideological purity, and libretto, music, dance, and design were repeatedly examined. Theatre or cultural officials, artists or policymakers, and specialists or amateurs turned up to rehearsals, sometimes unannounced. Private performances and dress rehearsals were held for select groups of constituents, like factory workers or Red Army officials, with a view not to polishing a production but to trialing it for the guardians of state-approved thought. Any ideological flaw, raised at any point, could jeopardize a production.[23]

At the Leningrad State Academic Theatre, the Artistic-Political Council for Ballet (Artistic Council) was an influential body that was charged, as its name implied, with monitoring the artistic and political quality of the repertoire. It oversaw repertoire selection, commissioned works, assessed productions, and fiercely debated artistic and ideological questions about ballet and its realization on the stage. Some individuals in these discussions were bureaucrats or workers whose only qualification was their perceived political reliability; they were meant to offer insights into the political value of repertoire, production teams, communications, publications, and other activities. Many members of the Council, however, had unassailable professional credentials. These included choreographers, musicians, artists, scholars, and intellectuals whose understanding of their fields, as well as interest in the components of ballet, enabled them to address complex artistic questions. Lopukhov played an enormous role. Ivan Sollertinsky, a stalwart of musical criticism and a leading figure of the Leningrad intelligentsia, enjoyed a position of influence on the Council, where his ideas and initiative (and sometimes his bullying) effected significant undertakings, including the libretto competition of 1929 that led to the commissioning of *The Golden Age*. Individuals came and went in these discussions, but some figures whose contributions appeared in the Theatre's internal records included the celebrated composer and musicologist Boris Asafyev, the theatre historian and critic Alexei Gvozdev, the preeminent ballet pedagogue Agrippina Vaganova, and other distinguished representatives of Leningrad's musical and theatrical arts. In 1929, Shostakovich also joined the Artistic Council, a step that witnessed to his professional standing and recognition as a composer for the stage. A central question for the Artistic Council during Shostakovich's tenure on it was what ballet repertoire to stage and how to convey artistic and political goals in the Theatre's productions.

The Repertoire

Ballet had suffered significant financial and ideological pressures following the Revolution. The constraints of war and privation had posed dangers to the ballet theatres and threatened to force their closure. Meanwhile, ballet's right to exist had been called into question by Revolutionary thought that rejected the genre's bourgeois legacy and long-standing connections to the Imperial court. In 1918, the ballet critic Aleksandr Pleshcheyev described an existential problem: "This season [was] a question of 'to be or not to be?' for ballet"—a question that was only resolved when "the new audience, the masses who flooded to the ballet after its emancipation from the *abonées* [bourgeois subscribers], adopted a firm position: it valued ballet and chose it as an accessible art."[24] If ballet's importance to the new Soviet state had quickly become apparent, what Soviet ballet would be was much less obvious. What topics would it take up, and what choreographic innovations would it consolidate or advance? How would it convey music, and what would the relationship between composer and choreographer be?

In dealing with these questions, Soviet ballet faced competing pressures: the need to resolve the genre's relationship to the classical legacy, to innovate in new forms of dance, and to produce works on topical themes. In response to the demands, two primary lines of development emerged. One aimed to revitalize the classical repertory by reworking the "old" ballets, and the other experimented with new forms and content by producing "new" ballets. At the same time, questions continued about ballet's contemporary relevance. How could ballet promote Soviet ideas leading to the transformation of Soviet culture? To what extent could old forms convey new content or what new forms would be necessary in order to accomplish this? One was a question of ideology and the other a question of genre. They were related but not identical.

The Soviet ballet theatre had inherited two choreographic traditions—the nineteenth-century ballets dominated by the Petipa repertoire and the early twentieth-century innovations led by Aleksandr Gorsky and Mikhail Fokine.[25] The contributions of Gorsky that remained in the Soviet repertory were his reworkings of classical ballets, in which he modernized dance and design and strengthened action and realism.[26] Meanwhile, the Fokine ballets that were performed in Russia emphasized the choreographer's ideas of modern beauty (*Chopiniana/Les sylphides*), the integration of "shifting images" in *commedia dell'arte* (*Le Carnaval*), and the stylization (*Une Nuit d'Égypt*), exoticism (*Islamey* and the "Polovtsian Dances"), or folklorism (*Jota Aragonesa*) of cultural elements.[27] Other choreographic ideas emerged in the work of particular dancers, like Isadora Duncan (who returned to Russia in 1921 at Lenin's invitation), and in the oeuvre of former Imperial dancers-turned-choreographers at the Bolshoi and former Mariinsky Theatres, like Boris Romanov, Leonid Leontiev, Aleksandr Chekrygin, and

Leonid Zhukov (all of whom were shaped by Fokine's ideas).[28] But the "old" repertoire dominated at the main theatres, where the "inertia of tradition" (in Ezrahi's phrase) as well as the robust appreciation of audiences ensured repeated programming of the nineteenth-century classics.[29]

Outside the main theatres, a great deal of experimentation took place, mostly in Moscow's dance studios, the most famous of which were Goleizovsky's Chamber Ballet and Nikolai Foregger's MASTFOR. Goleizovsky's "eccentric erotica"—by which his contemporaries referred to his use of Western ballroom dances like ragtime, tango, foxtrot, and shimmy—involved "ironically exaggerated gestures" derived from these popular forms.[30] Goleizovsky's interests were wide-ranging, however, and he also took up Constructivist ideas (*The Legend of Joseph the Beautiful*, 1925), gently satirized Romantic ballet (*Teolinda* to the music of Schubert, 1925), and engaged contemporary topics through images and symbols rather than narrative (*The Whirlwind*, 1927). Foregger's most famous contributions to experimental dance were his *Machine Dances* (1923) in which dancers enacted the movements of wheels, pistons, cylinders, pumps, and lathes.[31] While extremely disparate, the approaches of the 1920s shared a goal of reinvigorating dance with new forms and content. But the experiments were short-lived. Most remained in the dance studio, and only a few moved briefly to the ballet stage. Western ballroom dances, for example, would appear in *The Golden Age*, and machine-like movements would influence Lopukhov's avant-garde stagings of *The Nutcracker* and *The Bolt*.

In contrast to the experimentalism of Moscow's dance studios, the Bolshoi Theatre emphasized a conservative diet of classics. These were often lightly updated with new choreography or a political slant, but they were recognizably the Petipa "canon," and they hewed closely to the forms and structures of that repertory. The Bolshoi also produced some newly created Soviet ballets with contemporary settings and current topics. These were largely modeled on nineteenth-century story ballets, and they reiterated Petipa's codified formulas; they also mirrored the balletic collaborations of the Imperial period in which music was subservient to dance. *The Red Poppy*, the most (and only) influential new "Soviet" ballet, was regarded as a "watershed" in the genre for the way it adapted classical dance to revolutionary content.[32] Its story was inspired by contemporary events (as reported in a Soviet newspaper), its forms invoked classical ballet's set pieces (*pas d'action*, *divertissements*, and the like), and its music followed the choreography (often being written after the dance was set) and consisted of newly composed numbers as well as music recycled from other ballets.[33] As Souritz explains, The Red Poppy legitimated classicism as a foundation for Soviet ballet but also demonstrated the limitations of the old forms: "The Red Poppy proved that classical dance had the right to exist, particularly in the form of extended ensembles, complex choreographic structures, and the very form of the 'grand ballet' with divertissements. But the ballet also made it clear that it is impossible to limit dance to a copy of the old, that classical dance had to be enriched."[34]

Around the time that it produced The Red Poppy, the Bolshoi also contemplated bringing Sergei Prokofiev's avant-garde ballet Le pas d'acier to the stage, a Constructivist work that offered a Western view of Soviet modernism.[35] Both the Bolshoi and the Leningrad State Academic Theatre knew of this work, their awareness witnessing to Soviet consciousness of Western innovations. But after interviewing Prokofiev, the Bolshoi's administration deemed his views insufficiently ideological and refused to stage the ballet.[36] As the events illustrated, the theatre's repertory remained conservative, while "new" ballets—and their creators—were increasingly scrutinized for ideological correctness.

The situation in Leningrad was similar, but it also had distinctive emphases due to Lopukhov's influence and the innovative ideas he brought to both "old" and "new" ballets. Like the Bolshoi in Moscow, the Leningrad State Academic Theatre favored the classics. Performance lists recorded the dominance of the Petipa repertoire (and Gorsky's revivals) as well as the presence of Fokine's early works in the Theatre's productions.[37] A handful of new ballets were performed in the early 1920s (like Pavel Petrov's Solveig, 1922) but none entered the permanent repertory. Meanwhile, the Leningrad State Academic Theatre promoted dance experimentation in the work of the Young Ballet, whose performances took place at the Maly Opera Theatre—in other words, not on the city's primary ballet stage. Although the distinction in venue was important, the Young Ballet was supported by the Leningrad State Academic Theatre, which devoted choreographers, dancers, and resources to the experimental enterprises.

Through the 1920s, Lopukhov emerged as the most original choreographic voice in Leningrad. His first years as artistic director at the Leningrad State Academic Theatre were dominated by reviving, restoring, and preserving the "old" ballets. Amid this conservatism, however, Lopukhov's choreographies were notable for their experimentation and stylistic variety and for their illumination of crucial questions about the genre. Reviving the Petipa repertoire, Lopukhov aimed to purify it from the accretions of past productions, his most famous effort in this regard being his revival of *Sleeping Beauty* in 1923. Lopukhov was also interested in modern Russian ballets, especially Stravinsky's. He staged his own choreography of *Firebird* and produced *Pulcinella* and *Le Renard*. At the same time, he explored abstract, plotless ballet, such as his *Dance Symphony: Magnificence of the Universe* (staged at the Maly Theatre by the Young Ballet), which attempted to deal with "pure" dance. This search for the essence of the art form, over its content, was aligned with modernist (soon-to-be-labeled "formalist") impulses of contemporary ballet in the West. Returning to the model of story ballets, Lopukhov experimented with all-new, evening-length works. These used narrative content, which was sometimes political (and symbolic as in *The Red Whirlwind*) and sometimes fantastical (as in *The Ice Maiden* to music of Edvard Grieg). In a sudden and controversial development, Lopukhov returned to the nineteenth-century classics but re-choreographed them, using them as vehicles for new movements. His new choreography of *The Nutcracker* in 1929 fell into this category. The ballet was not well received, but it highlighted the era's twin impulses toward reinventing ballet classicism and innovating new choreographic language.

Lopukhov was deeply interested in new movement and new content, and under his purview a certain amount of balletic experimentation entered the Theatre's repertory. His ballet *The Ice Maiden*, for example, explored novel combinations of classical steps and acrobatic-gymnastic movements drawn from the popular stage. The famous "ring" motif in *The Ice Maiden* emblematized this fusion of balletic and non-balletic movement. As recorded in a famous photograph, the ballerina (Olga Mungalova) stood with her leg curved behind her body, encircling her head in a "ring." An analogous movement had appeared a few years earlier on the popular stage in "Sports Dance," a choreography by the modern dancers Mariya Ponna and Alexandr Kaverzin, who performed together in Leningrad from the early 1920s. Ponna had "stood on [her partner's] shoulders and, grasping the toe of her right leg with her left hand, pulled it up, forming a ring with her body, which closed over her head."[38] Drawing on such non-balletic movements, Lopukhov's fusion of classical steps with acrobatic feats and his responsiveness to ideas from the popular stage signaled the modern classicism of ballet in Leningrad under his aegis.

The Debates

The relation between form and content lay at the heart of this balletic experimentation in the Soviet 1920s. Questions over the future of Soviet dance were rooted in the nature of ballet itself—that is, in the tension inherent to the art form between narrative and poetic expression, between the advancement of drama and the poetry of "pure" dance.[39] These were long-standing questions of the genre, but they emerged in a new form in the Soviet period as aesthetic and political pressures confronted each other. As ideological constraints increasingly demanded messages that could be "read," however, ballet's virtuosic displays, ineffable meanings, or avant-garde movements would find no place in the future of Soviet dance.

The choreographic innovation of the early Soviet period represented an urgency for artistic reform that had begun in the pre-Revolutionary era. As this reform became politicized in the Soviet years, artistic debates in search of modernizing content and forms began to fuse with political questions about revolutionary messages and ideological purity. Ezrahi observes that Soviet ballet in the 1920s was created "in a political environment that questioned the right of ballet to exist and in a professional environment that was uncertain about ballet's future in Soviet Russia."[40] Neither classical models nor modern innovations seemed to offer acceptable directions for Soviet ballet. Critics of classical ballet deemed it overly decorative, while opponents of modern experiments found them insufficiently ideological. The solution—proposed not by the dance professionals but by critics like Sollertinsky and other writers—was "dramatic ballet" (*dramaticheskii balet*) or "choreographic spectacle" (*khoreograficheskii spektakl'*), which rejected classical or "pure" dance in favor of "plot-based pantomime."[41] This kind of ballet in which "dance only illustrated the action" laid the theoretical foundations for the genre of *drambalet*, which would be codified in the next decade.[42]

According to Soviet discourse, the central problem of Soviet ballet was the absence of new ballets on contemporary topics. This "crisis" of repertoire preoccupied the Leningrad State Academic Theatre, and its causes and solutions were fiercely debated in the pages of Leningrad's arts periodicals and in discussions of the Theatre's administrative bodies. A few ballets on revolutionary themes had appeared—like Goleizovsky's *The Whirlwind* in Moscow and Lopukhov's *The Red Whirlwind* in Leningrad—but only *The Red Poppy* remained in the repertoire. Beyond preserving the legacy of Russian ballet, the ballet theatres needed to create a successful model of

Soviet ballet. The question was what this ballet would be like. Artistically, the debate was divided between supporters of classical dance and proponents of dramatizing dance.[43] Ideologically, it centered on the messages that ballet conveyed. The libretto became the main focus of discussion, partly out of a commitment to strengthening ideology through narrative and partly out of a belief that new content would motivate new forms (which were theorized by Sollertinsky and his supporters as dramatized dance).[44] These artistic and political arguments became inextricable from one another in relation to Soviet ballet reform.

By 1929, more than a decade after the Revolution, Leningrad had produced no adequate model for Soviet ballet. To address the situation, the Theatre announced a libretto competition. The rules were drafted by Sollertinsky and called for an evening-length ballet on a contemporary revolutionary topic, to be conveyed not by classical ("abstract") dance but by new movements derived from sports, acrobatics, *fizkultura* (physical culture), and other activities of everyday Soviet life.[45] The winner was "Dinamiada" by Aleksandr Ivanovsky, a screenwriter for Soviet film. It was the scenario that became *The Golden Age*, and Shostakovich was commissioned to write the music.

Shostakovich and Dance

"Balletic Impressions"

Shostakovich's compositional interest in ballet had begun early in his life. His first published work was the set of *Three Fantastic Dances* for solo piano (March, Waltz, Polka, 1920–22), which recorded "balletic impressions" inspired by his younger sister's ballet lessons.[46] Originally published as his "Op. 1" (and later renumbered as Op. 5), the *Fantastic Dances* marked his debut as a composer.[47] Shostakovich programmed the *Dances* regularly on his piano recitals, and as a teenager, he accompanied Mariya Ponna as she interpreted the work in experimental choreography. Ponna was a former swimmer (who also held a record for jumping off Trinity Bridge into the Neva River), but she had become a music hall dancer with an aesthetic style influenced by Isadora Duncan.[48] Contemporary descriptions highlighted her athleticism, plasticity, and power in dancing: "Ponna bends, curls, twists, stretches. She flies into her partner's arms, wraps herself around his neck like a live snake, throws herself and falls to the floor in a bold pose, raises her leg at such a monstrous angle that it seems as if the head of the femur would pop out of the joint and the ligaments not withstand the stress ... All this, however, is ennobled by genuine plasticity and great feeling in the poses, as though almost every position could be reproduced in sculpture."[49]

According to spectators, Ponna's performance of the *Fantastic Dances* was thrilling. She arrived on stage carried aloft on her partner's shoulder, and then danced "in a light tunic, barefoot."[50] On the same program, she also performed choreographies to concert music by Mozart, Schubert, and Rachmaninoff—all accompanied by Shostakovich at the piano.[51] Both Ponna's costume and her inclination to choreograph concert music for solo performance linked her to Duncan's ideas.[52] Her experimental choreographies (usually created for her by her partner Kaverzin) influenced balletic experimentation in Leningrad for much of the 1920s, and resonances of her techniques were soon perceived in acrobatic qualities and sculptural poses on the ballet stage, particularly in Lopukhov's choreography.[53] Her avant-garde dancing could not have failed to impress a sensitive and insightful young composer like Shostakovich. He accompanied her twice for performances of his *Fantastic Dances*.[54]

Through his teenage years, Shostakovich eagerly attended the ballet, taking in both nineteenth-century and contemporary works. His friend Valeryan Bogdanov-Berezovsky (who had briefly accompanied the famous ballerina Olga Spessivtseva in rehearsals) was an important influence in cultivating Shostakovich's balletic experiences.[55] Shostakovich wrote regularly to Bogdanov-Berezovsky and to his girlfriend Glivenko about what he saw, documenting his impressions of classical ballets like *Giselle*, *Sleeping Beauty*, and *Don Quixote* as well as contemporary choreographies by Fokine, Lopukhov, and Petrov. Shostakovich loved Petipa's choreographies above all, finding *Sleeping Beauty* irresistible and admiring Tchaikovsky's score.[56] He was also discerning and appreciative of the dancers. He saw Spessivtseva in one of her final roles as "Giselle" in Russia before her departure for the Paris Opéra in 1924, and he extolled the "miracles" executed by her partner Viktor Semenov.[57] Seeing *Nutcracker*, he marveled at the "fantastic" (*skazachno*) quality of Balanchivadze's dancing, and when away from Leningrad, he urged his sister to follow Balanchivadze's performances and describe them in her letters.[58] Among contemporary choreographers, Shostakovich was not always moved by Petrov's and Fokine's ideas, but he noted Lopukhov's work and attended the choreographer's productions of classical ballets as well as anticipated new choreographies like *The Red Whirlwind*. By 1928,

Shostakovich's and Lopukhov's names appeared among the founding members of a "New Ballet Association," a group whose purpose was to "update" and "improve" the art of ballet by renewing its topics, music, dance, and design.[59] While it is not certain when Shostakovich and Lopukhov first met, they must have done so in these years when Shostakovich, still a student, was both a keen observer and an increasingly insightful critic of ballet.

Shostakovich enjoyed stimulating relationships among Leningrad's intellectuals and artists, and these connections deepened his links to the city's theatrical life and balletic milieu. By far his most important friendship was with Sollertinsky, which began in 1927 and was marked by mutual trust and a shared sense of humor. Sollertinsky expanded the young composer's musical knowledge—most famously by introducing him to the music of Mahler—while Shostakovich impressed his slightly older friend with creative wit and genius. Shostakovich's advancement as a composer for the stage was also supported by Sollertinsky's influence and writings. Sollertinsky published copiously, reviewing performances of Shostakovich's music and reporting on works in progress. As a member of the Artistic Council of the Leningrad State Academic Theatre, Sollertinsky exercised the force of his intellect and personality in shaping discussions and decisions, while his writings laid out the intellectual arguments for new directions in Soviet ballet. In this period, he also began writing a history of the Soviet theatre, whose first volume (published in 1933) charted ballet's development as a Soviet genre.[60] Given their close friendship, Shostakovich must have been aware of the topics occupying so much of Sollertinsky's time and intellectual effort. He was "impressed" by his friend's ideas about ballet, and their professional activities surrounding the genre sometimes aligned.[61] Not only did they serve on the Artistic Council together, but in the late 1920s, they both taught at the Choreographic Institute, where Shostakovich held classes in music theory and Sollertinsky lectured on the history of ballet.[62]

The Ballets

Shostakovich's encounters with ballet through the 1920s were shaped by the performances he saw, the artists he met, the discussions he joined, and the pressures he grasped in relation to Soviet ballet's artistic, dramatic, and political goals. In response to these influences, his own ballets would offer distinct perspectives on the creation of a new Soviet genre, yet all of them would accept the demand that Soviet ballet convey contemporary topics and correct ideology. *The Golden Age* was set in a Western city and presented an ideological conflict between Soviet sportsmen and bourgeois capitalists. *The Bolt* took place in a Soviet factory and celebrated Soviet industry and the power of collective renewal. *The Limpid Stream* was set on a collective farm and offered a snapshot of an idealized society of farmers, city dwellers, and national peoples. While their contemporary topics were important, the subject matter was also superficial, a kind of Soviet costume that dressed up important responses to the artistic questions of ballet reform.[63]

By the time Shostakovich began *The Golden Age* in 1929, he knew a great deal about the ballet repertory in Leningrad, both its emphasis on the classics and its urgency in trying to "Sovietize" ballet. But what none of the existing ballets at the Leningrad State Academic Theatre offered was a clear view of music's or the composer's role in the creation of a new Soviet genre. Each of Shostakovich's ballets would explore different solutions to this problem too as each aimed to navigate both older practices and modern emphases in ballet composition.

The "specialist" music of the nineteenth century (in which scores were "written to order") and the "modernist" model of the early twentieth century (in which "absolute" music permitted a departure from choreographic convention) offered divergent models for Soviet ballet.[64] In the early Soviet period, the "modernist" approach continued in the work of Leningrad's and Moscow's experimental choreographers. Lopukhov advocated "dance symphonism," which aimed for a direct correspondence between music and movement and pointed to the relationship between music and dance as a source of renewal for ballet.[65] He explored this idea in *Dance Symphony*, choreographed to the "absolute" music of Beethoven's Fourth Symphony. Although the ballet was performed just once, Lopukhov's ideas marked an important change in the role of ballet music in the Soviet repertoire; the consequences of his ideas, however, would not be explored deeply until later in the Soviet period.[66] Goleizovsky also valued "good" music but brought to his explorations not the intimate correspondence sought by Lopukhov but the influence of his teacher Fokine. Goleizovsky's evocatively titled *Scriabiana* and *Medtneriana* drew on pre-existing concert repertoire, using "absolute" music as a platform for choreographic innovation. At the same time, Goleizovsky was interested in new music and choreographed newly created scores for *Joseph the Beautiful* and *The Whirlwind*; he also discussed collaborations with Shostakovich on *The Golden Age* and *Stenka Razin*, though no partnership materialized.[67] In contrast to Lopukhov's and Goleizovsky's high view of music, Foregger saw music only as "rhythmical support" to dancing.[68] "Chopin and the drum are of equal value," he declared, as he employed percussion ensembles to accompany works.[69] By the end of the 1920s, however, the "modernist" approach was waning as dance studios closed and modernizing choreographers moved (or were moved) out of influential positions. Lopukhov's ideas had been the most original in the way they probed how musical structures might shape movement, but most experimental choreographies of the period did not innovate new relationships between music and dance.

Through his formative years as a young composer, Shostakovich encountered both "specialist" and "modernist" ballet music, as well as what Soviet critics considered "symphonic" examples from the repertoire. Sollertinsky, Asafyev, and other scholars advocated "symphonism" as a model for Soviet ballet. Although the term was not well defined (despite being much used), the ballet scores of Tchaikovsky and Stravinsky were held up as examples. Shostakovich insisted on a modern view of his score for *The Golden Age*, emphasizing that his music was not subservient to narrative but was intended to drive the dramatic action, and Sollertinsky described the score as "symphonic" for its large-scale forms and passages of profundity.[70] Shostakovich's music for *The Bolt* and *The Limpid Stream* was less complex. Instead of offering an independent, motivating force, as had parts of *The Golden Age*, it inclined toward older practices of ballet composition, in which music served the choreography, clarified the narrative, and sometimes recycled pre-existing music or quoted from (or alluded to) well-known works.

Shostakovich's ballet scores pointed to music's multiple roles in ballet—narrating story, creating setting, supporting dance, motivating movement—and to the composer's grasp of choreographic requirements. But they also highlighted a lack of clarity in the relationship between Soviet composer and choreographer. How would they work together? Whose decisions would take precedence? From what point of view would artistic judgments be made about music and movement? How would tensions between score and choreography be resolved? Shostakovich was forced to wrestle with these questions in each of his ballet scores. The most egregious mishandling of his music, as he deemed it, was in *The Golden Age*, where production decisions relegated his music to a secondary role and sometimes completely ignored the narrative or poetic implications of what he had written. By contrast, the most coherent correspondence between music and stage situations was achieved in *The Limpid Stream*—a score that Shostakovich did not like but on which he collaborated closely with Lopukhov, thereby gaining intimate knowledge of the choreographic and expressive requirements of the dances.

* * *

Shostakovich's path to ballet through the 1920s formed part of his broader compositional journey as a composer for dramatic genres. His collaborations across opera, ballet, stage, and film exposed him to the most cutting-edge ideas in Soviet theatre and cinema, while honing his compositional craft in art and popular styles. Meanwhile, the desire for "good" music was an enormous motivating factor in this period, and Shostakovich's success as a composer of art music lent prestige and significance to his theatrical contributions and brought him new commissions from Leningrad's theatres. Shostakovich accepted the commission for *The Golden Age* at the age of twenty-two and completed all three of his ballets before the age of thirty. The works attested to his grasp of the requirements of the genre as well as the demands of artistic reform and political pressures. None of his ballets would reach the maturity of some of his other works in this period (like the *First Symphony* or *Lady Macbeth*), but they would reveal his creative interests in and solutions for ballet composition. They would also highlight the unstable aesthetic and ideological conditions in which he worked.

Shostakovich created his ballets in a period in which every aspect of theatrical life was disrupted and contested. The repetitive renaming of institutions, the formation and dissolution of administrative structures, the introduction of new audiences and topics, and the swiftly changing reception of works were all factors that both undermined years of tradition and yet often effected remarkably little change. Unlike the later 1930s, in which scrutiny and condemnation were equally capricious yet much more intentional, this period of artistic life was shaped by chaotic uncertainty about what would be tolerated and what would be rejected. The only certainty was that art must align with new political realities *in some way*. In this environment, creative experiments existed in a space bounded by public tastes, institutional inertia, and ideological demands. The pressures were not necessarily in conflict with one another, and were even sometimes aligned, but it was often difficult to untangle in any particular instance how much influence one exerted above another. Like many other works of the period, Shostakovich's ballets illustrated these complexities as they took up long-standing artistic questions while navigating rapidly changing aesthetic and political realities.

2
Petipa's Legacy: *The Golden Age* and Classical Ballet

When Shostakovich received the commission for *The Golden Age*, his career prospects were bright, and he was enjoying a meteoric rise to the upper echelons of Soviet music. His First Symphony was being performed internationally. He was in demand as a composer and collaborator, and he had personal connections to Russia's leading artists in music, opera, theatre, and dance. While Shostakovich's astonishing output as a young composer spanned concert music and dramatic works, he composed for the stage with particular intensity in the late 1920s and early 1930s. Cultivating an interest in ballet, alongside other dramatic forms, he approached the genre initially as an enthusiastic spectator and increasingly as a music professional with meaningful contributions to make. He advised on ballet repertoire and contributed to aesthetic debates surrounding it while serving on the Artistic Council of the Leningrad State Academic Theatre. He also taught briefly at the Choreographic Institute, which prepared young dancers for professional lives on the Soviet stage. *The Golden Age* was a culmination of Shostakovich's balletic experiences and of his broader dramatic interests in his early career. It reflected his first professional experience composing for the genre of ballet, not to mention Leningrad's premiere ballet theatre, and it was a product of the period's many demands of Soviet dance.

The Golden Age premiered at the Leningrad State Academic Theatre on October 26, 1930.[1] Leonid Yakobson, Vasily Vainonen, and Vladimir Chesnakov choreographed the work, and Valentina Khodasevich designed sets and costumes. Audiences were enthusiastic, and some critics hailed the work's choreographic novelty and musical vibrancy.[2] But others wrote devastating reviews condemning the ballet for "bourgeois ideology" and a "strange mixture" of choreographic styles.[3] The ballet had moments of genius, and its score was compelling, but it lacked a unified creative vision. After nineteen performances, it was withdrawn from the repertoire.

Shostakovich's Ballets and the Search for Soviet Dance. Laura E. Kennedy, Oxford University Press.
© Oxford University Press 2025. DOI: 10.1093/9780197698082.003.0003

The *Golden Age* had been widely expected to advance the national endeavor of Soviet ballet by creating a successful model for the genre, but its creation and production exposed an array of challenges for Soviet dance. The problems were acute: Soviet ballet needed robust definition through a viable new repertory. Balletic questions through the 1920s had revolved around how to preserve the classical legacy while modernizing the repertory for the post-Revolutionary period, but no sustainable path of innovation had emerged. Ballet theatres had resisted change, and new balletic experiments had been short-lived. By the end of the 1920s, ballet in Leningrad was the subject of fierce debate. Sollertinsky, who was Shostakovich's friend and mentor and a figure of towering influence at the Leningrad State Academic Theatre, declared classical ballet a "dead, clichéd genre" and advocated "a radical rupture" with the past.[4] Though the language was inflammatory, it expressed a widely held sentiment that the classical repertory was insufficient to sustain the Soviet theatre and that a Soviet repertory had to move away from classicism's supposedly empty virtuosity and decorativeness. The question for the makers of Soviet ballet was how to make ballet "Soviet" and at the same time how to reconcile new choreographic directions with the genre's classical vocabulary. These debates about form, content, and narrative capacity converged in the creation of *The Golden Age*.

Created at the end of the 1920s, *The Golden Age* also captured that era's spirit of experimentation and possibility, as well as a view of modern Soviet culture as linked to, yet distinct from, Western counterparts. Broad cultural themes of the decade celebrated the modern and modernizing elements of Soviet life. During the period of the New Economic Policy (1921–28), Soviet artists and spectators enjoyed relative freedom and relaxed attitudes to cultural expressions. They explored new music, new visual languages, and new types of theatre, while experimenting with avant-garde art forms and contemporary topics. They also watched foreign films, hosted Hollywood stars, imitated Parisian dress fashions, performed jazz, held social dances, and entertained foreign musicians, artists, and dignitaries. By the end of the 1920s, however, Soviet life entered a transitional period as the relative permissiveness of the New Economic Policy was displaced by the factionalism and ambiguities of the Cultural Revolution (1928–32). Cultural products were summoned to participate in a radical shift, designed (in Katerina Clark's words) "to propel the populace to a truly socialist consciousness and way of life."[5] In this environment of crisis and change, *The Golden Age* was both an anticipated answer to urgent questions about Soviet ballet and a potential model of cultural orthodoxies. While illuminating the huge range of artistic options available to Soviet ballet by the end of the 1920s, the work became an example of the increasing constraints on how those options would or could be "read."

The Golden Age suggested the possibility of a new genre—Soviet ballet that engaged the classical legacy while grappling with the challenges of modern directions and the demand for contemporary relevance. It invoked formulas of classical ballet but reinterpreted those formulas in modern terms. Shostakovich's music took up the symphonic models of Tchaikovsky and Glazunov (points noted in the earliest reviews), while stage situations and elements of design critiqued images of the classical ballerina. Meanwhile, jazz idioms, ballroom dances, and sports themes juxtaposed everyday elements of modern Soviet life against the elevated grandeur of ballet's classical past. By subverting tropes of the Imperial and the Soviet periods, The Golden Age used the classical past as a source of inspiration but also signaled ideological orthodoxy: it attempted to preserve the legacy without being tainted by it.

Three narrative threads intersect in the creative history of The Golden Age. First, the story of the work's genesis and production illuminates the myriad pressures on ballet production at the Leningrad State Academic Theatre and also suggests something of Shostakovich's own expectations about the process of creating a ballet. Second, the surviving musical, dramatic, and choreographic elements of The Golden Age document the work's classical and modern interests, as well as the way these interests were situated within ideological parameters. Third, the reception of The Golden Age illuminated a complex historical and artistic situation in 1930 in which the creative urgency to "Sovietize" art seemed briefly to advance—but would ultimately be stymied by—progressive cultural pressures. Tracing this network of relationships, this chapter shows how The Golden Age aimed to solve pressing balletic questions while offering a model of modern Soviet classicism—a reinvention that paid homage to the past while maintaining currency with the political and artistic directions of the Soviet present.

The Production of 1930

The production of The Golden Age at the Leningrad State Academic Theatre in 1930 was a debacle. Practical challenges in administrating a newly restructured institution accounted for some of the disorganization, but much of the instability arose out of artistic questions about innovations in dance as well as increasing ideological scrutiny of the ballet repertoire, including how it was created and what messages it conveyed. At the same time, the libretto for *The Golden Age* was weak—a fact acknowledged when it was chosen—and it kept changing, making it difficult for any composer to know what to do. Shostakovich was commissioned to compose the music but found himself with no one to consult about what dances he was supposed to write. Meanwhile, infighting and power plays within the Theatre threatened to derail the ballet. No experienced choreographer would agree to take it on, let alone remedy it as it began to fall apart. The premiere was delayed for months. Multiple choreographers became involved, but nobody appeared to be in charge of making or implementing artistic decisions. Amid the chaos, Shostakovich's score was used in ways that he never envisioned; at times the production made nonsense of it. *The Golden Age* revealed artistic, practical, and ideological challenges that affected not only what the ballet was about but also how the creative team worked together (or failed to do so). The story of its production was one of scheming, factionalism, mismanagement, and revolt as members of the Leningrad State Academic Theatre sought solutions for Soviet dance while advancing their own personal and artistic agendas.

The Golden Age was born from a libretto competition in 1929 that called for ballet librettos on revolutionary topics. Announced by the Leningrad State Academic Theatre, the contest was meant to catalyze viable answers to long-standing questions about what Soviet ballet should be. The purveyors of the competition hoped to generate new topics (new content) that would prompt new approaches to dance (new forms), thus transforming the genre of classical ballet by marrying it to contemporary subject matter. Elizabeth Stern's account of the competition is particularly illuminating because it examines minutes from administrative meetings at the Leningrad State Academic Theatre. These records illuminate the competition's aesthetic and political conditions as well as Sollertinsky's role.[6]

The intended outcome of the competition was not simply a ballet with a Soviet story, but a new type of Soviet ballet itself. Yet libretto submissions proved weak—in fact, most were panned for having "no plot development and nothing interesting," for offering "fantasy in the style of Jules Verne," for being "difficult to stage," full of "absurdities," and "not even worth considering"—and reviewers grouched that they could have written better scenarios themselves.[7] Eventually, but unenthusiastically, "Dinamiada" by the screenwriter Aleksandr Ivanovsky was selected as the winner, and

Shostakovich was commissioned to write the music. No other members of the creative team were yet confirmed. Work on "Dinamiada" (soon renamed *The Golden Age*) began with a feeble libretto and only a brilliant composer who had never completed a ballet score.

Shostakovich was quickly dispatched to Moscow to persuade Kasyan Goleizovsky to stage the new ballet. But the renowned choreographer declined, suggesting instead that he and Shostakovich collaborate on a different project. Intrigued, Shostakovich wrote to Zakhar Lyubinsky, then director of Academic Theatres in Leningrad, and asked him to replace "Dinamiada" with two ballets of Goleizovsky—*Joseph the Beautiful*, which the choreographer had already produced with his experimental Chamber Ballet, and *Moral'*, for which Shostakovich was keen to write the music.[8] But, Shostakovich emphasized, if he ought to continue with "Dinamiada," he needed to know with whom to collaborate.[9] While nothing came of his request to change ballets, the correspondence revealed how little had been decided about "Dinamiada." It also indicated Shostakovich's expectation of working with a major choreographer at the forefront of experimental ideas. Unresolved by the meeting with Goleizovsky, Shostakovich's circumstances at the outset of his first ballet project foreshadowed the independence and creative isolation in which he would be forced to approach the score.

After Goleizovsky rejected "Dinamiada," the libretto was given to the dancer and choreographer Aleksandr Chekrygin in Leningrad. By the late 1920s, Chekrygin was known for highly successful productions of Western operas and operettas at the Maly Opera Theatre. But he was not known for successful ballets. Despite his pedigree in classical dance, including experience as Nicholai Sergeyev's assistant, Chekrygin had suffered a string of choreographic failures at the Leningrad State Academic Theatre. Souritz comments that he was "drawn towards sharp, sometimes grotesque forms" and that "his talent as a director" appeared in genres (like those at the Maly) that depended on "European revue, jazz, and eccentric dance forms."[10] How much Chekrygin contributed to *The Golden Age* is unclear, but the fact that he was invited to work on it—and that he remained involved in the production for months—suggests that his reworking of classical dance and his expertise in the "light genre" were consonant with the goals of the new ballet.

No single choreographer was ever in charge of *The Golden Age*, a situation that was driven partly by ideology and partly by infighting, and that endlessly frustrated Shostakovich.[11] Through the 1920s, ideological commitment had elevated the notion of "collective choreography" as an ideal of

Soviet ballet. Leningrad's weekly publication *Rabochii i teatr* (*Worker and Theatre*) recorded many such collective approaches and promoted the practice to the public.[12] Some new ballets, like *The Red Poppy* (first produced at the Bolshoi), involved multiple choreographers, while new productions of "old" ballets were sometimes divided up and acts distributed among different choreographers. The choreography of *The Golden Age* was intended as a similar collective effort, and the press regularly updated readers on which choreographers were expected to contribute.

Unfortunately, the names kept changing. On December 8, 1929, for example, *Zhizn' iskusstva* announced Lopukhov and Chekrygin as "balletmasters" for *The Golden Age* (then still "Dinamiada"), Emmanuil Kaplan as *regisseur*, and Aleksei Ermolayev, Vakhtang Chabukiani, and Yakobson as "co-directors from the ballet youth."[13] But within a fortnight, Lopukhov refused to work on the ballet, and a meeting of the Theatre Directorate was called. Without luminaries like Lopukhov or Goleizovsky, the directorate decided to assign the ballet to young choreographers only—now selected as Yakobson, Vainonen, and Chesnakov—and to depend on Lopukhov's mentorship of them. The list of participating choreographers continued to shift for months, with new names added and others dropped, and Lopukhov declined any responsibility for the production.[14] Ultimately, Vainonen and Yakobson choreographed most of the ballet while Chesnakov contributed a single dance.[15]

Shostakovich was deeply unhappy with the situation and wrote to Lyubinsky in February 1930 insisting that the collective assigned to *The Golden Age* was "unable to cope" with his ballet and that the production "[could] only be carried out by the distinguished balletmaster Lopukhov."[16] Given Lopukhov's refusal to stage the work, the composer demanded an end to the production along with the return of his score and the termination of his contract. Instead of granting his requests, however, the Theatre pressed ahead and the situation continued to deteriorate. Rival factions developed around Lopukhov and Kaplan. Shostakovich refused to work with Kaplan. Lopukhov disparaged Kaplan's dramatic understanding of ballet.[17] But Lopukhov was in turn accused of undermining the young choreographers and of exploiting the situation in order to get "the production handed over to him."[18] (Stern suggests that Lopukhov was not only being blamed for failings in *The Golden Age* but that his enemies within the Theatre saw the situation as an opportunity to get rid of him.[19]) The director of the ballet troupe was particularly incensed about the "abnormal conditions" for his dancers, and many members of the company complained in person to the Artistic Council.

By May 1930—almost a year after he had accepted the commission and six months since he had completed the score—Shostakovich was furious. Abandoning his earlier opinion of Kaplan, he endorsed the *regisseur*'s efforts, along with Vainonen's, calling them "heroes" for "working in such an atmosphere."[20] But he was outraged at the theatre's power plays and disorganization, at the "completely unbelievable accusations" against members of the creative team, and at the Artistic Council's inept leadership.[21] In a statement to the Council, he fumed: "I am taking back my score and there can be no discussion whatsoever of my further work at the former imperial ballet—I stress *imperial* ballet."[22] For Shostakovich, the production of *The Golden Age* had all the hallmarks of the worst abuses of theatrical life. Instead of reflecting Soviet reforms, his ballet had been derailed by petty jealousies, personal agendas, self-serving activism, and bureaucratic mismanagement. He never got his score back (to this day, half of it remains in the Mariinsky Music Library). Instead, after months of delays and difficulties, *The Golden Age* premiered, and was withdrawn, in a single season.

The situation surrounding the production of *The Golden Age* would have been challenging for an experienced ballet composer; it was clearly vexing for a young composer who was writing a ballet for the first time. Whatever his talents or his confidence, Shostakovich wanted input on his first ballet, and his letters to the administration of the Leningrad State Academic Theatre documented his requests for guidance and his frustrations. Shostakovich's expectations for the process of creating a ballet probably arose from practices he observed at the Theatre and perhaps from what he knew of the nineteenth-century ballet repertoire, as well as from his own recent collaborations in film (*The New Babylon*) and stage plays (*The Bedbug*) where he worked closely with critically acclaimed directors. However his expectations were shaped, they were clearly unmet in the creation of *The Golden Age*. He enjoyed little, if any, guidance or collaboration as he composed. He struggled to get basic information about the dances. His concerns over the rehearsal team—some of whom, he pointed out, lacked experience in ballet and even in the basics of running a rehearsal—went unheeded. His insistence on experienced professional involvement achieved nothing. And his attempts to withdraw his score were thwarted.

An important consequence of this breakdown in communication was that the score and the libretto for *The Golden Age* never truly matched. As Daniil

Petrov, a contributing editor to the *New Collected Works* edition, comments, the ballet's scenario was "constantly being elaborated and even thoroughly revised," and "there was never a full music text of the ballet that entirely corresponded to the original version of the libretto."[23] In other words, there was no early score based on the original libretto, nor was Shostakovich's final score based entirely on the published libretto. When the scenario changed, his music was recycled, and at times he was forced to write new dances without an updated scenario from which to work. During the production process, he also saw his music rearranged, used, and interpolated into new stage situations in ways over which he had no control. His music was used inexpertly and naively, as though it could be recycled to any choreographic purpose. Some infelicities between score and stage arose because the scenario was not worked out at the beginning and kept changing as Shostakovich composed, but many were connected to the production process, after the score was finished and out of Shostakovich's hands. *The Golden Age* was arranged out of the work that Shostakovich imagined he was composing into the work that eventually appeared on stage.

While the "specialist" composers of ballet's past might not have been surprised at the situation, Shostakovich complained repeatedly about a superficial approach to his music and a tendency to "take liberties" in production.[24] His frustration was not just over a cavalier attitude to ballet music but over a misunderstanding and misappropriation of aesthetic goals. He had completed his score a year before *The Golden Age* reached the stage and well before the choreographic team was finalized. His relative independence (and isolation) in the compositional process created the circumstances in which he produced a musically cohesive score free from interference or external demands. His vexation then grew at what he saw as a fractured realization of his creative concept. Shostakovich was deeply frustrated with the production of *The Golden Age*, and his professional relationship with the Leningrad State Academic Theatre grew tense.

Soviet "Classical" Ballet

Despite the fraught production that undermined artistic cohesion in *The Golden Age*, components of music, dance, and design continued to illuminate the work's creative resources and showed how Shostakovich and his fellow artists aimed to fashion this Soviet ballet. *The Golden Age* opens at an industrial exhibition in a Western capitalist city, where "Fascists" (bourgeois visitors) parade ostentatiously while the Soviet soccer team attends unobtrusively. Diva, the favorite dancer of the decadent crowd, arrives at the exhibition's music hall and dances for her admirers. She tries to flirt with the Soviet Soccer Captain, but he politely refuses her advances. Outraged at the perceived slight, provocateurs slip incriminating documents into his pocket, and he is arrested. Sports games begin at a workers' stadium; the centerpiece is a soccer match. But when two characters rush in to tell the Soviet team what has happened to their Captain, the sportsmen leave the stadium. A scene at the music hall ensues. Diva dances with the leader of the Fascists, who is now disguised as the Soviet Soccer Captain, but Western workers and Soviet sportsmen expose the farce and the Fascists flee. The ballet ends with a dance of the Western and Soviet workers.

The Golden Age was meant to be funny—and its libretto was certainly silly—but the humor was embedded within a serious test of the genre's capacity for artistic innovation and political content. The libretto of *The Golden Age* was ideologically correct; it advanced a message of class conflict and moral bankruptcy, even if those topics were blatant to the point of farce. The theme was timeless—two opposing forces signified good and evil, or virtue and vice—but the moralities were political: virtue was proletarian (and Soviet) and vice was bourgeois. A fundamental tension emerged, however, between the ideological requirement (to advance a political message) and the need for artistic invention (to evolve the genre of ballet). The goals were meant to be synchronous, and sometimes they aligned—for example, in the ballet's designs, which visually distinguished characters and their politics. But at other times, the disparate impulses made strange bedfellows as each aesthetic component was expected to convey ideological distinctions. What was at stake in *The Golden Age* was ballet's ability to "perform" Soviet themes.

The visual components of *The Golden Age* successfully served up the ballet's moralities with images of decadence, hypocrisy, and self-indulgence for bourgeois characters but modesty and restraint for proletarian figures. In Khodasevich's costume sketches, bourgeois characters are sumptuously, but often scantily, clad. A sketch of Diva's costume reveals the ballerina in next to nothing, her bikini leaving little to the imagination. A photograph of the ballerina Olga Yordan in this costume shows that she was not quite as exposed as Khodasevich's drawing suggests—her top is a bandeau and her skirt is opaque—yet the outfit is the scantiest in the ballet. In another photograph Diva (Yordan) wears a sparkling flapper dress, whose sequins, beaded cascades, and feathered plumes convey the voluptuous pleasures of the 1920s. Her admirers are ostentatiously dressed too, like the Mime Artists in black velvet tops, tiered skirts, rosettes, and glamorous hats. These characters are cosmopolitan, wearing clothes that reject utility and nationality. Other costumes ridicule religion; the ballerina's outfit for the "Tango" (Act III), for example, consists of a black cross suggestively (and only) covering her intimate parts, while she carries a rosary as a fashion accessory. Still other costumes critique the tropes of the nineteenth-century ballerina: pointe shoes; the implication of a tutu; high, elegant hair; an open, elongated pose. One such design shows a ballerina inside a hat box, tied up with bows as though she is a present.[25] But she is both constrained and absurd. She cannot move properly in such a costume; she is a decoration at best, an object of voyeurism at worst.

Soviet characters, by contrast, wear simple clothes in everyday styles with red stars that distinguish their politics and their nationality. Khodasevich's design for the female soloists in "Soviet Dance" features a knee-length, A-line dress with black-and-white panels, red trim, red accessories, and a red kerchief tied behind the head in a sign of revolutionary commitment.[26] The traditional style and simple elements reject eroticism, pretension, and cosmopolitanism. Similarly, sportswomen dress in practical clothing suited to their activities and roles. One sketch shows a green-and-white outfit for seven sportswomen. (The color scheme is identical to the palette of the hat-box costume, inviting the viewer to juxtapose strongly contrasting perspectives on the female image.) These sports ballerinas are no gifts to be gawked at, like the ballerina in a box. They are strong, sensible, and contemporary—part of a team. Such costumes are simple and functional, obliterating difference and reinforcing images of decency, unity, and collective identity.

Shostakovich explained that his score participated in this blunt characterization by musically juxtaposing the "unhealthy eroticism" of bourgeois culture with the "healthy calisthenics and sports" of a classless society.[27] Popular musical styles denoted Western characters through ballroom and music hall numbers, while "proletarian" music (without these Western-inflected idioms) accompanied Soviet characters. Shostakovich's explanation rationalized his use of popular musical idioms, but it also belied the actual complexity of his score as well as the variety of narrative and expressive purposes that his music served. The practice of creating soundscapes—that is, sound imagery whose qualities suggest a characteristic setting and its attributes—was well established in ballet music and had been explored extensively and inventively in Tchaikovsky's ballet scores. Meanwhile, the use of popular Western dance forms on the stage aligned with contemporary practices in Soviet theatre, where music hall styles were often codes for satire. Shostakovich's score reflected musical-dramatic precedents, while nudging viewers toward political interpretations.

The topics of *The Golden Age* are disparate, sometimes confusing, and easily dismissed because of the facile ideology within which they are packaged, but they are important because they illuminate what was permissible and possible in Soviet ballet at the end of the 1920s. *The Golden Age* includes references to nineteenth-century classical ballet, to sports, and to popular (music hall) dancing. Acts I and III depict bourgeois lifestyles and make significant references to the repertoire of classical ballet, a fact that suggests how dependent the "new" ballet was on the "old" repertoire. At the same time, the use of the "old" is ideologically permissible in these acts because it is connected to modern bourgeois activities (like ballroom dancing). Act II takes up the topic of sports. The theme mirrored contemporary cultural discourse that elevated sports as a product of the *fizkultura* (physical culture) movement and as a means of social and personal transformation. The pastiche of elements in *The Golden Age*—including the multivalent references yet blunt politicization—spoke to the complex demands on this ballet. The work faced the pressure of ideologically driven content, the tension of "old" and "new" balletic components, and the complexity of fusing elements of the past with images of the present.

Each act of *The Golden Age* addresses these tensions differently. Act I reinterprets formulas of classical ballet by incorporating but disguising Petipa's codified forms. Act II examines sports as a metaphor for Soviet values, and Act III deals with images of the modern age conveyed in a *divertissement* of dances. Of course, "old" and "new," or classical and modern, elements are not discrete from each other but intertwined. The *divertissement* in Act III, for example, transforms a nineteenth-century formula with twentieth-century ballroom dances. While recognizing the interwoven themes throughout the ballet, the ensuing discussion takes up the acts in order, for the sake of narrative coherence, and aims to illuminate the ballet's perspectives on classicism and modernity.

Act I: Ballet Classicism

Act I opens with a confrontation between Fascists and Soviets at "The Golden Age" exhibition. Civic authorities, bourgeois visitors, entertainers, and Fascists mingle with local workers and the Soviet soccer team, but a series of entertainments—including a racist boxing match whose outcome is fixed by a bribe—reveals the moral gulf between the bourgeoisie and the proletariat. Events polarize the two groups, and the police intervene as social unrest erupts. The next scene is set in a music hall, where the "golden youth" dance a foxtrot as they await Diva. Their favorite enters to widespread admiration, "men eagerly kissing her hand" and "women admiring her toilette" before she dances for her admirers.[28] When the Soviet football team arrives, Diva is fascinated with its Captain but cannot interest him. The Fascists are incensed. As conflict is about to break out, the Soviet Captain raises his team's soccer ball in a sign of collective commitment to a higher and healthier cause, but in hysteria the Fascists take it for a bomb and collapse in terror, at which absurdity the Captain and his team leave the situation with quiet dignity. The act ends with a foxtrot-fugue in which the bourgeoisie expend their emotions in frenzied dancing. The ideological conflict is ridiculously caricatured, but the musical force of this act is far more complex than the scenario suggests.

Diva's arrival in Scene 2 features the first important sequence for the prima ballerina, a *pas d'action* that offers one of the ballet's most profound and aesthetically unified passages. The stage situation, the choreographic conventions, and the music invoke the Petipa repertoire with a subtlety that suggests dependency on and homage to the classical past. While the scene relies on a codified form (the *pas d'action*) from classical ballet, however, the references are disguised. Dances are infused with new movements, important dances belong to the "wrong" characters, and the music de-familiarizes the dance procedures. The classical conventions are undoubtedly practical, building on centuries of choreographic vocabulary, but their presence is "justified" by ideology that links "classicism" to "bourgeois" entertainment. In other words, only Diva as a bourgeois character dances what a classical ballerina would dance.

The standard components of a *pas d'action* are an *entrée*, *Adagio*, variation, and coda. Diva enters to important introductory music (*entrée*) and then dances a supported *Adagio*, a variation, and a *pas de deux* with her partner (the Fascist) that ends with a coda for *corps de ballet* (Table 2.1). The arrival

Table 2.1 The *pas d'action* embedded in Act I, Scene 2.[29]

Act I, Scene 2	Components of the *pas d'action*
No. 8: Dance of the "Golden Youth"	*Entrée* (piccolo clarinet from R115)
No. 9: Dance of Diva (*Adagio*)	*Adagio*
No. 10: Appearance of the Soviet Football [soccer] Team and Diva's Variation	*Variation* (at R145)
No. 11: Soviet Dance	
No. 12: Diva Asks the Leader of the Soviet Team to Dance with Her	
No. 13: Dance of Diva and the Fascist & Scene	*Pas de deux* Coda (at R180)

of the Soviet soccer team, followed by the "Soviet Dance," provides the dramatic link between Diva's presentation (*entrée* and *Adagio*) and her virtuosic display (variation and *pas de deux* with coda) designed to attract the attention of the Soviet Captain. Dances for *corps de ballet*, arranged around the *pas d'action*, confirm the classical formula.

While the components of a *pas d'action* are embedded in the scene, they are wittily masked. Diva arrives on stage (*entrée*) to the accompaniment of trombone slides and a saxophone solo—instruments that the Soviets associated with jazz in the 1920s.[30] The piccolo clarinet takes up a virtuosic solo featuring scalar runs in 32nd-notes, followed by spiky leaps at half speed that are reminiscent of the ballerina's pointe work. A piccolo flute echoes the runs before the piccolo clarinet returns to end the section with cadenza-like flourishes. In the Petipa repertoire, the introduction to the *Adagio* was conveyed almost exclusively by the harp, and Shostakovich certainly knew this. Giving the passage to the piccolo clarinet, as he did here, distorts both the classical formula and the character. As the beloved dancer of the Fascists, Diva is the "wrong" character to have this music, and the sardonic quality of the solo instruments (which Shostakovich used to parodistic effect in other works too) underscores the irony.

Diva's *Adagio* then opens with a long-breathed melody in the soprano saxophone over simple chords in the bass. The saxophone enters with a sustained note, then sweeps upward into a lyrical melody to launch Diva's dance. The music observes the characteristic formula of a classical *Adagio* (clear rhythm, thin texture, prominent melody line), but the sound of the saxophone entirely alters the color and character of the dance. The instrument associates Diva with jazz while the languorous quality of the music characterizes her as seductive and sensual. By the late 1920s, jazz was considered "bourgeois eroticism" in Soviet Russia, and many purveyors of culture viewed the saxophone with particular suspicion; some even wanted to ban it.[31] In this context, the use of the saxophone in Diva's *Adagio* was provocative for its sound, idiom, and associations. By all accounts, the choreography reinforced the subversive connotations. Soviet sources reported a fusion of "classical techniques" with "salon dances" and "typical foxtrot" gestures.[32] The description suggests a classical dance subverted with non-balletic movements, a mixture of art and popular idioms that parallels the intimations of the music.

Amid the obvious modernity, Diva's *Adagio* contains the ballet's most significant classical reference—an allusion to the "Rose Adagio" of *The Sleeping Beauty*, an association that recalls the splendor of Princess Aurora only to reveal the seductive glamor of the modern Diva. The classical reference is established in two ways. First, the choreographic situations for the two *Adagios* are similar: the prima ballerina is introduced to a circle of admirers, which include potential suitors, none of whom is the ballerina's real interest. Second, Shostakovich's music for Diva evokes Tchaikovsky's for Aurora. Both *Adagios* are introduced by *entrées* with solo cadenza-like passages (for harp in *The Sleeping Beauty* and for piccolo clarinet in *The Golden Age*) ending on a B-flat dominant 7th chord. Both are in E-flat major. Both are in four (12/8 and 4/4). Both begin with almost the same accompaniment gesture—a rising, arpeggiated E-flat triad—and both sequence two repetitions of it. The melodies in both variations then begin on the downbeat, with a sustained note, before departing in different directions on beat 3. Clearly, there are differences too. The melody in *The Sleeping Beauty* is played in grand gestures by the strings and falls through a 7th in the first bar; the melody in *The Golden Age* emerges in the solo saxophone and rises through an octave. However, the placement, preparation, key, meter, accompaniment, seriousness of presentation, and, above all, the strong vocality of the melody lines create a strikingly similar effect. Shostakovich's Diva is an Aurora for the Jazz Age.

The allusion to the "Rose Adagio" is brief, but it sets the serious tone of Diva's *Adagio*, a quality that is sustained through a ten-minute form. Sollertinsky singled out this dance for praise, calling it "beautiful," "profound," and "symphonic."[33] It was for music such as this that he saluted

Shostakovich as the next Russian ballet composer, deserving of the mantle of Tchaikovsky and Stravinsky. Lest audiences be seduced by her character, however, the libretto instructed them to see Diva's dances as "erotic," and Soviet writers assured readers that no one was meant to "admire" the dances but rather to understand their "sarcastic attitude."[34] Yet it is hard to wring ridicule out of the elegiac tone of Diva's music. Whatever the silliness of the scenario, there is nothing frivolous about Shostakovich's presentation of Diva. Her *Adagio* is without question the apex of the dramatic and poetic writing in the ballet.

Diva is morally bankrupt, however, and her character is elaborated through the rest of her *pas d'action*. Her Variation (No. 10, from R145) recalls the harmony and timbre of the *entrée*. Like the introductory music, it implies the key of G minor, features spiky woodwind solos and sweeping 32nd-note gestures in the piccolo, and includes a near-quote of the *entrée*'s cadenza-like ending.[35] Although the Variation is metrically regular, as it must be for dancing, it sounds unpredictable due to wide leaps, changing solo instruments, and abrupt shifts in timbre and tempo. The musical portrait suggests an erratic, fickle, yet captivating character. After an ensemble dance for the Soviet Team (No. 11) and a short exchange possibly in pantomime (No. 12), the *pas de deux* for Diva and her partner (No. 13) seemingly returns to the sincerity of the *Adagio*. The restrained tempo, thin textures, color changes, and carefully chosen sonorities of the solo instruments—clarinet and English horn at the beginning, followed by *obbligato* parts for flute, oboe, saxophone, and solo violin—project emotional intimacy. But a brash coda interrupts (R180), undermining any presumption of emotional depth, and closes the *pas d'action* with a scene of revelry. Diva's *pas d'action* in Act I is a revelation of her character. She is sensual, erotic, winsome, capricious, unstable, and almost irresistible (except to an upstanding Soviet sportsman). Moreover, hers is the only role in the ballet that is characterized in such a sustained and multi-dimensional fashion, the complexity being conveyed entirely in Shostakovich's music.

Diva's presentation in Scene 2 reinforced the centrality of classicism in Soviet ballet, but it also highlighted a desire to disguise and update the classical model. The scene joined elements of the academic classical past to modern sounds and movements, a conjunction in which both past and present were reinterpreted yet both were given a place in Soviet ballet. Classicism appeared in the codified forms of the nineteenth century and in allusion to the Tchaikovsky/Petipa repertoire. Modernity was evident in the contemporary topic, setting, costumes, and sounds. The intertwined classical and modern elements created a collage of ideas overlaid with reductive ideological explanations. In fusing classical forms with modern steps and Soviet messages, this scene explored how to align the demands of the genre—that is, to reconcile classical technique and dramatic expression— with the ideological requirements of the Soviet context, in which art was expected to advance political "realities."

While Act I contained *The Golden Age*'s most sustained exploration of "Soviet" classical ballet, it was also the least cohesive act in the work and the least understood by contemporary audiences. Shostakovich blamed "oversophisticated" dances for spectators' muted reactions.[36] Yet another difficulty was surely the range of relationships between music and stage situations. At times the music strongly correlated with what took place on the stage, as in the *pas d'action* of Scene 2. In such passages, the music narrated with a descriptive power that illuminated what was relevant to the stage moment and what meanings were advanced. At other times, however, score and stage action did not align. Music written for one purpose was recycled to another and, in the change, lost any descriptive relevance. This was especially true of dances in Scene 1 (see Appendix A). Act I contained some of the most successful as well as some of the most egregious examples of "Sovietized" classicism. The difference between the best and the worst dramatic moments depended on the approach to Shostakovich's music—whether it was used for the purpose for which it was written (like Diva's *pas d'action*), or whether it was wrested to altered stage situations over which the composer had no control (like many dances in Scene 1).

Act II: Sports

Act II shifts from bourgeois topics to the theme of sports. The libretto describes a wafer-thin plot revolving around the unlawful arrest of the Soviet Soccer Captain (Scene 3). Between his detention at the beginning of the act and the disclosure to the Soviet team at the end, nothing "dramatic"—or plot-based—happens. Instead, Act II focuses on sporting contests and performances (Scene 4), among which the central event (one dance) is a soccer game. An ever-present connotation in the libretto urges the audience to find decadence in individualism but decency in collective (team) work.

The topic of sports in this act intersected with contemporary emphases in ballet both in Russia and abroad. A fashion for sports was common in ballet in the 1920s, not only because the theme was eminently suitable for adaptation to the stage but also because it had the potential to generate new forms of dance. At the same time, sports emblematized modernity, and sporting activities occupied a place in the everyday life of modern societies. Yet the topic of sports operated differently in Western and Soviet ballet. In the Western repertoire, as Garafola has explained, sports and physical culture were "rife with suggestions of privilege."[37] The tennis game in *Jeux*, the acrobats in *Parade*, the roller rink in *Skating-Rink*, the athletes in *Les biches*, or the vignettes of tennis, golf, acrobatics, and bathing in *Le train bleu* projected an "aura of chic modernity."[38] Sports were an important theme of the "lifestyle modernism" that preoccupied Western ballet in the 1920s.[39]

In Soviet repertoire of the same period, artistic representations of sports were usually associated with the avant-garde. Many experimental Soviet choreographies incorporated sports and related physical activities like gymnastics and acrobatics. New movements derived from sporting activities offered fresh choreographic vocabulary by simplifying "'outdated' classicism" or by stylizing portrayals.[40] Lopukhov's *The Red Whirlwind* included gymnastic exercises reminiscent of Dalcroze movements, while his stagings of *Le Renard* and *The Ice Maiden* featured acrobatic combinations, as did some of Goleizovsky's contemporary ballets like *Whirlwind*.[41] Other avant-garde explorations included Meyerhold's plays, particularly his biomechanics with principles derived from acrobatics and sports.[42] Meanwhile, the topic of sports appeared regularly in the Soviet visual arts, catalyzing Constructivist experiments in painting as well as new trends in fashion, textile, and even household designs.[43]

While Soviet sporting themes served a practical purpose in updating artistic vocabularies, they also carried ideological goals. In his extensive studies of sports in visual culture, Mike O'Mahony explains that sports in Soviet society reflected the *fizkultura* movement emblematizing "civic duty" and the transformation of the "Soviet New Person."[44] Sports were not the province of a bourgeois elite but an activity in which every Soviet person participated and through which "Soviet" values of "discipline, teamwork, honesty, and patriotism" were demonstrated.[45] The Soviet state mounted both competitive sports (games) and theatrical events (sporting parades), making sports a ubiquitous element of the modern Soviet experience and promoting them as a practice and a product of Soviet culture.[46] The materials and objects of Soviet sports became central to depictions of new Soviet realities—and moralities—not only in the stadium but also on the stage.

Several Soviet ballets took up sports themes, and a number of these works explored the topic of soccer specifically. Soccer was the Soviets' favorite sport; games drew huge crowds, and the soccer jersey became a symbol of modernity for Soviet youth.[47] In 1924, a "mass dance" on soccer was staged at the Moscow Choreographic School. A few years later, Asaf Messerer's experimental solo "The Soccer Player" (1929) earned him the sobriquet "the Chaliapin of ballet."[48] In 1930, the ballet *Futbolist* (The Soccer Player), a full-length work by Igor Moiseyev and Aleksandr Tsfasman to a libretto by Viktor Kurdyurov, was staged at the Bolshoi Theatre. It was an exact contemporary of *The Golden Age*, and the librettos are so similar—sports games, a soccer match, class conflict, bourgeois consumerism, a Dandy and a Lady, the Lady's attempted seduction of an upstanding Soccer Player—that one wonders who plagiarized whom.[49] In any case, the topic of sports in *The Golden Age*, with a soccer game at the central point, was not only contemporary for the Soviet stage; it was also an opportunity to theatricalize a national obsession.

The Golden Age was one work to participate in a wave of artistic responses that took up sports as a symbol of Soviet modernity and cultural transformation. The ballet's original title "Dinamiada" emphasized its sporting credentials and almost certainly evoked contemporary associations, like the Dynamo Stadium (the massive sports stadium built in Moscow in 1928) and the Dinamo Moscow soccer club (which made the Stadium its home).[50] Meanwhile, the activities of Act II would have resonated with recent events like the First Workers' Spartakiad, an international sporting event hosted at Dynamo Stadium in 1928. Designed as a Soviet alternative to the Olympics, the Spartakiad recruited international competitors—including soccer teams from England and Uruguay who were ultimately eclipsed by a winning Soviet team—and a plethora of visual culture produced during and after the games promoted the variety and superiority of Soviet sports.[51] The first Spartakiad marked a "watershed" in how Soviet sporting activity was officially cultivated and represented, and the games catalyzed artistic representations of *fizkultura* topics in Soviet life.[52] Resonances in "Dinamiada" would have been hard to miss.

While the soccer subject is the best-known element of *The Golden Age*, a wide range of sports were on display in Act II, and the effect must have been visually and choreographically breathtaking. The libretto lists "boxing, discus-throwing, tennis, fencing, volleyball, basketball, javelin-throwing, and shot put."[53] Meanwhile, a marvelous range of sketches includes costumes for these sports plus more like skiing, ice-skating, swimming, soccer, biking, race-walking, motorcycling, and *fizkultura* activities. Act II features sports contests and a sports procession, showcasing the competitive and performative nature of sports. Unlike other examples of sports in Soviet ballet, the topic was not treated satirically (as soccer was in the "modern exaggerated hobby" of *Futbolist*[54]), nor did sports-derived movements simply update choreographic language and stylize character (though, of course, they did that too) as in the Lopukhov repertoire. Rather, *The Golden Age* displayed a panoply of sporting activities, presenting sports for participant and spectator, competitor and performer, in line with the competitive and theatrical emphases of Soviet politics.

The sports scene was choreographed by Yakobson and operated as plotless ballet.[55] Yuri Broderson, one of the ballet's sharpest critics, berated Yakobson for this "plotless dance," while reluctantly commending the choreographer for "fresh" and "technically sophisticated" ideas.[56] Photographs from rehearsals record some of Yakobson's concepts.[57] In one image, Galina Ulanova appears in a stunning gymnastic pose, executing a backbend from Konstantin Sergeyev's stomach. In a second photograph, Ulanova and another ballerina are suspended between the knees of male dancers, while arms and legs extend in sharp, straight lines. In a third picture, Ulanova stands rigid, feet flat and parallel with arms outstretched, as four male dancers surround her on bended knee, their arms again in straight lines. Based on these photographs, the Soviet scholar Galina Dobrovolskaya has suggested that Yakobson's choreography was intended to break classical positions.[58] More recently, Janice Ross has argued that the images emphasize "athletic bodies arranged aesthetically . . . as if Yakobson were taking the proletariat vocabulary of daily actions, done by real people, and grafting them onto a classically trained cast."[59] Both Dobrovolskaya's and Ross's readings underline the stylized muscularity and athleticism in Yakobson's choreography, and both astutely emphasize formal innovation over narrative significance.

Footage from a television broadcast in 1965 shows the "Sports Quintet" (No. 24 in the *New Collected Works* edition) for the Western Komsomol girl and four sportsmen, as reconstructed by Yakobson for Alla Osipenko and members of the Kirov ballet.[60] The footage begins at R356 in the score. The ballerina stands at the back of the stage, her feet parallel and together, while the four sportsmen enter individually with jumps and pirouettes. The ballerina advances in movements that resemble swimming strokes, and she executes a series of sporting movements while supported by the sportsmen. Held aloft, her body parallel to the ground, she moves her arms and torso in an imitation of swimming and diving. The sportsmen return her to her original position at the back of the stage, and each of them then leaps across the stage as discus- and javelin-throwers. The ballerina advances again and mounts the "balance beam." This is the moment captured in the photograph of Ulanova in a backbend over Sergeyev's supine body. Her hands are on his raised, extended leg; her supporting leg is straight, her free leg bent at the knee as though in preparation for a flip. In the footage from 1965, the sportsmen "rock" the ballerina and her "beam," creating the illusion of motion. In the next sequence, two male dancers extend their arms straight at shoulder-height and a set of "high jumps" begins. The dance culminates with the ballerina "thrown" aloft, where she is held standing, upright and rigid, by two sportsmen. In a set of heart-stopping "falls," she rotates through 180 degrees and "falls" fully backward; she is caught and "thrown" up again to fall fully forward. The rhythm of swinging and falling calls to mind the uneven bars of a gymnastics routine. (The "falls" are also evocative, however inadvertently, of those in Balanchine's choreography for "The Unanswered Question" in *Ivesiana* of 1954. Of course, the effect is very different in Balanchine's work, given the remote, abstract quality of Ives's music, but the movement is analogous.)

Shostakovich's music for the "Sports Quintet" is not rendered in full in the 1965 footage, but some relationships between the music and the dance remain discernable. The music suggests qualities of movement (such as precision, expansiveness, elevation), while changes of tempo, texture, and instrumentation correlate with changes in the sport represented. At the beginning of the sequence, the ballerina's advance across the stage in "swimming strokes" is accompanied by a cheerful, staccato tune, played by the first violins in four-square rhythms. The simple melody outlines the interval of a perfect 4th and revolves around the 6th scale degree (D) in the key of F major; its opening motive recurs three times, with the third iteration inverted. The passage is spirited but uncomplicated, its simplicity and predictability conveying orderliness and precision. The footage continues at R359, where a change in texture, gesture, and articulation supports the ballerina's "swimming" and "diving." At the *Andantino poco allegretto* (R367), the tempo broadens, the tessitura is high, and the rhythms are occasionally syncopated. Harmonically, the music arrives on an E major 6/4 chord (R367) and immediately wanders into new harmonic territories (R367–369). This passage is choreographed for the javelin- and discus-throwing of the male sportsmen, followed by the ballerina's gymnastic "beam" routine. The expansive character of the music, the subtle undermining of meter, and the harmonic instability create an effect of suspended time, as though the music extends the actions on the stage, amplifying the throws and elaborating the gymnastics. A *Più mosso* at R369 accelerates the pace for the "high jumps" while triplets in the upper register intensify the rhythmic energy. Broadening again into a closing *Andantino* (R370) and returning to the key of F, the music seems to elongate time, range, and volume for the heroic finale of the ballerina's "swings" and "falls." Despite being a truncated version of Shostakovich's score, the music in the 1965 footage closely follows the stage situation, mirroring emphases in the action and conveying not just the athletes' movements but also the quality that those movements suggest.

Khodasevich's designs for this scene underscored its daring elements as the dancers appeared in fashionable modern swimming costumes. Galina Ulanova and Olga Mungalova both performed the role of the Komsomol girl. Khodasevich's sketch for Ulanova's costume showed a bright yellow swimming suit, with two wide bands of red and orange above the waist and a yellow swim cap and yellow ballet shoes completing the effect. (Mungalova's costume was the same but in blue; Khodasevich also created a set of matching swimming costumes for the four sportsmen.) A photograph of Ulanova wearing Khodasevich's costume suggests how closely it was modeled on contemporary bathing suits of the 1920s. The style, not to mention the use of bathing suits on the ballet stage, also echoed Coco Chanel's bathing costumes in *Le train bleu*. The resonance was probably unintentional, but it underscored the ubiquity of topics involving modern life and fashion in ballet of the 1920s. Even a Komsomol girl had a Chanel-style bathing suit. The vibrant costume "falling" through the air at the end of the Sports Quintet must have been sensational.

Over thirty years after the premiere, Shostakovich recalled Act II with special satisfaction. Commenting on its unity of components, he described the "harmonious" and "dynamic" effect; the audience was so enthusiastic, he remembered, that at times he could not hear his music for the applause.[61] Above all, he found his music "transformed" in Yakobson's choreography: "It seemed to me that Yakobson and I were born for the first time in art, and my music sounded like a new composition in the choreographic interpretation."[62] Enhancing the effects were Khodasevich's "memorable" designs, especially the "yellow scenery and costumes [that appeared] like patches of sunlight."[63] Khodasevich's yellow costumes for the "Sports Quintet" would certainly have merited such a description. The surviving sources for Act II suggest a unique cohesion of music, dance, and design in this part of the ballet and help to account for its popular success.

The sports topic in *The Golden Age* brought "Soviet" life and values—or an idealized version of those—into focus. At the same time, it drew on new visual and choreographic vocabularies, offering new content and forms through Yakobson's "plotless" dances. It also displayed contemporary fashions in sport and leisure clothing and used music to extend and complete the stylized images on stage. The sports topic was consonant with contemporary ideological emphases promoting sporting activity as a component of Soviet culture and signifying post-revolutionary commitment. In *The Golden Age*, as in contemporary cultural products of the period, the depiction of sports on stage permitted avant-garde ideas while promoting state-sponsored pursuits. *The Golden Age* was not simply a "soccer ballet" but a ballet that displayed the full range of sports—and their ideological and moral significance—for the modern Soviet experience.

Act III: The Modern Age

Act III of *The Golden Age* shifts away from sports and returns to the preoccupations of Act I: the conflict of opposing politics, the transformation of classical balletic models, and the sounds of modern music and popular idioms. The act opens in a music hall with a *divertissement* of ballroom dances characterizing pleasure-seeking pastimes (Scene 5). The only "intrigue" (if the word may be pardoned) concerns Diva and her partner, the Fascist, who is in disguise as the Soviet Soccer Captain. The ruse is that the characters (and what they represent) have been reconciled, yet the scam is quickly exposed (Scene 6). The Soviet Soccer Captain is released from prison, and the Western Komsomol girl strips the Fascist of his disguise. While exposure panics the bourgeoisie, the ballet ends with a "dance of solidarity" between Western workers and the Soviet team. Dramatically, the dénouement is the exposure of the Fascist and the routing of his supporters, but ideologically, the ending was never in doubt. Because of this, the final act lacks dramatic tension and relies on the music for interest and inventiveness.

The music hall setting of Act III recalls the "bourgeois" pursuits of Act I and returns Diva and her admirers to the stage for ballroom dancing. The social critique in this act would not have been lost on Soviet viewers. Although the critic Broderson condemned the music hall forms as a vector for bourgeois ideology, popular dances on the theatrical stage regularly signaled satire in early Soviet theatre. Satire was a dominant theme in the Soviet 1920s. As Julie Curtis has shown in her study of the subject, the use of satire was intimately connected to "cabaret, music hall and variety [shows]," where appropriate political targets were "capitalist vices" and "consumerist behavior."[64] In the latter half of the decade, a debate emerged over the ongoing place of satire in a post-Revolutionary context. Detractors held that satire was "redundant" and meaningless in a classless society, while proponents—notably Meyerhold—emphasized satire's seminal role for "propaganda purposes."[65] Debate over the role of satire and the way it could be justified in Soviet theatre was regularly emblematized by use of the foxtrot and related popular dance music. Among the most famous examples was the foxtrot in Meyerhold's production of *The Bedbug* to music by Shostakovich. In the play, dancing the foxtrot symbolized the corruption of the main characters.[66]

Who danced the foxtrot was also important in Soviet discourse. In *The Golden Age*, the offending parties were the "golden youth" (Act I) or the revelers around Diva (Act III). The moral implications were supposed to be clear. The "golden youth," or *zolotaya molodozh'*, were a social entity frequently targeted by Soviet critique; the term for them was widespread and linked to social dancing and suspect politics. Soviet writers elaborated the hedonism of the "golden youth" who "dance the foxtrot so well ... [and] drink champagne in cut-glass goblets."[67] Moreover, efforts toward the moral improvement of Soviet young people rejected the "golden youth" as an anti-type of proletarian youth; the "golden youth" were those who failed to promote a classless society.[68] In early Soviet histories, the term also denoted counter-revolutionary parties in the French Revolution (like those responsible for the death of Jean-Paul Marat) and thus established a European reference point.[69] In Soviet discourse of the 1920s, the "golden youth" signaled specific contemporary concerns, not only anxieties about modern, Western influences but also ideological and cultural questions about what constituted—and what ought to be excluded from—a Soviet future.

Tapping into these ideas, the music hall in *The Golden Age* stood for pleasure-seeking and self-indulgence and satirized "negative" characters. Writing music for a premise so thin might have been frustrating for Shostakovich. His manuscripts suggest that he was less certain of the dramatic content and organization of this act than he was of other parts of the ballet, and he left some dances untitled, which he did not do in other parts of his score.[70] Whatever the problems he faced, however—and they were certainly both dramatic and practical—his inventiveness lay in creating musical relationships and sound pictures that elevated his music beyond the trivial events of the libretto. The "golden" individuals of *The Golden Age* explored a realm of glittering possibilities that were portrayed through dazzling orchestrations, modern instruments, and special effects.

Act III opens with a *divertissement* that elaborates the qualities of the "golden" life (Table 2.2). The form itself is derived from the nineteenth-century classical *divertissement*, which was rationalized in a ballet as public entertainment, often a wedding or communal celebration. Like the classical precedent, the Act III *divertissement* of *The Golden Age* is a celebratory gathering in which a new union is fêted (in this case, a supposedly new union between Diva and the Soccer Captain). Twentieth-century tap, tango, polka, waltz, and cancan supplant the nineteenth-century tarantella, waltz, and galop. In a nod to the classical structure, the *divertissement* in *The Golden Age* ends with the cancan (No. 33), a descendant of the galop that typically closed the nineteenth-century *divertissement*.[71] The use of modern ballroom forms in *The Golden Age* took account of ballet's long relationship with ballroom dance. The Act III *divertissement* relied not on Parisian or Imperial ballrooms of the past, however, but on the modern ballroom where urbane social dancing was cultivated in contemporary societies.

Shostakovich's music makes sonority the organizing principle of this scene and brings cohesion and distinctiveness to the dances. The sonority here is not the fairytale sound imagery of *Sleeping Beauty*, the child-like pictures of *Nutcracker*, or the rustic village life of *Coppélia*, but the sound of sumptuous

Table 2.2 The *divertissement* of Act III.

Act III, Scene 5	Dances of the *divertissement*
No. 28: Chechotka (Tap Dance)	*Tap*
No. 29: Tango	*Tango*
No. 30: Polka "Once Upon a Time in Geneva"	*Polka*
No. 31: The Touching Coming-Together of the Classes with a Certain Degree of Fakeness	*Waltz*
No. 32: Entrance of Diva and the Fascist, Their Dance	*Exotic dance*
No. 33: Cancan	*Cancan*

modernity—a modern fantasy that tests the genre's capacity for fresh characterization. Part of the modern sound arises from the harmonies, which are often unexpected and always shifting. Flatted-5th scale degrees are frequent, as are modal mixtures and layering of tonal and modal elements. Each dance in the *divertissement* also has a distinctive character shaped by rhythm and color. In the tap dance (No. 28 in the *New Collected Works* edition of the score), irregular patterns and unexpected silences emphasize rhythmic disruption, which is punctuated by sparkling tunes from the xylophone and brash announcements from brass and percussion. The sultriness of the tango (No. 29) derives from its relaxed tempo, characteristic rhythmic accompaniment, decorative flourishes, idiosyncratic motives, and kaleidoscopic colors. The dance is flamboyant, but it is also sophisticated, a sense of consequence and intricacy being conveyed through textural and harmonic density, overwrought motifs, and a highly chromatic melodic line. The polka (No. 30), by contrast, is straightforward, with cheeky tunes in piccolo instruments and even cheekier interruptions from the brass.

Glittering instrumentation is the *divertissement*'s most memorable quality. The saxophone returns to a prominent role. Its smooth sound conveys the languorous atmosphere of relaxed indulgence. In the "languid waltz" (No. 31), so termed in the libretto, muted strings in triplets summon a ghostly effect, as of shadows in a dimly lit ballroom, while the flexatone in the waltz's *Andante* section suggests a strangeness that is both glamorous and outlandish. Shostakovich also used the flexatone in his contemporary film music for *The New Babylon*, where, according to Titus, the instrument sounds "when love, sincere or insincere, is made apparent."[72] Whether it has the same meaning in *The Golden Age* is not certain, but its highly unusual sound juxtaposed against a humble waltz tune suggests overwrought sensibility. Diva and the Fascist's dance (No. 32) implies a strongly exotic flavor in its tonal-modal juxtapositions (the implication of d minor with flatted 2nd and 4th scale degrees), metrical manipulation (the 6/8 dance alternating between triple and duple subdivisions of the bar), the tambourine strikes and the imitation of castanets (the percussion hits on beats 3 and 5 of the bar), the guitar-like flourishes in the inner voices (rendered by the woodwinds), and the violins' syncopated, expressive melody line (suggestive of vocal improvisation). Meanwhile, the xylophone interjects in many dances, solidifying meter and sharpening brilliance at every appearance. The *divertissement* exoticizes the sounds of modernity. Like the classical *divertissement*, it creates distinctive sound imagery that is explored in variety and depth. Reinventing the classical *divertissement*, however, it fashions the balletic atmosphere out of new and modern intonations.

The final scene of the ballet (Scene 6) abandons the intonations of the music hall and turns darker and more serious with dissonant, harmonically ambiguous language. The dances move through serious, popular, charming, and unpredictable episodes. The quick changes and often overblown orchestration suggest busy action on the stage, including scenes of *corps* dancing and possibly some pantomime. The routing of the bourgeoisie takes place to a rousing fugue (a counterpart to a fugue that closed Act I), while the final "dance of solidarity" restores order through metrical, textural, and harmonic clarity. Broderson was critical of the final scene, calling it "a strange mixture of the Polovtsian Dances and Walpurgis Night."[73] The comment was mostly directed at incoherent choreographic decisions (in Broderson's view), but the evocative suggestion, summoning the exoticism of *Prince Igor* and the dark forces of *Faust*, underscored qualities of fantasy and confusion in this final scene. Shostakovich left the dances of Scene 6 untitled in his manuscripts, but he must have worked to some guidance as to their events and character, especially the emotional trajectory from ambiguity to triumph, which is convincingly conveyed in his music.

Act III returned to many of the preoccupations of Act I, taking up setting, characters, and styles from earlier in the ballet and reengaging the motif of transforming classical models. Musically, the *divertissement* was the focal point of the act. Shostakovich's inventive response to the classical *divertissement* asserted his grasp of the form and of the musical cohesion achieved in the best nineteenth-century examples. At the same time, his music reshaped the classical *divertissement*, disguising the model and creating a new soundscape for Soviet ballet. The choreography for Act III is not known, and contemporary sources say little about it; but given the many links to Act I, it seems likely that the *pas* (or steps) in this act continued the fusion of classical and ballroom steps explored earlier in the ballet. Meanwhile, the ideological message, emphasized by the libretto, rejected the dazzling world depicted so vividly in the music. This tension between what the music projected and how audiences were supposed to react—that is, between irresistible charm and required rejection—added to the confusing array of impulses that this ballet was meant to satisfy. While aiming at unequivocal political messages, *The Golden Age* actually portrayed the perplexing state of Soviet modernity and its many anxieties about the place of the past in the construction of the future.

New Directions

The Golden Age ushered Shostakovich into a new role as ballet composer. His score documented his knowledge of the ballet repertoire, the subtlety of his allusions, and the projection of dramatic meaning and emotional intimacy in his music. It also summoned the shade of Tchaikovsky, occasionally in specific allusion and pervasively through a ballet score filled with characteristic sound, descriptive musical detail, and the evocation of the style and spirit of a time. *The Golden Age* was arguably Shostakovich's best ballet score, yet the ballet that Shostakovich wrote and the ballet that the Theatre produced were never fully reconciled as a unified work. As Shostakovich's frustration mounted during the ballet's production in 1930, he distanced himself from his work and tried to abandon it. Instead of cancelling the production, however, the Leningrad State Academic Theatre offered him a new commission: *The Bolt*, to be created in collaboration with Lopukhov. Shostakovich accepted, although he privately expressed skepticism over the new libretto.[74] But Lopukhov endorsed it and the composer set to work. While financial considerations may have influenced Shostakovich's decision to sign another contract with the Theatre, *The Bolt* also seemed to promise precisely what *The Golden Age* had failed to deliver—a coherent creative vision for Soviet ballet, developed between a gifted composer and an experienced choreographer.

The Golden Age also illuminated the many artistic and political pressures on Soviet ballet at the end of the 1920s. One of the most complex concerns was ballet's relationship to the past. Stylistically, what language, in both music and dance, remained essential to the art form? Artistically, what represented innovation, not imitation? Ideologically, how should the past be treated, and if it could not be abandoned, how could it be reinterpreted? On the surface, *The Golden Age* was about the present—a cheeky modern tale of Soviet virtue—but beneath the surface, it was indebted to the past. In music, dance, and design, it depended on and critiqued the legacy of Russian ballet classicism. While *The Golden Age* attempted to conform to prevailing cultural orthodoxies, its ideological conformity was also a veneer for a sustained look at the classical past. Ultimately, *The Golden Age* demonstrated early Soviet ballet's dependence on the classical vocabulary in addition to its impulses in other directions altogether. The work used the techniques of the past to look at the present, while also using present artistic concerns to transform past practices.

At the same time, *The Golden Age* took up the question of how to represent modernity in a highly conventionalized genre (a challenge common in both Soviet and Western ballet repertoire of the 1920s). It proposed scenes in the sports stadium and the music hall—situations from daily life that were familiar and recognizable and that offered ways of enriching ballet's classical vocabulary with contemporary sounds and movements. The two settings emblematized different values, of course. Sports represented the transformation of Soviet culture while the music hall depicted the vanity of self-indulgence. Shostakovich's score, moreover, contributed to—and often largely created—the depiction of modernity through fresh orchestrations, popular idioms, modern instruments, and special effects.

The Golden Age did not solve the crisis of Soviet ballet, but it offered a series of perspectives on what Soviet ballet could be—classical, contemporary, Soviet, and modern. In his next two ballets, *The Bolt* and *The Limpid Stream*, Shostakovich together with Lopukhov would explore new models, a modernist and a Romantic ballet, respectively, each examined through a Soviet lens. The ballets would not survive on the Soviet stage, just as *The Golden Age* did not, but they would continue to trace Shostakovich's reassessment of traditional practices in relation to the genre. Most significantly, they would reveal his creative imagination as he elaborated, refined, and aimed to transform Soviet ballet in fresh and innovative ways.

3
Amateur Dramatics: *The Bolt* and Modern Ballet

Shostakovich composed *The Bolt* for much the same theatrical milieu as *The Golden Age*. The two ballets premiered in the same season, at the same theatre, six months apart (October 26, 1930, and April 8, 1931, respectively), and both were expected to generate new forms and content for ballet by linking artistic reform to ideologically correct topics. The collaborative team for *The Bolt* was new, however. Tatiana Bruni and Georgy Korshikov designed sets and costumes, Viktor Smirnov wrote the libretto, and Lopukhov created the choreography. The Leningrad State Academic Theatre had high hopes for *The Bolt* and started making plans for similar works should the ballet "prove a success."[1] But it failed and was withdrawn after a single performance.

The Bolt tells the tale of a drunken factory worker, Lyonka Gulba, who sabotages a lathe. As the ballet opens, workers prepare for the day with an exercise routine in the factory's changing room. Lyonka Gulba slouches in from a drinking session. New lathes are installed in the factory, and an amateur concert—featuring those who promote Soviet production and those who undermine it—celebrates the setting-up of a new workshop. Lyonka Gulba gets drunk with his friends and is fired from his job. In a nearby village, dances and demonstrations take place. While everyone is distracted by the entertainments, Lyonka Gulba dreams up a plan to sabotage the factory and convinces a young boy, Goshka, to insert a bolt into one of the new lathes. Boris, leader of the shock workers, overhears the conspirators, but Lyonka Gulba hits him over the head, almost knocking him unconscious. Goshka then carries out the sabotage. As Boris tries to intervene, he gets locked inside the factory workshop, and Lyonka Gulba tells the guards that Boris has sabotaged the lathes. Regretting his part in the plot, however, Goshka confesses the truth. Lyonka Gulba is arrested, and the ballet ends with another amateur concert at the factory club.

Contemporaries attributed the failure of *The Bolt* to this banal libretto. Just two months before the premiere, Shostakovich mocked it privately to

Sollertinsky: "Comrade Smirnov read to me his story for the ballet *At the New Machine*. The content is very topical. There was a machine, then it broke down (the problem of wear and tear). Then it was mended (the problem of depreciation), and they also bought a new one. Everyone then dances round the new machine. Apotheosis. The whole thing takes three acts. Comrade Smirnov and I remain friends."[2]

While Shostakovich's music won some praise as the best part of the production, critics unanimously condemned the story's banality, sarcasm, and lack of dramatic relevance. They derided "schematic" characters, "ridiculous" antics, and "childish" events; they also decried the embeddedness of "old" classical forms within supposedly "new" Soviet ballet and condemned *The Bolt* as "parody" and "mockery."[3] To these assessments, scholars have since added accounts of the rapidly shifting aesthetic and political pressures of the period and have shown how *The Bolt*, like *The Golden Age* before it, attempted to meet requirements that were obsolete by the time the works reached the stage.[4] *The Bolt* was absurd, and it was a casualty of cultural policies whose direction few could predict.

While *The Bolt* was unsuccessful as a Soviet ballet, however, it was important for the way it explored relationships among ballet, popular media, and contemporary art forms. It attempted to marry classical ballet with avant-garde and political art. In doing so, it created a plethora of associations that were bizarre and confusing. Some elements of *The Bolt* recalled standard components of classical ballet (a story in three acts, character dancing, *divertissement*). Alongside these, the ballet emphasized features that were unconventional for the genre but that displayed revolutionary content and modern materials (factory setting, current events, poster art, characters as puppets). Looking outside the genre of ballet, *The Bolt* also drew on elements of Soviet amateur theatre, particularly performing groups like the Theatre of Working-Class Youth (TRAM), Blue Blouse, and Living Newspaper performances. Like amateur stage works of the period, the ballet was meant to be funny. It adopted a humorous, satirical tone about topics pertinent to Soviet youth, and it waded into a debate between amateurism and professionalism that occupied Soviet dramaturgy.

This chapter examines these diverse and competing influences on *The Bolt*. To do so, it explores the work from three perspectives—cultural context, artistic resources, and creative decisions. First, the cultural milieu contextualized the ballet's topic of sabotage. The topic featured prominently in national conversation and was motivated by contemporary events in

Soviet Russia. Second, *The Bolt* drew on both "high art" and "popular art" and navigated a tension between ballet as a professional art form and amateur theatre as a popular form. In doing this, the ballet explored both how amateur art could be professionalized (by being brought under the aegis of an Academic Theatre) and how professional art could be made more accessible (by incorporating "unrehearsed" forms). An "amateur" aesthetic pervaded *The Bolt* and posed fundamental questions about what Soviet art and artists could be. Third, *The Bolt*'s music, design, and choreographic elements illuminate how dances were situated within the ballet and how the work portrayed modern Soviet life and society. In its emphatic commitment to everyday settings (factory, village), ordinary experiences (collective events), and artistic encounters (amateur performances), the ballet examined an ongoing conundrum of Soviet life: a conundrum between what people *should* want and what they *did* want. *The Bolt* put forward a model in which this tension could be reconciled, but only within an ideological orientation. In its cultural synchronism, aesthetic tensions, and creative components, *The Bolt* was a Soviet "modern" ballet fashioned out of artistic contradictions and political propaganda.

The Milieu

In 1931, *The Bolt* was eminently topical and in tune with subjects of national interest. Soviet Russia was in the midst of the First Five-Year Plan (1928–32), a policy that aimed at the rapid industrialization and forced collectivization of the country. As the Great Depression engulfed Western economies, the First Five-Year Plan saw the proliferation of factories, heavy industry, and new technologies in Russia. Settings and enterprises associated with industry became subjects of national conversation and cultural production. At the same time, the perils of sabotage were constantly discussed, and propaganda urged perpetual vigilance to safeguard Soviet achievements. In 1928, the story of the Shakhty Trial reverberated through the Soviet press. Scores of engineers in Shakhty (Eastern Donbas) were arrested on charges of conspiracy and sabotage and brought to Moscow for trial, where almost all were convicted.[5] Newspapers covered the events in detail, and the subject of sabotage preoccupied Soviet life, emblematizing the threats to Communism. "Saboteurs" and "wreckers" were sought and suspected everywhere.

The Shakhty trial marked a watershed in Soviet culture, ending the permissiveness of the New Economic Policy (NEP) and inaugurating the militancy of the Cultural Revolution. The events inflamed a fierce conflict aimed at eliminating "bourgeois specialists" and establishing "proletarian hegemony" in all areas of Soviet endeavor.[6] As the historian Sheila Fitzpatrick explains, the Shakhty trial "put the loyalty of the whole intelligentsia in doubt" and launched "an onslaught . . . on privilege and established authority."[7] The ensuing cultural conflict, she writes, "described a political confrontation of 'proletarian' Communists and the 'bourgeois' intelligentsia, in which the Communists sought to overthrow the cultural authorities inherited from the old regime. The aim of the Cultural Revolution was to create a new 'proletarian intelligentsia.'"[8]

Cultural officials defined the fight as a crusade "against bourgeois elements that are supported by the remnants and survivals of the influence, traditions, and customs of the old society."[9] As militant rhetoric filtered through society, powerful proletarian voices hailed the "battle against sabotage" in every area of Soviet life, and citizens were summoned to a new culture war.

A critical expression of the cultural conflict between "bourgeois" and "proletarian," or "specialists" and "workers," emerged in a debate over professionalism and amateurism in the arts. Which was more valuable, more authentically "Soviet"—art produced by professional institutions that cultivated "specialist" training and expertise, or amateur artistic enterprises that promoted the talents and tastes of "workers"? In relation to staged works, such questions pitted "big" theatre for large-scale professional productions against club theatre for factories, cafés, and other non-professional venues. For ballet, the problem was acute. Not only was the art form historically linked to the "old" bourgeois social order, but dancing itself required specialist training. Ballet emblematized professionalism.

The Bolt touched on all of these cultural flashpoints. It portrayed Soviet industry and told a tale of sabotage. It was a work for the professional stage, but it featured amateur theatricals as part of the plot. It presented the conflict between high art and popular art, between a professional genre that depended on specialism and skill and amateur forms that celebrated spontaneity, improvisation, and lack of finesse. In doing so, *The Bolt* raised conundrums. Was a ballerina a skilled professional dancer or a worker who danced? Did ballet raise cultural standards or perpetuate a cultural establishment? Did it require professional performance, or should such boundaries be broken down? Was ballet elite or popular, specialized or spontaneous, rehearsed or improvised? And where did amateurs belong? *The Bolt* explored the "political confrontation" of the Cultural Revolution through a work that juxtaposed professional ballet with the elements of popular and amateur art.

"High Art" versus "Popular Art"

The Bolt's varied and often incongruous elements arose from the huge variety of contemporary sources, both artistic and popular, Soviet and Western, on which it drew. Earlier avant-garde experiments in dance formed one sort of precedent for *The Bolt*. Some experimental approaches, like Nikolai Foregger's *Machine Dances* (1922), had been pioneered in Moscow's dance studios. Others were anticipated, but not realized, at the leading ballet theatres, like Aleksandr Mosolov's ballet *Steel* (1927) and his expected contribution to the ballet *The Four Moscows*, commissioned by the Bolshoi Theatre in 1928. Still other avant-garde ballets had been created abroad but were known in Russia, like Prokofiev and Massine's *Le Pas d'acier* (1927). Moreover, new dramatic genres, as well as radical approaches to traditional theatre, became extremely popular in the early Soviet period. As new stages proliferated and competed with long-established venues, amateur theatre and its subgenres of small forms wielded enormous influence. *The Bolt* was a product of these unusual dynamics. It combined the "high art" of ballet with avant-garde experimentation and with the "popular art" of amateur and political forms.

"High Art"

One of *The Bolt*'s most anticipated contributions was to be its treatment of the industrial theme. The subject of industry was not only topical in Soviet theatre, but through the 1920s, it had consistently been associated with modernism. Foregger's *Machine Dances* were among the earliest experimental works based on industrial processes. In Foregger's choreography, performers imitated the movements of machines—a choreographic concept echoed in the "machine dances" in *The Bolt* (although, according to Bruni, these were not actually performed at the premiere).[10] Other dramatic works exploring industrial topics included Vladimir Deshevov's opera *Ice and Steel* (*Lyod i stal'*), which premiered at the Leningrad State Academic

Theatre in May 1930 and included an act set in a metal factory. A few years earlier, Deshevov had also written incidental music for *Rails* (*Rel'sy*, 1926), using experimental techniques to evoke mechanized sounds.[11] Mosolov's *Iron Foundry* (*Zavod: Muzyka mashin*) from his ballet *Steel* (*Stal'*), as well as his projected opera *The Dam* (*Plotina*, 1930), similarly envisioned industrial themes on the stage.[12] In each of these works, the industrial topic was linked to modernist experimentation. Deshevov's modernist music helped to evoke the mechanized sound of machines, hammers, gears, or whistles, while Mosolov's *Iron Foundry* famously incorporated a metal sheet into the orchestral timbre to create the din of heavy machinery. (The score for *Steel* disappeared in 1929, but the music for *Iron Foundry*, its final episode, survived and was widely known. Mosolov was also expected to write futuristic music for the ballet *The Four Moscows* for the Bolshoi. His portion of the ballet was to be set in the year 2117.[13]) None of these works survived on the stage, and some were never performed. But the industrial topics were important for the way they reflected Soviet modernity and prompted artistic experimentation in conveying the noise of modern life. *The Bolt*'s industrial theme aligned with this trend of Soviet modernism.

The conditions for a ballet like *The Bolt* had been set, moreover, by the libretto competition of 1929, which had aimed at "Sovietizing" the repertoire. The competition guidelines had even suggested "industrial culture" as a possible topic for a new ballet.[14] As Elizabeth Stern has shown, two submissions for the libretto competition shared affinities with *The Bolt*: these were *Zavod* (Factory) and *Nash put'* (Our path), both of which proposed ballets on industrial themes. The libretti were rejected by the Leningrad State Academic Theatre, but reviewers nonetheless expressed excitement at the possibilities that the settings and subjects might offer, and Lopukhov declared himself keen to choreograph "dances on the factory floor."[15] Adopted in 1930, a year after the libretto competition, *The Bolt* was not part of that contest, but it expressed many of the competition's ideals and offered another chance at "Sovietizing" ballet. Its perceived relevance and potential impact resonated with the artistic and political agenda of the Leningrad State Academic Theatre.

The Bolt's industrial topic also had a reference point in the avant-garde experiments in Constructivism that had appeared in Soviet and Western ballet through the 1920s. In that period, Constructivist ideas had been available to Soviet ballet primarily through stage design. Although no truly Constructivist ballet was ever created in Russia, several examples of

Constructivist ballet sets were made through the 1920s, and these were uniformly associated with experimental works.[16] The aesthetic components of Soviet Constructivism on the ballet stage included functional designs, "supra-emotional" systems, glorification of the industrial process, and the imitation of machines.[17] While not a Soviet ballet, the most notable Constructivist ballet of the period was *Le Pas d'acier*, danced by the Ballets Russes in Paris in 1927 and considered (for a time) for productions at both the Leningrad State Academic Theatre and the Bolshoi Theatre in Russia. *Pas* had an industrial setting and explored a "utilitarian aesthetic" in an effort to stage "Soviet ideals."[18] Scholars have called the ballet "the most provocative treatment of industrial themes in the modern canon" and have highlighted the insights it provides into "a brief, volatile and highly formative period of contact between the Western avant-garde and post-Revolutionary Russia."[19] There is no evidence that *Pas* influenced *The Bolt* directly, although Lopukhov and Bruni probably knew of the ballet and certainly knew of its Constructivist aesthetic. The parallel between *Pas* and *The Bolt* lay in the fact that an industrial topic and Constructivist style played a role in both works, albeit to varying degrees. Both ballets attempted to capture the stylistic impressions of an idea—an approach at the heart of the modernist model—and both produced strange juxtapositions of banal activity and technological fantasy.

Some of Bruni's designs for *The Bolt* also exhibited Constructivist ideas through geometric forms, blocks of pure color, emphasis on machines and industrial projects, and the dissolution of boundaries between figures and objects. This was especially true of her décor for Act I, in which humans not only worked machines but also took roles as parts of those machines (such as human figures posed to represent parts of a crane, wires, and pistons).[20] Yet Bruni's designs relied on other sources too, especially the iconography of amateur theatre and political art. The visual aesthetic of *The Bolt* was not unified by a single style but drew on multiple contemporary sources, as did the choreography and the music.

"Popular Art"

Soviet political art and amateur entertainment exerted an enormous influence on *The Bolt*, forming part of the modernity—or the experience of the ordinary Soviet person—that was the subject of the ballet. Scholars have long recognized a link between *The Bolt* and Soviet propaganda art and have described the ballet (pejoratively, it is true) as "archetypal agitprop," "a caricature of proletarian dramaturgy," a "consciously 'bad'" ballet, and a "satirical comedy show" modeled on proletarian theatre.[21] The labels rightly connect *The Bolt* to political and amateur art. In this context, it is helpful to grasp how widespread, accessible, and popular such art was in Soviet Russia as well as the ways in which this art symbolized the modern Soviet experience.

Amateur theatre was one of the most prominent forms of Soviet political art. As Lynn Mally has shown, the entertainment was hugely popular and served multiple purposes in amusing audiences, educating them politically, and shaping dramatic repertoire.[22] Amateur stages showcased topical issues through the "theatre of small forms." Performers and spectators largely comprised Soviet youth. Stories were often adapted from headlines and news bulletins and delivered in club performances or skits, where their improvisational nature allowed them to be malleable and versatile, quickly adapted to topical issues. Amateur performances were small in scale, partly because money was scarce, rehearsal time limited, and performance spaces and actors poorly equipped. But small forms were also politically useful because they confronted the central conflict of the Cultural Revolution—specialism versus amateurism. Amateur theatre rejected the professionalism of "big" theatre.[23] Ironically, however, avant-garde theatre was increasingly attracted by improvised amateur forms, and a rich exchange arose as professional thespians promoted, directed, and sometimes performed in club shows. Vsevolod Meyerhold was an important supporter.[24] He not only helped to train club theatre directors, but he also staged club performances at his own theatre, notably, the play *The Shot* (1929) for which Shostakovich wrote the music.

Amateur theatre emphasized the day-to-day events and concerns of Soviet life. This made productions accessible and informative as well as useful tools of social transformation. Performances had a sense of immediacy because they dealt with news and current events, not dramas of the past. One of the most popular theatrical forms was the "living newspaper," which told the news through satirical sketches, bright placards, exaggerated costumes and props, and lively routines of singing, dancing, and pantomime.[25] The skits blended traditions of Russian folk theatre—even the puppet Petrushka appeared occasionally—with popular topics of urban life drawn from cinema and café cultures. The most famous "living newspaper" group, the Blue Blouse (named for their *bluzi*, or blue work shirts), performed news headlines, turning them into vignettes about local, national, and international events. Hugely popular and widely imitated, the Blue Blouse inspired amateur "living newspapers" in drama clubs, factories, and trade unions across Russia. The paradigm of "living newspapers" even animated a number like the "Naval Disarmament Conference" in *The Bolt*, a scene that "performed" a current event using satire, exaggeration, and distortion.

Amid an explosion of amateur theatricals in the early Soviet period, the Theatre of Working-Class Youth (TRAM) in Leningrad emerged as the best-organized and most influential group. Its productions established a genre of theatre whose shared and repeated conventions were reiterated in many contemporary works. TRAM put on plays that "explored the joys and sorrows of Soviet youth" as well as the "complex urban cultures" that these young people had to navigate.[26] Stories mostly presented young people caught between the virtues of Komsomol living and the temptations of other attractions (hooliganism, the Soviet underworld, fashionable NEP lifestyles), and works typically ended with characters rejecting anti-Communist "error" and reembracing the Komsomol community. The propaganda value of such stories was clear. Yet beneath the simplistic plots, politicized virtues, and predictable outcomes, these plays used stock characters and situations as "social masks" to explore the things that mattered to Soviet youth.[27] In the 1920s and early 1930s, these youth were the *first* truly Soviet generation, a cohort that reiteratively explored questions of what it meant to be Soviet.

The plot of *The Bolt* mirrored the conventions of TRAM plays, especially the opposition between Komsomol virtue and anti-Soviet hooliganism as well as the restoration of waverers to the Komsomol community. In particular, *The Bolt* evoked two famous TRAM creations: the character of Crazy Sashka (who appeared in living newspaper skits) and the play *Factory Storm*. Crazy Sashka was a stock character—a wayward factory worker who was repeatedly tempted by hooligan elements and liable to scrapes.[28] In one of TRAM's most successful productions, Crazy Sashka was the main character in an eponymous play in which he was enticed by hooligan friends until he finally rejected hooliganism and returned to the Komsomol. In another play, *Factory Storm*, a drunken worker arrived late to work, got fired from his job, and in revenge arranged for his hooligan friends to beat up a Komsomol leader. Resonances with *The Bolt* are obvious in the mischief of the drunkard (Lyonka Gulba), the restoration of a conflicted character (Goshka), the persecution of a Soviet youth (Boris), and the triumph of the collective. Much has been made of the ballet's terrible plot—and indeed, it proved terrible for the ballet—but it reflected the types of stock plots and situations that regularly delighted audiences of Soviet amateur theatre.

Soviet poster art was another prominent genre of political art that influenced *The Bolt*, especially some of the ballet's visual resources. By the early 1930s, the visual propaganda of Soviet posters played an important role in the political education of the populace. In her study of Soviet political posters from this period, Victoria Bonnell explains the Bolshevik dichotomy that divided society into two groups: "positive" types who advanced a classless society and "negative" types, or "enemies," who hindered it.[29] Soviet propaganda posters regularly caricatured these divisions and satirized "bad" characters. Among the "negative" types were "workplace villains" who shirked, idled, cadged, or even betrayed the collective enterprise but were usually "considered redeemable" with sufficient political guidance.[30] These were, for the most part, the kinds of villains presented in *The Bolt*. Some of these villains served no narrative function in the ballet, but they appeared on stage as visual reminders of the social order. Their derivation from contemporary visual iconography would have been clear.

The idea of exploring popular art in ballet also had parallels, however inadvertently, in Western avant-garde ballet. As Lynn Garafola has explained in relation to that repertoire, the Western aesthetic emphasized "a style culled from various avant-garde sources and applied to an extended range of balletic contexts."[31] Those avant-garde sources fractured perception, or defamiliarized what is intuitively familiar, by filtering it through popular art forms, mechanization, caricature, and parody. In Massine's *Parade* (1917), for example, popular culture that was normally taken at face value in its original context was presented in a "high art" context where no one was sure whether to be entertained or offended. The subversive quality in the modernist approach of Diaghilev and his circle differed sharply from the earnestness of the Soviet aesthetic, yet the artistic tools that the Soviets used were sometimes very similar, as they were in *The Bolt*. The ballet juxtaposed contradictory, even antithetical, elements: classical ballet and amateur theatre, dancers *en pointe* and dancers as puppets, avant-garde art and poster art, the professional stage and the factory floor. In setting up these relationships, *The Bolt* brought low-brow art to the professional stage and scanned the modern Soviet world, particularly its popular entertainments, for material. The fusion of classical dancing and forms with the mechanization of the factory and the caricature of low-brow art was meant to appeal, instruct, and innovate. *The Bolt* aimed to evoke a kind of authenticity or realism as it expressed a preoccupation with everyday Soviet life, an appetite for contemporary artistic trends, and an urgency in ideological communication.

Soviet "Modern" Ballet

The Bolt's tale of the "saboteur" at the factory is populated with representatives of Soviet society's desirables (Young Pioneers, Komsomols, Red Army men) and undesirables (the Drunkard, the Malingerer, the Bureaucrat, and other proxies for anti-Communist debauchery and corruption). These caricatures prompted a range of artistic representations that drew on both avant-garde and everyday artistic elements. Music fused high- and lowbrow genres. Humans danced as characters, as life-sized puppets, and as machines. Costumes evoked Soviet propaganda posters, and some designs featured Constructivist elements. The components of music, dance, and design in each act suggest much about how the story was told and what kinds of ideas were projected aurally and visually.

ACT I: The Factory

Throughout Act I, the music characterizes individuals (like Lyonka Gulba), groups of characters (workers and shirkers), social situations (revelry), and social types ("undesirables" who obstruct collective work). What is absent is any hint at the inner emotional life of characters or any exploration of individual feeling. There are no primary dance roles, no primary relationships between characters, and no balletic formulas that allow for the projection of intimacy (such as an *Adagio* or *pas de deux*). The characters in Act I are one-dimensional, part of colorful vignettes of Soviet society. The act establishes a carnivalesque atmosphere in which many types of characters appear and their place in the social order is explained.

The events of Act I are arranged in four scenes in the factory's changing room and workshop. In Scene 1, workers exercise to a radio broadcast before heading to the factory floor. Musically, their training routine is organized by changes in meter (5/4, 3/4, 2/4) and key (G major, C major, F major). Disrupting the orderliness, Lyonka Gulba stumbles into the changing room just after his colleagues leave. Displaced downbeats suggest his tipsy steps, while fragmentary phrases in the solo English horn and bassoon outline an unsteady path (No. 4). Sparse textures, changing meters, unexpected silences, dark sonorities, minor tonalities, and dissonant harmonies create an atmosphere of uncertainty and menace, a foreboding ambiguity. This opening scene establishes a familiar conflict in ballet: the tension between an ordered reality and a threat to that reality. With the installation of the lathes in Scene 2, new characters appear, including the clerk Kozelkov, whose self-indulgence is symbolized by his fondness for the foxtrot, and a group of cleaners, who are announced incongruously by a trumpet flourish. The centerpiece of the scene is an amateur concert celebrating Soviet production and exposing Soviet society's "undesirables." Following the entertainments, Scenes 3 and 4 contrast workers and hooligans. The carousing of Lyonka Gulba and his friends takes place to highly episodic music (No. 15), which includes, among other striking images, a passage of oscillating chords, high pedal tones, and modal mixture reminiscent of the drunken Shrovetide revelers in *Petrushka*.[32] Lyonka Gulba and his friends get thrown out of the factory. This is the event for which Lyonka Gulba will take revenge.

The "workshop concert" in Scene 2 is the central episode of Act I, and it epitomizes the ballet's tension between professionalism and amateurism. The concert fuses a *divertissement* for character dancing (a typical balletic formula) with political poster art (or visual propaganda). The dramatic premise is that an amateur entertainment is put on by and for factory workers so that what happens here is not part of the ballet's story (which centers on Lyonka Gulba's disaffection) but is part of a performance-within-a-performance (a device that Shostakovich and Lopukhov would use again, to great effect, in their next ballet). The concert features four dances: an "intermezzo" for the Saboteurs, character dances for a Bureaucrat (who does no work) and a Blacksmith (who works at double speed), and a final *corps* dance for members of the Komsomol and Young Pioneers (Table 3.1). In the 1931 libretto, the dances for the Saboteurs, the Bureaucrat, and the Blacksmith are identified as "poster" or "placard" (*plakat*) dances. The reference is to satirical poster art that caricatured "good" and "bad" traits in a socialist society.

Musically, the dances of the *divertissement* vary in meter, mood, melodic figuration, orchestration, and instrumental color to create individual portraits (Bureaucrat, Blacksmith) or to sketch the attributes of groups (Saboteurs, Soviet youth). The Saboteurs' intermezzo (No. 10) conveys clumsiness and ineptitude. The trumpet leads the first theme, which is in C major and 4/4 time and features staccato leaps outlining diatonic chords. The tune seems foursquare and predictable, but it is disrupted by syncopation

Table 3.1 Act I, Scene 2, Nos. 10–13: The "workshop concert" (*divertissement*)

The dances as labeled in the *New Collected Works*	... as listed in the 1931 libretto	... rendered as a *divertissement*
No. 10: The Saboteurs (Intermezzo)	"poster-interlude"	Intermezzo
No. 11: The Bureaucrat	"poster-dance"	Polka
No. 12: The Blacksmith	"poster-dance"	"Spanish" dance
No. 13: Entry of the Komsomol Members and Dance of the Young Pioneers	"production march"	March

that "limps" or "falls" onto beat 2 and by a tuba that blunders into "wrong notes" (C# in the key of C major). The dance's second theme (R89) opens in the solo clarinet in A-flat major and 3/4 time, but the clarinet only manages a four-note fragment that is repeatedly interrupted by shimmering trills and disjunct motives handed off through the woodwinds. Nothing is consistent melodically, harmonically, or timbrally, as though the music—unable to complete its ideas—suggests futility and foolishness.

After the intermezzo, the Bureaucrat dances a polka (No. 11) that features extreme contrasts in timbre and register. A nimble piccolo tune juxtaposes with spiky accompaniment from the bassoon while impatient slides from the trombone occasionally upset the delicate texture. The trombones take control in a brash interlude, but the intrusion is short-lived and the piccolo-bassoon dance returns. The contrast of delicacy and bombast suggests ineffectiveness and belligerence. In the 1931 production of *The Bolt*, the awkwardness was reinforced visually by the Bureaucrat's costume, which featured a bald man with black round-frame glasses, a gray jacket, and huge stacks of filing folders for trousers. It must have been difficult to move—and surely impossible to dance—in a costume that "drowned" the Bureaucrat in his own materials.[33]

The Blacksmith's dance (No. 12) is exotic in its shimmering tune, minor mode, and castanet-like rhythms. After an introduction for strings and xylophone establishing F-sharp minor, the piano takes the lead with a glistening melody played in oscillating octaves over accompaniment from woodblocks and percussion. The oscillation in the tune gives the impression of double speed while drum crashes on the downbeat mimic the sound of hammer blows at the forge. Like much ballet music for character dances, there is a suggestion of diegetic components here (the onomatopoeic "hammer blows"), as though the Blacksmith's activities produce part of the musical texture. Contemporary reviewers singled out this dance for criticism, interpreting it as "parody" of a "positive" character, a worker who operates with speed and efficiency.[34] Yet the music has a foreign flavor, its F-sharp minor tonality and castanet-like accompaniment recalling elements of the "Spanish dance" in Act III of *Swan Lake*. Perhaps unluckily, it exoticized an ordinary character in a classless society—a hard worker.

The final dance of the *divertissement* is a *moto perpetuo* for Komsomol youth that gives way to a march for Young Pioneers (No. 13). Members of the Komsomol enter the stage to whirling 16th-note passages. The music's minor tonality rests on a first-inversion chord, not the tonic root; the slight instability permits harmonic flexibility that pivots seamlessly to different keys before ushering in the Young Pioneers' dance in C major (R132). Their rousing finale closes with celebratory tunes in the brass over the full panoply of orchestral writing. Clarity of rhythm, key, meter, and melodic ideas emphasizes the vigor yet orderliness of Soviet youth.

While the music created these vivid cameos, figures or "types" derived from Soviet poster art appeared on stage as part of the concert. In Bruni's sketches, their costumes, props, and poses emphasize visual clichés associated with "undesirable" social qualities. The Truant/Shirker (*Progul'shchik*) wears a gray suit with orange-and-yellow socks and scarf. He holds a flower in one hand and a silver-topped cane in the other, and sports a large nose (with especially large nostrils for picking, according to notes on the sketch). His clothes and accessories are incongruous, emphasizing idleness and inconsistency. The Drunkard (*P'yanitsa*) appears in lop-sided cap, striped shirt, and patched trousers, clutching a bottle in one hand as another protrudes from his pocket. His attire echoes the stereotypical dress of the hooligan in Soviet amateur theatre and thus connects him to an underworld rejected by socialist society.[35] The Malingerer (*Byulletenshchik*) presents exaggerated injuries. His head is bound up with a scarf that obscures his face while his right arm and leg are in casts. Incongruously, he holds a crutch that is clearly useless to someone with injuries in all the places he has sustained them. The Flyer (*Letun*, sometimes translated "Job-Changer") wears blue work coveralls with wings on his backside. His arms are extended as though in flight, his pose and costume emphasizing capriciousness and unreliability. The Opportunist (*Opportunist*) holds a briefcase and wears a gray suit with a showy red bow on the shoulder, as well as red spectacles and red shoes. An annotation on the sketch notes that he has "no nose, no mouth, no eyes, no ears"—he is quite literally a blank. The Bungler (*Golovotyap*) is inept and ridiculous, represented in Bruni's sketch as a figure with a block of wood for a head, yet dressed in fancy evening clothes (bright blue tuxedo jacket, black bowtie, and trousers) and holding a trumpet in his hand. The Counter-Revolutionary (*Kontrrevolyutsioner*) wears bulging green breeches and a gray jacket with silver buttons, recalling the uniform of a Tsarist officer. Whereas most of the "undesirables" are workplace offenders lacking sufficient political education, the Counter-Revolutionary is a political subversive, and thus an implacable foe of Soviet enterprise.

The amateur concert in Act I contained individually distinctive, and occasionally novel, elements of music, dance, and design. Each dance was a witty vignette. While the music characterized particular qualities or activities (like the Blacksmith's work at the forge), it featured standard dances of the balletic *divertissement*, updated and modernized with popular idioms and instrumentations. Little is known about the choreography, but costumes could not have allowed for standard balletic movements. Many would have permitted only clumsy movements and gestures. In fact, some were designed to inhibit movement altogether; several sketches even showed characters in decidedly non-dancing footwear. The amateur concert in Act I stylized the kinds of theatrical events that took place in Soviet factories and other small-scale, non-professional venues. Most significantly, the scene translated contemporary ideas from the popular arts to the ballet stage and, in doing so, tested the elements of popular art within the "serious art" of ballet.

ACT II: The Village

Act II takes place on a Sunday afternoon in a village. Some people attend church; others join a political rally. Lyonka Gulba and his friends drink at a bar and hatch the plan to sabotage the factory. The public gatherings in the village rationalize a *divertissement* that occupies most of the act and parodies individuals and groups (a priest, Kozelkov, Goshka, parishioners, hooligans). The music is clever, often witty, but never serious. Some of it prefigures cameos in *Lady Macbeth*, like the priest in the ballet who succumbs to dance music (as another priest does in the opera) rather than carrying out the duties of his office with any kind of solemnity or decorum. A few numbers from Act II were reused in *The Limpid Stream* and subsequent works, a fact that underscores the recyclable nature of this music and its detachment from dramatic significance.

One of these musically striking but malleable dances is the tango for Kozelkov and his friends at the end of the act (No. 29). The music has the standard features of the Spanish dance—heavy syncopation, habanero rhythm, chromatic tunes, sultry mood, passionately expressive episodes (marked *espressivo molto*). Its exotic flavor derives from its "foreignness," its glamorous mystique, and denotes cosmopolitanism and self-indulgence (as the tango and ballroom dances did in *The Golden Age*). Dramatically, however, the tango has no relevance. It does not further a relationship, deepen a character, or clarify motivation. It simply supports the moralizing message of the stage situation: the dangers of subversive influences. The tango is one example (among several in *The Bolt*) of clever music that could suit different purposes.

Winsome and well crafted, the tango enjoyed an afterlife in subsequent works into which Shostakovich recycled it. He used it in *The Limpid Stream* immediately before the cross-dressing scene in Act II, a scene that parodies Romantic ballet's fantastical encounters in the forest between human "lovers" and ethereal "sylphs." In that position, the exotic dance, redolent of forbidden expression, presaged the transgressive encounters that formed the moral, narrative, and artistic heart of *The Limpid Stream*. Shostakovich also included the tango in the ballet suite for *The Bolt* and in a cabaret scene for the ballet-pastiche *The Young Lady and the Hooligan* (1962).[36] His reiterative use of this dance probably suggested some partiality for the music and certainly illuminated how detachable it and dances like it were from *The Bolt*. This observation does not diminish the music but asserts its charms, while also recognizing how Shostakovich deployed (and preserved) some of his ballet music in new contexts.

ACT III: The Club

One Soviet critic memorably described *The Bolt* as an "intrigue confined to five minutes of havoc in the third act."[37] These "five minutes" involve Goshka's sabotage of the lathe and the comeuppance of Lyonka Gulba. A final celebratory scene then takes place in the factory club, where an amateur concert, paralleling the one in the first act, parodies politically undesirable (and potentially subversive) social elements.[38] The concert comprises an extended *divertissement* in two parts, the first for members of the club brigade and the second for Red Army men.[39] In a cheeky nod to nineteenth-century "grand ballet," *The Bolt* ends with a "Final Dance and Apotheosis," which, like the apotheosis of grand ballet, reasserts the political order.

The club brigade's concert (Nos. 34–39) is the most interesting part of Act III for its musical variety and its political summary of contemporary events and social categories. As in Act I, the topics, visual elements, and political stance draw from the practices of amateur theatre. The premise for including this "concert" in the ballet is quite literal: amateur theatricals *did* take place in factories (and other places), and these were the sorts of small-scale skits that might be encountered there. The dances emphasize an ideological message by depicting bourgeois immoralities (presented by the club brigade in Act III) and celebrating Soviet virtues (displayed by the Red Army men).[40] The reiterative approach to marking "negative" versus "positive" values reflects ideological circuity in which all events aim at the same message.

Table 3.2 lays out the structure of the concert in Act III. The club brigade performs six dances: the Naval Disarmament Conference, the Aesthetic Young Lady, the Yes-Man, the Drayman, the Textile Workers, and the Colonial Slave Girl. Respectively, these dances expose hypocrisy in international politics (Naval Disarmament), formalist tastes of the bourgeoisie (Aesthetic Young Lady), compromise over principle (Yes-Man), exploitation of the worker (Drayman), futility in capitalist labor (Textile Workers), and capitalist oppression (Colonial Slave Girl). A dance for the *corps de ballet* follows, rationalized in the libretto as a dance for the Komsomols, presumably their collective response to the individuality just on display (No. 40). Closing the *divertissement*, the dances of the Red Army men feature divisions of the Soviet military.

The dance of the "Naval Disarmament Conference" (No. 34) parodies the topic of disarmament—a bizarre reference for a ballet, to be sure, but a subject of national and political significance in Soviet Russia. Disarmament had occupied a central place in global diplomatic relations after World War I. Through the 1920s, a series of international conferences had taken place in the United States and Europe, culminating in the World Disarmament Conference in Geneva in 1932. A central issue through the decade was the "policy of naval arms limitation," agreed in 1922 by the world's leading naval powers.[41] The dance of the "Naval Disarmament Conference" in *The Bolt* gave the nod to this event. (The same event was in view in "No. 30: Polka (Once upon a Time in Geneva)" in *The Golden Age*.)

Table 3.2 The "club concert" (*divertissement*) of Act III.

Act III, Scene 7, Nos. 34–39 and No. 42 (NCW)
The Club Brigade No. 34: The Naval Disarmament Conference (*hypocrisy*) No. 35: The Aesthetic Young Lady (*formalism*) No. 36: The Yes-Man (*conventionalism*) No. 37: The Textile Workers (*futility*) No. 38: The Drayman (*exhibitionism*) No. 39: The Colonial Slave Girl (*exploitation*)
Nos. 40–41 in the NCW is a dance for *corps de ballet* (the Komsomols) probably with some pantomime for Goshka's confession.
Red Army No. 42. Red Army Dances - Infantrymen and Artillerymen - ADAC (Association for Defense, Aviation, and Chemistry) Members - Bicycle Infantry - Red Army soldier & Red Navy man - Airmen - Budyonny Cavalry Corps

By the early 1930s, disarmament was widely understood in Russia as ideological shorthand for Soviet morality and capitalist vice. The Soviets participated vigorously, albeit cynically, in disarmament talks. "On every possible occasion," wrote one analyst, "[they] energetically stressed the urgent need for total disarmament"; yet ideologically, the Soviet position maintained that "disarmament is possible only in a socialized world" and that capitalists use disarmament to prepare "war under the cloak of pacifism."[42] The Soviets' repeated calls for total disarmament were intended to expose "all proposals stemming from non-Soviet countries . . . as hypocritical gestures . . . insincere and meaningless" and to demonstrate that "the abolition of war [is] possible only with the fall of capitalism."[43] Moreover, in Russia, the First Five-Year Plan had mobilized an internal policy shift toward rearmament for "the defense of socialism" against "all and any attempt at military intervention from the outside."[44] So important were these issues in Russia that they were not just recorded in Soviet papers, diplomatic documents, and manifestos, but they were also advertised in cultural enterprises and popular entertainments. When *The Bolt* (and *The Golden Age* before it) raised the topic of disarmament, the ballets acknowledged an acute contemporary issue through which Marxist dogma and Soviet policy were regularly expressed.

The dance of the "Naval Disarmament Conference" is a march-to-nowhere. Its opening motif (descending through a minor 3rd, A-flat–G–F) occurs over alternating major-minor triads in the low brass and repeats seven times with the same harmony, pitches, and patterns; only the orchestration is altered (in a manner reminiscent of changing-background variations). Disparate musical ideas appear between recurrences (a heraldic trumpet call, bluesy trombone slides, jazzy syncopation), but the music keeps returning to the same motif, creating an obsessive repetition beyond which no progress is made. During this number, exaggerated figures caricatured the world's major naval powers—the American, French, English, and Japanese fleets. These figures appeared on stage as life-size puppets.[45] The "American fleet" sported a top hat, smoked a military rocket in place of a cigar, and flaunted an American flag and heavy weaponry on his rotund belly. He epitomized the conventions of Russian visual propaganda in which "the fat cigar-smoking capitalist in a top hat" was a standard image.[46] The "French fleet" appeared in a submarine costume, a reference to the power of the French submarine fleet, which was not only the largest in the world in the early 1930s but also boasted the biggest and most advanced submarine of the time (the *Surcouf*).[47] The "English fleet" wore the costume of a dreadnought, the battleship that exemplified the fighting power of the Royal Navy and that had precipitated a naval arms race among world powers in the early twentieth century.[48] The figure of the "Japanese fleet" held a heavy cruiser—Japan's leading ship design in the 1920s—in claw-like steel hands while guns protruded from shoulder lapels and the character grimaced through enormous fangs.[49] These costumes were designed for show, not for movement, and their military arsenals satirized the topic of disarmament.

After this striking opening, the club concert continues with a set of character dances. The "Aesthetic Young Lady" (No. 35) explores "formalist" devices through disjunct musical elements. Blaring dissonances give way to an elegant waltz, which veers into the burlesque before dissolving into astringent dissonance and ending raucously in an uncertain key. Melody, harmony, meter, style, and syntax are confused—a picture of "incoherence." Entirely different, and utterly conventional, the "Yes-Man" (No. 36, also translated as the "Conciliator" or "Compromiser") emphasizes predictability. The xylophone dominates with a diatonic melody in eight-bar phrases. As Morrison has noted, the tune stresses "cadential agreement" but also suffers brassy interruptions suggestive of circus music.[50] The variation is distinguished by its sparkling timbre and its simplicity of melody, rhythm, and harmony, as well as its emphasis on the tonic E minor, the key in which the xylophone enters every time. Just before the end, the xylophone veers out of character to hammer out an F major triad (R624). But just as abruptly, it gives up, and the dance closes with three repetitions of a perfect cadence in E minor. The musical portrait is of a character who belabors points of agreement and avoids putting a foot wrong. The dance of the "The Textile Workers" (No. 37) is a *moto perpetuo* that suggests bustling activity and the spinning of machines. The choreography for this dance was innovative, according to Soviet descriptions. The dancers rose and fell (that is, stood and knelt) while their arms moved back and forth like the parts of a loom.[51] A rehearsal photograph shows two rows of dancers arranged on the stage, the front row kneeling, the back row standing, and the dancers' arms linked as though forming a "chain" or "rod." (That is, each dancer's left hand holds the next dancer's left elbow, creating a straight line. Each dancer's right arm is then folded up toward her chest and can open outward and close again to her body. Contemporary photographs document the use of the hand-to-elbow "chain" and its association with mechanistic motion in other contemporary Soviet productions, e.g., "Machine Dance" performed by the Moscow Ballet School in 1931.[52]) "The Drayman" (No. 38) dances a heavy-footed march, reinforced by snare-drum tattoos, trombone glissandi, and brassy tunes. The music's most distinctive element is a relentless, whip-like accent on the downbeat, which creates a sense of heaviness and effort, even cruelty.[53] "The Colonial Slave Girl" is depicted by wandering passages of uncertain meter, harmony, and melodic direction followed by an exotic interlude whose dissonance and timbres recall evocations of the East in the Russian balletic tradition. The sense of weightiness and vague menace in this variation underscores the plight of the victim.

After a closing *divertissement* for Red Army men (which need not tax the reader's patience), Act III ends with an "apotheosis" that parodies conventions of nineteenth-century ballet while affirming the "right" political order in this Soviet ballet. The tradition of apotheosis in ballet was rooted in the genre's courtly origins where the final apotheosis served as a political act exalting the king. In both the *ballet de cour* and the *masque* of the early modern period, the "apotheosis of the king" presented the glorification of the king as a ballet's "inevitable result."[54] Through the dance reforms of the eighteenth and nineteenth centuries, the ballerina, rather than the ruler, emerged as the central figure of ballet and thus the subject of apotheosis. In French Romantic ballet, this apotheosis was achieved emblematically in the death or ethereal afterlife of the ballerina's character (as in *La sylphide* or *Giselle*). In the grand ballets of Petipa, the vision of the ballerina was also inextricably linked to a "political vision" of the well-ordered state.[55] Important apotheoses in the Russian repertoire were found in *La Bayadère, The Awakening of Flora, Swan Lake, Nutcracker, Raymonda,* and other ballets. The most spectacular example of all was *The Sleeping Beauty*. "A grand spectacle, four hours long, with a prologue, three acts and an apotheosis," writes Garafola, "*Beauty* was a summation of the conventions elaborated over the course of the century."[56] When "apotheosis" was reiterated in *The Bolt*, albeit humorously, the convention was a familiar part of the genre and would have been recognized as such. *The Bolt*'s apotheosis highlighted ballet's political and artistic legacy and reaffirmed the work's central subject: the well-ordered state. In a manner reminiscent of grand ballet, the closing scene of *The Bolt* offered a kind of exalted court drama—now a Soviet court—featuring the "desirables" and "undesirables" of the kingdom, each in their rightful place.

More than fifty years after the premiere of *The Bolt*, the Soviet art historian Grigoriy Levitin described the final scene as "a gigantic panorama of the achievements of the Soviet Union."[57] Levitin identified this monumentality in Bruni's stage set, which featured a backdrop of primary colors and an artistic rendering of the enormous Volkhovstroi dam (a major industrial project that had been constructed near Leningrad during the First Five-Year Plan).[58] The sense of massiveness on the stage must have underscored the elaborate display of apotheosis.

The *divertissement* and the apotheosis of Act III, however, posed an impossible contradiction: amateurism versus spectacle. They attempted to combine the small, spontaneous forms of amateur theatre (club concert) with the summative, polished spectacle of the final act (apotheosis). Improvised genres undercut monumentality, and grand spectacle jostled awkwardly with small-scale intimacy and lack of refinement. The parody of the final scene arose from this juxtaposition of incongruous elements. Years after the premiere, Lopukhov claimed that the creative team for *The Bolt* had specifically pondered the novelties of amateur theatre and political posters (that is, Blue Blouse "living newspapers," TRAM performances, ROSTA windows) and brought these into the ballet. Scholars have sometimes pondered whether Lopukhov was satirical in such statements, or at least engaging in doublespeak to account for *The Bolt*'s failure.[59] Whatever Lopukhov's thoughts were privately, *The Bolt*—and particularly its final scene—drew on the improvised, spontaneous qualities of Soviet amateur theatre and in doing so challenged the pageantry of other balletic components. The contradiction lay in using professional ballet to execute amateur theatrics and, conversely, in inserting improvised forms into specialized dance. The approach emphasized *The Bolt*'s "amateur" aesthetic in which the unpolished and the non-professional—that is, the opposite of the refined and well-rehearsed—were an artistic goal.

* * *

The Bolt explored how to give formal, material, and artistic expression to contemporary ideological values. Formal balletic elements included dancers on pointe, *corps* dances, and set pieces (*divertissement*, apotheosis). Material elements drew on the visual culture of popular art. Artistically, the ballet experimented with things that would not normally be done on the ballet stage (dancers as machines, giant puppets, figures that could not dance). The incorporation of visual propaganda and agitational theatre into *The Bolt* enhanced the ballet's ideological credentials and brought Soviet concerns about political purity, social virtue, and economic advancement into dialogue with contemporary artistic developments. The ballet was well crafted in each component (witty music, innovative movements, original designs) and it was unique for the way it combined the sum of its parts (an industrial topic, classical forms, amateur theatre, and political iconography). But even though such individual elements were often successful in other art forms, they failed to cohere in a satisfactory way in *The Bolt*. Moreover, the ideological orientation superseded, and at times overwhelmed, the work's artistic components.

The Bolt was a type of political allegory, and in that respect, was linked to other political ballets in the genre's history. A political component had been pervasive in court ballets, where an intimate correspondence often existed between current events and the way those were parodied on the stage. The political allegory in these ballets was clear, and their symbols were neither subtle nor contested. Whether consciously or not, *The Bolt* reached back to this balletic model that had long been abandoned. It examined dangers to the Soviet political order and offered depictions of the well-ordered state and superior political positions. In doing this, the ballet asserted a way of orienting Soviet life and of understanding the Soviet person's place within it.

The Bolt did not succeed as either an artistic or a political work, however, and the debacle had significant consequences for Lopukhov and Shostakovich. The Leningrad State Academic Theatre removed Lopukhov from his position as artistic director and replaced him with Agrippina Vaganova, who was then teaching at the Choreographic Institute, and Sergei

Radlov, whose expertise lay in stage plays and operas. Radlov promised to overhaul *The Bolt*, but no revisions began, and by June 1931 the ballet had been abandoned. Yet Shostakovich salvaged some of the music, turning a handful of numbers into a ballet suite (Op. 27a) and reusing several more in *The Limpid Stream*. After *The Bolt*, Shostakovich did not work again with the Leningrad State Academic Theatre but came to prefer collaborations with the Maly Opera Theatre, which he found to be more adventurous in its approach to his dramatic works.[60] His next and most significant dramatic endeavor was his opera *Lady Macbeth*. Riding the triumph of that work, he committed to another ballet with Lopukhov: *The Limpid Stream*.

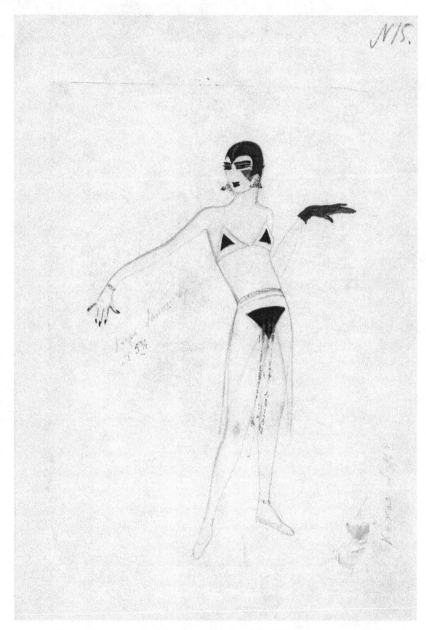

Plate 1 Valentina Khodasevich's costume sketch for "Diva" in *The Golden Age*. The St. Petersburg State Museum of Theatre and Music, 1930.

Plate 2 Valentina Khodasevich's costume sketch for female soloists in "Soviet Dance" in *The Golden Age*. The St. Petersburg State Museum of Theatre and Music, 1930.

Plate 3 Valentina Khodasevich's costume sketch for Western sportswomen in *The Golden Age*. The St. Petersburg State Museum of Theatre and Music, 1930.

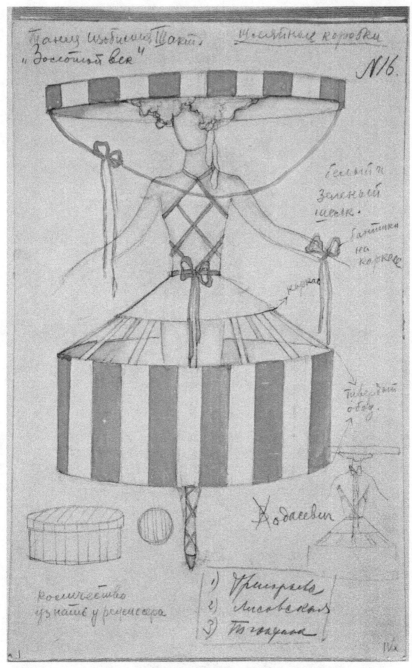

Plate 4 Valentina Khodasevich's costume sketch for character in a hatbox ("Dance of Plenty") in *The Golden Age*. The St. Petersburg State Museum of Theatre and Music, 1930.

Plate 5 Front cover of the program booklet for *The Limpid Stream*. Mikhailovsky Theatre [Leningrad: Ivan Fedorov], 1935.

Plate 6 Zinaida Vasilieva as "Zina" in *The Limpid Stream*. Mikhailovsky Theatre [Leningrad: Ivan Fedorov], 1935.

Plate 7 Mikhail Bobyshev's costume sketch for collective farm workers in *The Limpid Stream*. Mikhailovsky Theatre [Leningrad: Ivan Fedorov], 1935.

Plate 8 Mikhail Bobyshev's costume sketch for collective farm workers in *The Limpid Stream*. Mikhailovsky Theatre [Leningrad: Ivan Fedorov], 1935.

Plate 9 Mikhail Bobyshev's sketch for the set of Act I in *The Limpid Stream*. Mikhailovsky Theatre [Leningrad: Ivan Fedorov], 1935.

Plate 10 Mikhail Bobyshev's sketch for the set of Act II in *The Limpid Stream*. Mikhailovsky Theatre [Leningrad: Ivan Fedorov], 1935.

Plate 11 Mikhail Bobyshev's sketch for the set of Act III in *The Limpid Stream*. Mikhailovsky Theatre [Leningrad: Ivan Fedorov], 1935.

Plate 12 Vladimir Dmitriev's costume sketches for the *dachnitsa*, or dacha-dweller's wife, in the Bolshoi production of *The Limpid Stream*. Bolshoi Museum, 1935.

Plate 13 Vladimir Dmitriev's costume sketches for *narod*, or national peoples, in the Bolshoi production of *The Limpid Stream*. Bolshoi Museum, 1935.

Plate 14 Vladimir Dmitriev's costume sketches for "Zina" in the Bolshoi production of *The Limpid Stream*. Bolshoi Museum, 1935.

Plate 15 Vladimir Dmitriev's costume sketches for members of the collective farm community in the Bolshoi production of *The Limpid Stream*. Bolshoi Museum, 1935.

4
Soviet Sylphs: *The Limpid Stream* and Romantic Ballet

In the mid-1930s, Shostakovich reached the height of his early career with the international sensation of his opera *Lady Macbeth of Mtsensk District*. The opera premiered in 1934 at the Maly Opera Theatre in Leningrad. Over the next two years, it enjoyed three Soviet productions and ran for almost two hundred performances in Leningrad and Moscow, while also being staged in major opera houses across Europe and the Americas. Months after *Lady Macbeth*'s premiere, with every door open to him, Shostakovich chose to commit to a new project—the ballet that became *The Limpid Stream*. It was to be based on a libretto by Lopukhov and Adrian Piotrovsky, with choreography by Lopukhov and designs by Mikhail Bobyshev.

The Limpid Stream enjoyed enormous success upon its premiere at the Maly Theatre on June 4, 1935.[1] Audiences flocked to see it, the auditorium filled at every performance, and ecstatic reviews commended the ballet's music and choreography.[2] Shostakovich's music garnered the highest praise, with critics comparing it to "the best traditions of dance music from Strauss to Glazunov"; they noted its "sparkling" and "brilliant" charm, its "rich, colorful, melodic" qualities, its "symphonic" moments, its "beautifully orchestrated" character, its "realistic" music, and its masterfully written dances.[3] Lopukhov's choreography was applauded too for its "virtuosity" and unabashed return to "classical technique."[4] The ballet's one flaw, critics said, was its libretto. Some deemed the story "weak," "unlucky," even "insipid"; yet most tempered any disapproval with the judgment that music, dance, and design "neutralized the impact" of narrative limitations.[5] (Only Sollertinsky, the ballet's harshest reviewer, found fault with most components of the work.) *The Limpid Stream* was hugely popular, and in a move that seemed to seal its fortunes, the Bolshoi Theatre commissioned a Moscow production within months.

On November 30, 1935, the ballet premiered at the Bolshoi, a month before *Lady Macbeth* was also produced at the theatre in a third Soviet production.[6] On December 3, Stalin attended a performance of *The Limpid Stream* on the night of its premiere with an all-Bolshoi cast.[7] That same evening the theatre hosted a delegation of visiting Cossacks from collective farms along the Don River. Presumably, Stalin did not criticize the ballet privately; at least press coverage remained positive. And the Don Cossacks wrote a note thanking the Bolshoi for an unforgettable evening (of course, seeing Stalin was the most unforgettable part, but they enjoyed the ballet too). In a sign of particular favor, the Bolshoi then programmed *The Limpid Stream* on Stalin's birthday, December 21.[8] Such a rare honor was a powerful reminder of the ballet's perceived significance. But the triumph was short-lived. On February 6, 1936, just days after denouncing *Lady Macbeth* ("Muddle instead of Music"), *Pravda* published a devastating review of *The Limpid Stream* ("Balletic Falsity"), accusing the ballet of disregard for "verisimilitude" to Soviet life. The work was withdrawn from the repertoire. Lopukhov lost his job, and Shostakovich never wrote another ballet.

The circumstances surrounding the condemnation of *The Limpid Stream* are well documented and illuminate the watershed events of 1936 that profoundly altered Shostakovich's creative life. But before those events took place, the ballet occupied a central position in Soviet dance and in Shostakovich's creative approach to it. *The Limpid Stream* embraced the national initiative of creating Soviet ballet but did so uniquely, departing from the dominant emphases of other Soviet ballets of the period and even of Shostakovich's own earlier attempts in the genre. It did not employ experimental forms (like the movements from sports, gymnastics, or mechanical operations that had appeared in the composer's earlier ballets), nor did it include popular styles (music hall numbers or ballroom dances), and it certainly did not conform, or even attempt to conform, to the soon-to-be-dominant genre of *drambalet*. Dressed up in Soviet costume, *The Limpid Stream* was Soviet only in the most cosmetic sense. It was, in fact, a ballet about ballet—a work that created a network of references to the scenes and sounds of ballet's past and used these as sources of inspiration, parody, and allusion. *The Limpid Stream* was modeled on the genre of Romantic ballet. It invoked and parodied familiar Romantic conventions and situated those humorously within a Soviet setting.

The Limpid Stream came into being during a volatile epoch in which a sea change in thought and policy reshaped every aspect of artistic life and redefined the role of the arts in Soviet culture. In the early 1930s, the Cultural Revolution ended (1928–31) and High Stalinism dawned (1932–41). High

Stalinism aimed at "extreme cultural centralization" and the canonization of socialist realism as cultural "method" and doctrine.[9] In the arts, socialist realist endeavors were supposed "to provide legitimizing myths for the state," not by mirroring reality as it was but by constructing reality as it would become.[10] But the ideology remained ill-defined, and its implications were opaque. How precisely was the party line to be defined in each of the arts? The question was acute in relation to ephemeral and ineffable art forms like music and dance. *Drambalet* became the genre of ballet associated with socialist realism and the "correct" expression of ideological goals. But the process of codifying and elevating *drambalet* took time, and the ballets that were ultimately hailed as exemplars of the genre (*The Flames of Paris*, 1932, and *The Fountain of Bakhchisarai*, 1934) largely achieved their status in retrospect. *The Limpid Stream* was written in this fluid period of political and aesthetic change, as socialist realism was being advanced ideologically but before it took definitive form, and as the exemplars of *drambalet* were being created but before they were fixed as the future of Soviet dance.

In this milieu, *The Limpid Stream* marked an artistic, cultural, and professional achievement in Soviet ballet, at least for a time. Its creation and reception charted evolving artistic concerns alongside a shifting political landscape and many practical challenges. A rich set of musical and theatrical materials chronicles the creative history of *The Limpid Stream* and offers insights into the work's artistic goals and cultural relevance. These sources document *The Limpid Stream*'s engagement with the genre of Romantic ballet and trace the reinvention of Romantic conventions within a Soviet topic. They also reveal the ballet's place within its artistic milieu and in Shostakovich's and Lopukhov's individual careers. Ultimately, they record its success and failure in the national enterprise of Soviet cultural production. This chapter situates *The Limpid Stream* as the final act in Shostakovich and Lopukhov's collaborations toward a model of Soviet dance and demonstrates how the work reimagined Romantic ballet, aiming to reconcile it with the demands of Soviet realism, contemporary balletic needs, and new artistic and political priorities.

Soviet "Romantic" Ballet

The Limpid Stream is set on a collective farm (*kolkhoz*) in the North Caucasus, where a farming community welcomes a group of ballet artists from the city. The intrigue centers on three couples: Zina and Pyotr from the collective farm, a Classical Ballerina and her partner the *Danseur* from the city, and an old dacha dweller and his simpering wife. Zina and the Ballerina recognize each other from ballet classes long ago, and the two friends share a "lesson" as Zina recalls her long-neglected training. Fascinated by the city Ballerina, Pyotr develops a crush on her, leaving Zina hurt and jealous. At the same time, the old dacha dweller starts chasing the Ballerina too, while his wife makes flirtatious overtures to the *Danseur*. Eventually, the young people from farm and city decide to teach those with wandering eyes a lesson. Pyotr must be restored to Zina, and the dacha dweller and his wife must learn the absurdity of their dalliances. Zina dresses up as the Ballerina and dances a *pas de deux* in disguise with Pyotr. The Ballerina dresses up as the *Danseur* and holds a "tryst" with the dacha dweller's wife. At the apex of absurdities, the *Danseur* dresses up as the Ballerina—a "sylphide," as the libretto says—and meets the dacha dweller in the woods at night. But the "lover" kills his "sylphide" by mistake, and everybody ends up with the right partner in the end. The ballet closes with a tour-de-force of dances that celebrate both the plentiful harvest (of enormous Soviet vegetables) and restored relationships.

The Limpid Stream was a Soviet "Romantic" ballet, a work dressed in a Soviet story but performing and parodying the tropes of ballet's Romantic era. Many elements of *The Limpid Stream* were familiar Romantic conventions—sylphs in the moonlight, disguised identities, *travesty* dancing, national dances, and realism of the *mise-en-scène*. Moreover, like many Romantic ballets, the central characters of *The Limpid Stream* danced the role of dancers in order to give the story greater verisimilitude. Zina (a former ballerina) and the Classical Ballerina and *Danseur* were dancers "in life" and "on stage" who together represented Soviet cultural and collective enterprises. (Underscoring the realism, the characters of "Zina" and "Pyotr" were named for Zinaida Vasilyeva and Pyotr Gusev, who performed the role of the principal couple.) Meanwhile, the ballet's original title, "The Two Sylphs," alluded to Romantic ballet's most famous types of characters.[11] Of course, the title changed (multiple times); but the Romantic model remained, and its surviving components in the source record illuminate how the principles of Romantic ballet were approached and subverted in this work.

The Limpid Stream engaged three primary Romantic conventions: national dance (Act I), the realm of the sylph (Act II), and explanatory borrowing (Act III). Moreover, each of these components was reinterpreted as "Soviet" and as "real" in a manner that parodied the Romantic precedent.

National elements were derived from Soviet Russia's ethnic people groups in the Caucasus. The realm of the sylph was not supernatural but was populated with "real" Soviet ballet dancers. And the borrowing, or interpolation, in Act III served a narrative purpose (resolving conflicts on the collective farm) while also linking *The Limpid Stream* to other famous productions in the storied history of Russian ballet. *The Limpid Stream*'s most obvious, sustained, and coherent Romantic reference occurred with the sylphs in the forest in Act II. In order to follow the narrative, however, it is helpful to look at the acts in order and to explain how the Romantic components in each are constructed on the stage and in the music.

Act I: National Dance, Shakespearean Shores

Act I opens at a small railway station in the Kuban, where the artists from the capital arrive to join harvest celebrations on the collective farm and perform for the local community. Zina and the Classical Ballerina dance together, and Pyotr's eyes begin to wander after his wife's friend. When the ballet troupe meets the larger farming community returning from the fields, spontaneous dancing breaks out as Kuban "fieldworkers" and city "artists" show each other their entertainments.

The meeting of city dwellers and collective farm residents is the narrative situation for the use of national, or character, dance in Act I.[12] Locals and farmworkers perform folk-like dances, while city people—not only the ballet troupe but also the dacha-dweller and his wife, who are only part-time residents in the country—perform classical dances. A *divertissement* of classical and character dancing is labeled "genre dances" in the libretto and includes a Waltz for the Classical Ballerina, a Chaconne for the dacha dweller and his wife, a Russian *plyaska* (communal dance) for the men, a *khorovod* (round dance) for the women, a "warlike" Cossack dance (per the libretto), and a few paired dances for soloists (milkmaid and tractor driver, accordion player and schoolgirl) (Table 4.1).[13] These dances serve three narrative functions. First, they chart the interaction between city and farm communities that leads to Pyotr's flirtation, Zina's heartbreak, and a determination by the "young people" to restore right relationships. These are the events that set the story in motion. Second, the genre dances build excitement as they culminate in the fast and furious dance for mountain Cossacks and Kuban fieldworkers. Third, they provide emotional and structural

Table 4.1 The *divertissement* of Act I, Scene 2, Nos. 9–16 in the *New Collected Works* edition of the score.

Dances of the *divertissement* (as laid out in the *New Collected Works*)	Stage action as laid out in the 1935 libretto
No. 9: Russian Dance	*Plyaska* (communal dance for "inspectors" on the farm)
No. 10: Chaconne[14]	An "ancient chaconne" (dacha dweller and his wife)
No. 11: Young Girls' Dance[15]	A so-called "*khorovod*" (in fact, a recycled number from *The Bolt*)
No. 12: Milkmaid and Tractor Driver's Dance	Pair of soloists (milkmaid and tractor driver)
No. 13: Ballerina's Waltz	*Waltz* for the Classical Ballerina and *Danseur*, which mesmerizes Pyotr and the Dacha Dweller
No. 14: Comic Dance	Pair of soloists (schoolgirl and accordion player)
No. 15: Caucasian Tribesmen's and Kuban Fieldworkers' Dance	A "warlike" dance evocative of a *hopak*
No. 16: Exit	Exit of *corps* and soloists

balance because they contrast with the mock serenity of the "forest scene" in Act II and mirror a tour-de-force of communal dancing at the harvest festival in Act III.

Musically, the national dances are generic, using popular idioms and not attempting authenticity. The *plyaska* is energetic with repeating rhythmic figures and brittle orchestration (No. 9). The Cossack's "warlike" dance (No. 15) is generalized through duple meter, a major key, and a frenzied character (reminiscent of a *hopak*). A "weavers' *khorovod*" originally featured some evocation of the choral singing associated with this genre.[16] But the dance was excised from the score and replaced with "Dance of the Textile Workers" from *The Bolt*, which was retitled "Young Girls' Dance" in *The Limpid Stream* (No. 11). The libretto continued to call it a "*khorovod*," however, a fact that suggests just how much national qualities were conferred by fiat. Without the choreography, it is impossible to know the steps of these dances, but the choreographic result was not ethnographically accurate, as many reviewers attested. Instead, dances were probably stylized according to contemporary practice. Character dancing conveyed local color, and certain steps invariably appeared, no matter what country or tradition was represented. As texts of the period explained, such steps "[took] on as many colors as [they were] changed by the musical accents and temperaments of the people dancing."[17] In *The Limpid Stream*, as in Romantic ballets, the idea of national components was reinforced by the libretto and by visual elements on the stage.

Costumes were a chief means of communicating national qualities in *The Limpid Stream*. Vladimir Dmitriev's sketches for the Bolshoi production depict a plethora of characters in traditional dress. In one sketch, labeled simply "*narod*" (national people), two figures are painted in cloth trousers, smocks, and striped robes. One wears an enormous sheepskin hat (a Cossack *papakha*), and the other, a round hat trimmed with fur (similar to a *borik*). Other sketches feature the enormous *burka* overcoat of traditional dress as well as the Cossack *cherkeska* (or *chokha*), a woolen coat sewn with cartridge belts at the chest and fixed with a *khanjali* dagger on a silver-studded belt—details that Dmitriev's drawings faithfully reproduce (Plate 13). Production photographs from the Maly also show male dancers in *kubanki* (round hats), embroidered shirts, and wide trousers tucked into leather boots. They are captured in a flat-footed, pugilistic pose as they advance across the stage in high boots with arms and fists raised in stylized preparation for a fight. Such particulars of dress, rendered with sufficient precision to identify their components, evoked the idea of the Soviet Union's national peoples.

The national components in *The Limpid Stream* helped to establish the ballet's setting in the North Caucasus and the national ethnic groups of the local community—Cossacks, Uzbeks, Georgians, Russians, all of whom were identified in production materials. This emphasis on Russia's national peoples and their involvement in Soviet enterprises tapped into a contemporary concept of *narodnost'* ("people-mindedness"), which was a cornerstone of socialist realist ideology as well as a regular component of Soviet stage productions in the 1930s.[18] Moreover, the North Caucasus was romanticized in the ballet; it offered a literal yet exotic location that functioned much as the Scottish Highlands did in *La Sylphide* or the Polish village in *Coppélia*. Soviet writers were sensitive to this stylized reality. As the dance critic Viktor Iving noted, "This Northern Caucasus [in *The Limpid Stream*] appears on the stage with the same geographical convention as the 'deserted seashore in Bohemia' . . . [in] *The Winter's Tale*."[19] The "violation" of "realism," he continued, included male dancers in Caucasian costumes and female dancers in Russian ones, with national dances ending up as exoticized as the "Polovtsian Dances" in *Prince Igor*.[20] While Iving judged *The Limpid Stream* a success for its musical and choreographic achievements, his complaint about a Shakespearean seashore was evocative: it associated the collective farm in the North Caucasus with ethnographic fantasy. The critique underscored the romantic (and romanticized) quality of the ballet's national components.

The Limpid Stream served up realism, local color, and an imagined cultural essence of Soviet Russia—a kind of Soviet exoticism. In this, the ballet recalled the emphases of the nineteenth-century Romantic repertoire. National components, whether real or invented, were "markers of authenticity and suppliers of local color" in Romantic ballet, a kind of visual shorthand that distilled the salient features of setting and culture for "the impression of a well-wrought verisimilitude."[21] In the heyday of Romantic ballet at the Paris Opéra (1830–50), as described by Marian Smith, designers of sets and costumes were sometimes sent to the locations in which ballets were set in order to "have the experience that would make it possible for [them] to create an aura of authenticity in [their] stagings."[22] Composers were expected to "create a sense of place" in national-sounding music.[23] Dancers occasionally turned to native performers for coaching, and choreographers distilled "a certain repertory of markers" in the *pas*, understanding that these "function[ed] emblematically, reinforcing the spectators' sense that they were somehow gaining access to the essence of a culture or nation."[24] In short, Romantic fashion called for "as much verisimilitude as possible" in the rendering of national components.[25] *The Limpid Stream*'s emphasis on Russia's national peoples updated this kind of Romantic realism with a Soviet setting and suggested how the conventions of Romantic ballet also satisfied Soviet aesthetics.

When *Pravda* condemned the ballet, however, some of its harshest criticism fell on the work's national components. It derided the ballet's "doll-like" (inauthentic) approach and contrasted this with "authentic" national dances performed by actual folk groups in other productions: "On the same stage of the Bolshoi Theatre, where dolls painted 'to look like a collective farmer' break down, real collective farmers from the North Caucasus have recently shown the amazing art of folk dance; in that, there was an individuality characteristic of the people of the North Caucasus."[26] *Pravda*'s critique pressed ideological requirements that were very different from the aesthetics governing Parisian ballet of the 1830s and 1840s; but, ironically, though no doubt unwittingly, the complaint about "realism" and "inauthentic" national components echoed the criticisms of a host of French Romantic ballets. In fact, *Pravda* advocated precisely the remedy that critics of French Romantic ballet had advised—namely, travel to the location in question in order to create "realism" out of ethnographic study.

The presentation of Russia's national peoples in *The Limpid Stream* was ideologically useful because it created a colorful, and politically correct, depiction of an ordered Soviet reality comprising artists and farmworkers, city dwellers and mountain folk. At the same time, the national components emphasized realism in opposition to fantasy and, in doing so, reinforced the dualism inherent in the Romantic model. The "reality" of the collective farm existed in counterpoint to the illusions and delusions that would unfold in the next act.

Act II: Soviet Sylphs, the Marxist Forest

The Limpid Stream's most obvious exploration of Romantic ballet takes place in Act II, where the "sylphide"—the cross-dressing male dancer—meets the dacha dweller in the forest, and where Zina, dressed as the Classical Ballerina, meets Pyotr. The Ballerina dressed as the *Danseur* also holds a "tryst" with the dacha dweller's wife. The meetings with the old couple are full of pranks, but the rendezvous between Pyotr and Zina is tender and romantic. After the trysts, in which the guilty parties are tricked by their "lovers," the Ballerina-dressed-as-the-*danseur* "demands satisfaction" from the dacha dweller for his attentions toward the "sylphide." A duel ensues. The Ballerina aims and misses; the dacha dweller then aims but, hearing a bang somewhere, thinks he has fired, and he watches in horror as his "sylphide" falls to the ground dead. He rushes away, and the unharmed "sylphide" springs up to join the pranksters in a delighted dance.

The "forest scene" is the heart of *The Limpid Stream*'s reimagination of Romantic ballet. Its references cross music, dance, design, and narrative to create the work's most coherent engagement with, yet inversion of, Romantic conventions. The "forest scene" contrasts with the ordered norms of the collective farm and permits the encounters that cannot take place in that society. Moreover, the scene appropriates the Romantic forest and its occupants for the Marxist enterprise. It reinvents the Romantic forest as a material reality in which Soviet sylphs are "real" (Zina) or "imagined" (the *danseur en travesti*) but never supernatural.[27] In this Soviet forest, the false reality of idle imagination is epitomized by the false "sylphide," while the true reality of the

Soviet collective is embodied by Zina, who is both ballerina and collective farm worker.

Bobyshev's set design for Act II renders the scene in soft colors with undulating patches of blue and green.[28] In the foreground are the trees and bushes in which "sylphs" flit and tryst with "lovers." In the distance, schematic shadows, silhouetted peaks, and a glistening stream evoke a moonlit valley. The scene contrasts strongly with the colorful sets and daytime activities of Acts I and III. Bobyshev's sketch for Act I, for example, is a riot of orange and gold, showing the fruits of a plentiful harvest and a stage full of farm workers dressed in jewel-tone colors. A festive set for Act III depicts young people whirling on swings under trees laden with fruit, the women's pink and orange dresses splashing bright dabs of color against a green and gold background. The scene is lively and full of energy. Contrasting with these vibrant settings, Act II is wholly different—an empty stage, muted colors, eerie stillness, a sense of suspended time, of another realm.

Photographs from the Maly production show the "sylphs" of this realm in iconic poses. In one photograph, the *travesty* dancer, in white tutu and *pointe* shoes, lies under a tree, gazing at "her" admirer and gesturing into the distance with a bouquet. In another, a sylph appears in a tree just out of its lover's reach. The characters are Zina and Pyotr, and the pose is an unmistakable visual reference to the French ballet *La Sylphide*, in which the sylph floats up into a tree to show her lover a bird's nest. Lopukhov knew *La Sylphide* in Petipa's choreography and possibly in August Bournonville's too; his reference takes in French, Danish, and Russian Romantic traditions.[29] But there is no "supernaturalism" in the allusion, and any dualism between "real" and "unreal" is firmly situated within Soviet values.[30] Soviet sylphs are not "ethereal" creatures, but flesh-and-blood workers. The false "sylphide" is a creature of idle fantasy—an old man's lustful imagination as he relaxes at his dacha contributing nothing to the collective enterprise. The real "sylph" is Zina.

Costuming also signals these values, allowing us to recognize or "know" the characters even as they are expressed through a comparatively limited range of choreography. A promotional photograph for the Maly production shows Zina (Vasilieva) in a stylized arabesque in Act II. She wears white flowers in her hair and a long, white dress, which—according to the story—she has borrowed from her friend the Ballerina. She is, quite literally, "in costume." Among Bobyshev's designs for the Maly production, this dress is unique in its lightness and romantic elegance, and it contrasts strongly with the costumes of other female characters. Older women on the farm wear simple blouses, skirts, and kerchiefs, rendered in dull colors and basic geometric patterns. Younger women's dresses echo the palette of folk designs in bright pinks, reds, oranges, and yellows. Meanwhile, the "city wear" of the visiting ballet troupe is businesslike—matching striped suits for the Classical Ballerina and her partner, and a stylish coat, hat, and clutch for the Classical Ballerina (her traveling clothes for the train journey). In a "borrowed" costume of poetic elegance, Zina fits into the midnight realm of the forest and most fully inhabits her role as "sylph." She is both the ballerina her husband imagines and the wife he does not recognize.

Dmitriev's costumes (for the Bolshoi) also emphasize the moral standing of characters. Here, Zina wears a simple, white A-line dress. Its shape, style, and long skirt match the dresses of the female farm workers; but the white color sets Zina apart, both visually on the stage and morally as she represents the ideal union of Soviet cultural and collective virtue. What is most notable about this white costume is its utter simplicity and lack of decoration. It is a sensible Soviet tutu that allows Zina to take part in the collective enterprise. Other costumes reject Soviet virtues. For instance, the dacha dweller's elderly wife dresses in styles absurd for her age and social place. In one sketch, she is shown in a day dress with puff cap sleeves, ruffled skirt, and an impossible hour-glass waist. In another, she wears flounces and bows—a dress appropriate at a social tea, but totally out of place on a collective farm or in any Soviet space. She is dressed to entertain and be entertained, like an aristocrat. Her costumes emphasize her transgressive bourgeois values, both practical (as she clearly spends money on her clothes) and sexual (as she pursues partners rather than seriously devoting herself to moral causes).

While costuming and mise-en-scène in Act II contain many Romantic references, it is the music that offers the most compelling treatment of Romantic models. The Act's two *Adagios* offer good examples (Table 4.2). One parodies a Romantic *pas de deux* (No. 25: Arrival at Rendezvous) and the other functions in every respect as a typical Romantic component (No. 29: Pyotr and Zina in Ballerina's Costume). The first *Adagio* (No. 25) ushers in the travesty "sylph" over a harp cadenza, followed by a long, lyrical melody played by a solo French horn over thin accompaniment. But the *Adagio* is rudely interrupted by popular idioms that disrupt the "dreaminess" with overwrought orchestration, band-like textures, and banal licks. The

Table 4.2 Act II, Scene 3, Nos. 25–32 in the *New Collected Works* edition.[31]

Dances in two sets, grouped according to the 1935 libretto	Stage action
Set 1: Playing Jokes on Old Dacha Dwellers	
No. 25: Adagio. Arrival at Rendezvous	The dacha dwellers, the two Classical Dancers (in disguise), and the tractor driver appear on stage. Identities get mixed up, and interruptions in the music mark interruptions in the interactions between characters.
No. 26: Waltz. Variation of Male Dancer in Woman's Dress	Variation for the false "sylphide" (the *danseur en travesti* who is pursued by the dacha dweller)
No. 27: Variation of Ballerina in Her Partner's Costume	Variation for the Classical Ballerina (who is pursued by the dacha dweller's wife)
No. 28: Coda	Coda for soloists and others
Set 2: *Pas de deux* for Zina and Pyotr	
No. 29: Adagio. Pyotr and Zina in Ballerina's Costume	*Adagio* for Pyotr and Zina-in-disguise
No. 30: Plotters' Dance	A group of young people (the conspirators) dance
No. 31: Zina's Variation	Variation for Zina
No. 32: Coda	Coda for Zina and Pyotr

juxtaposition of musical styles signals the absurdity in the stage situation (the old man's fantasy of a "sylph") even as it parodies a Romantic *pas de deux*, making the tropes of that passage both comical and ridiculous.

The second *Adagio* in Act II is far more serious, more "real" (No. 29). It opens the *pas de deux* between Zina, in disguise, and Pyotr, as the narrative moment revolves around their relationship. Pyotr has arranged a tryst with the Classical Ballerina, but Zina—at her friend's insistence—turns up instead and Pyotr fails to recognize her. At this point in the story, Pyotr is confused about his feelings for two very different women (another Romantic trope), and this *pas de deux* reestablishes the proper relationship between him and Zina, at least for the audience. Pyotr must learn that his fantasies of a ballerina are, in fact, fantasies of his own wife, and we will all learn that there is no difference between a Soviet ballerina and a collective farm worker.

Zina and Pyotr's *Adagio* opens with the same music that introduced their first dance in Act I (No. 2). The repetition tells us that Pyotr is dancing with Zina, although he does not know it. In contrast to the music for the *travesty* sylph, Pyotr and Zina's *Adagio* proceeds in an uninterrupted flow of lyricism, containing the cues of the Romantic *Adagio* in length and quality of melody and in the vocality of the solo instrument. The solo here is played by the cello in its middle and upper ranges. In color, character, and tone, the passage is highly evocative—for example, of the cello solo in the Act II *pas de deux* from *Sleeping Beauty* or the viola solo in the Act II *pas de deux* from *Giselle*. Like its Romantic counterparts, Zina and Pyotr's *pas de deux* confirms the characters' relationship. At the same time, the sustained lyricism and unbroken character of the music imbue their *Adagio* with the intimacy, sincerity, and elevated tone of the Romantic model. One Soviet critic described this dance as "elegiac and romantically dreamy," evoking *Solveig* balletically and Grieg musically (a comment referring to Lopukhov's staging of *Solveig* as *The Ice Maiden* to Grieg's music in 1927).[32] While the critic pondered Soviet references, his central insight was that the passage looked back to scenes and music from the genre's past. The intuition was accurate. The *pas de deux* of Act II reached deep into ballet's past, exploring how Romantic conventions could be reimagined with Soviet topics.

The "forest scene" in *The Limpid Stream* is the ballet's moral and narrative center, the pivot between the "real world" of national dance and the new "reality" that will emerge from the confrontations in the forest. Moreover, the forest at night is a quintessentially Romantic location, and the "forest scene" in *The Limpid Stream* offers the work's most significant reimagination of the Romantic ballet. In ballets like *Giselle*, *La Sylphide*, or *Sleeping Beauty*, the forest stands in direct contrast to the ordered life of "reality" (the town, city, or court) and is the catalyst for encounters with the supernatural. In *The Limpid Stream*, the forest occupies a parallel position; it contrasts with the ordered "reality" of the collective farm and offers a space in which the rules of that "reality" are suspended. Of course, there are no supernatural beings in the Marxist forest, but it remains a realm that is not properly arranged, a realm in which characters may transgress, whether emotionally or physically, their proper roles—the *travesty* dancer in female dress, the dacha dweller and Pyotr in illicit dalliances, Zina in disguise. Within the Marxist forest (and the Romantic forest), there is no doubt about how things will turn out. But there is a suggestion that they might not turn out rightly, and this generates the tension that provides the moral anchor for the narrative, as well as the dramatic denouement.

Act III: Classical veils

Act III of *The Limpid Stream* returns to the collective farm and resolves the confusion of the forest by revealing the identity of the "sylphs"—the real and the false one—and by restoring the right partners: Zina and Pyotr, the dacha dweller and his wife, and the Classical Ballerina and the *Danseur*. Zina and the Ballerina dance in veils (or masks) before an audience on the collective farm. Pytor is entranced. Rushing forward as the dancers remove their veils, he recognizes his wife and shamefacedly begs her forgiveness. Meanwhile, the dacha dweller realizes that one of the dancers looks like the "sylphide" whom he inadvertently shot in the forest. Recognizing that he has been tricked for his own good, he follows Pyotr and Zina's example and reconciles with his wife. The ballet ends with a celebratory dance for the entire cast.

This reconciliation of relationships is also a reconciliation of real and imagined realms, and it is mediated through an interpolation from Léo Delibes' ballet *Sylvia*, a work that had premiered at the Paris Opéra in 1876 and been produced at the Imperial Theatre in 1901 by Lev Ivanov and Pavel Gerdt. The centerpiece of Act III of *The Limpid Stream* is a *pas d'action* with an *Adagio* for the three couples, three solo variations for the "real" dancers (the *Danseur*, Ballerina, and Zina), and a coda. This is the revelation scene in which the identities of the characters are revealed, and it involves veils, disguises, disclosure, and reunion. In scenario and stage situation, the scene echoes Sylvia's veiled dance before Aminta in Act III of *Sylvia*. The libretto for the Imperial production of Delibes' ballet describes an exotic setting, veiled girls, and Sylvia's dance: "A galley approaches the seashore...the veiled slave girls dance, hoping to charm Aminta. He remains indifferent but with the appearance of one more slave girl, her face covered by a veil, Aminta's heart guesses that it is Sylvia. He removes her veil, uncovers her face, and recognizes Sylvia as his beloved."[33]

The libretto for *The Limpid Stream* suggests an allusive situation in an exotic mountain valley. Like Aminta recognizing Sylvia in the removal of her veil, Pyotr recognizes the woman he loves and is reunited with her. Of course, being a good Soviet, he also grasps her true identity in the Soviet enterprise. "Two dancers, dressed exactly alike, appear on stage, their faces hidden by veils. Their dance over, Pyotr, unable to restrain himself, rushes towards them ... They raise their veils and the secret is out. Pyotr, who sees one of the ballerinas is his wife, timidly begs her forgiveness. They are finally reconciled. Pyotr sees that his modest Zina is both a first-class worker and a marvelous ballerina."[34]

Shostakovich's music confirms the reference with a pizzicato variation that recalls Delibes' "Pizzicato" for Sylvia. (Shostakovich's dance was, in fact, titled "Pizzicato" in the Maly *répétiteur* and the conductor's score but is published as "No. 41: Ballerina's Variation" in the *New Collected Works*. The name change obscures the relationship.) Of course, the strongest aural connection between Shostakovich's and Delibes' music is timbre: the pizzicato strings. But there are parallels too in melodic, rhythmic, and expressive relationships. Shostakovich's variation is marked *Allegretto*, like Delibes' *Allegretto ben moderato*. After a seven-bar introduction, Shostakovich's melody, like Delibes', opens with a falling perfect 4th (B-flat to F, the same pitches that launch Delibes' dance), then rises through arpeggiation that echoes the broken-chord patterns of Sylvia's variation. Meanwhile, the rhythmic profile is an alternation of eighth and quarter notes, paralleling the alternation of note values (sixteenths/eighths) in Delibes' music. Of course, there are differences too. Shostakovich's variation is in B-flat minor, whereas Delibes' is in E-flat major, yet the change of key and mode in no way undermines the allusion. On the contrary, in pacing, placement, timbre, tempo, rhythmic relationships, and melodic resonances, Shostakovich's pizzicato variation vividly recalls Sylvia's dance.

Since this is the moment of recognition and reunion, we might expect that Shostakovich's "Pizzicato" would be for Zina, whom Pyotr recognizes as she removes her veil and with whom he is reunited. But it is not. It is danced by the Classical Ballerina. In other words, the interpolation does not reenact the narrative of *Sylvia* (lovers reuniting) but suggests a subtler and more dramatically coherent allusion. The interpolated ballet becomes part of the story of *The Limpid Stream*, a "real" ballet being staged on a collective farm. According to the libretto, the Classical Ballerina dances on "an improvised stage" erected in the meadow. "All seats are taken" as the spectators—and particularly Pyotr—watch the show. The stage within a stage imbues this moment with the air of a performance. Not only is the Ballerina's "Pizzicato" seemingly diegetic, as though we are hearing the music to which she is actually dancing—and wondering fleetingly if she is "Sylvia"—but the moment also reinforces the narrative by clarifying her "real" and "stage" roles. At the same time, it illuminates for Pyotr and the audience all that has taken place and reaffirms our understanding of the events. The Classical Ballerina dances what classical ballerinas dance. Moreover, as a Soviet ballerina, she dances in the line of great Russian ballerinas, not only the Imperial ballerina Olga Preobrazhenskaya, who danced the role of "Sylvia" to much acclaim in 1901, but also—cementing the association with ballet modernism—the Fokine ballerinas Anna Pavlova, who programmed Sylvia's *divertissement* most frequently, and Tamara Karsavina, who re-created the role at the Imperial Theatre in 1916.[35] In these relationships, the Classical Ballerina extends the legacy of Russian ballet into new Soviet roles.

The evocation of *Sylvia* also connected *The Limpid Stream* to a notorious incident in the life of the Imperial Theatre. The 1901 production of *Sylvia* was an unhappy one, beset by acrimony and in-fighting, and heavily criticized in the press (despite praise for the performers). It provoked a bitter dispute between Diaghilev and the Imperial Theatre, as Diaghilev was first given creative control of the ballet, only to have his authority rescinded after detractors among his colleagues threatened revolt. *Sylvia* had been Diaghilev's own choice for his first theatrical production. When Serge Volkonsky, director of the Imperial Theatres, initially authorized Diaghilev's role, the aspiring impresario had gathered around him a constellation of artists, several of whom would later become part of his Ballets Russes (including Léon Bakst, Aleksandr Benois, and Nikolai Legat). When Volkonsky backtracked on his promises, however, the fight that ensued—"the *Sylvia* debacle," as Diaghilev's biographer terms it—led directly to Diaghilev's "category-three dismissal" from the theatre's staff.[36] *Sylvia* was thus a ballet of great significance to the Imperial Theatre and to ballet in Russia. Not only had it involved a very public scandal, but in fracturing certain relationships and cementing others, the Imperial production had catalyzed a realignment of forces that resulted, just a few years later, in the birth of Russia's most radical new company.

If Lopukhov or Shostakovich pondered resonances with "*The Bolt* debacle"—Lopukhov's dismissal from the former Imperial theatre, his founding of a new troupe, and his rival ideas for Russian dance—they left no record of their thoughts. In any case, the interpolation from *Sylvia* was important for what it accomplished in *The Limpid Stream*. It functioned dramatically by conveying what was happening both on the stage and on the stage within the stage. In this explanatory role, it paralleled the use of musical borrowing in Romantic ballet, where interpolated music and dance were extremely common. Borrowed music helped to emphasize the narrative and (as Smith has explained) "invested ballet scores with special explanatory power."[37] This was precisely the role of interpolation in *The Limpid Stream*, as the allusion in music and stage situation underscored the narrative and reaffirmed the Romantic model. Moreover, the interpolation from *Sylvia* connected *The Limpid Stream* to conventions, traditions, performers, and productions that had shaped both the Imperial and the modernist history of Russian ballet. It also connected Lopukhov and Shostakovich to a balletic tradition that passed from ballets like *Sylvia* into divergent traditions of Russian dance and now onward to Soviet ballet. These evocations and reinventions of the past staked a claim for *The Limpid Stream* as the inheritor of Russia's balletic legacies and as the future of Soviet modernism.

The Artistic and Professional Milieu

The State of Ballet

The allusions and ambitions of *The Limpid Stream* reflected much about the ballet's contemporary artistic milieu and the professional context in which the work came to be. *The Limpid Stream* was created in a window of balletic endeavor when the artistic environment and political scrutiny of artistic messaging were changing yet new priorities were not yet fixed. The work was both product and victim of fluid aesthetic demands. It explored topics and forms that seemed "safe"—classical dancing on a collective farm—but it would be condemned as "inauthentic" and "formalist." Moreover, the ballet was produced in a new professional context, the Maly Theatre, a balletic setting wholly different from the Leningrad State Academic Theatre and a situation that involved Shostakovich and Lopukhov in fresh artistic and practical challenges. Almost everything about Shostakovich and Lopukhov's final collaboration—from the cultural conditions to the state of ballet, the theatrical teams, and even their own respective professional standings—differed from their earlier circumstances. Such an altered environment had a profound effect on *The Limpid Stream* and its place in the balletic milieu, where its humorous pastiche and gentle parody emerged as one kind of experiment (among several) being made in Soviet ballet.

The balletic environment of the early 1930s was less experimental and less fractured than it had been in the 1920s. The cohesiveness of several new Soviet ballets in this period—including *The Limpid Stream*—was at least partly a reflection of paths abandoned, lessons learned, and loyalties realigned through the previous decade. Yet broad questions remained about how ballet could, and should, participate in cultural policy. These matters became acute as the ideology of socialist realism advanced and, with it, an emphasis on state control and prescription of cultural products. As ballet theatres and critics attempted to parse what socialist realism meant for dance, certain themes emerged: ballet would be narrative-driven, it would involve full-length works, and it would aim at dramatic and psychological realism derived from literary genres. These principles applied both to revivals of the classical repertory and to newly created works. Soviet ballet, new or old, was supposed to convey ideologically correct content through dramatically rich stories told in psychologically compelling scenes of music, dance, and design.

Ballet's response to socialist realist aesthetics was *drambalet* (literally, "dramatic ballet" or ballet that offered ideologically correct dramatic narrative), the first exemplar of which was *The Flames of Paris*, produced at the Leningrad State Academic Theatre in 1932.[38] Contemporary critics saw *drambalet* as a robust response to the "ballet wars" of the previous decade, yet not as the only possible response. In 1933, a year after *The Flames of Paris*, Sollertinsky still spoke of a "wide, unblazed trail" open to Soviet choreography, and important and artistically meaningful explorations of dance continued.[39] Although Soviet dance history would retrospectively portray *drambalet* as the decisive and inevitable path of Soviet ballet after *The Flames of Paris*, the actual situation was more complex. Indeed, the broadest question of the early 1930s was not how to create *drambalet* (though that became the answer), but it continued to be how to Sovietize ballet—a goal that required an ongoing search for potential models.

Romantic ballet persisted alongside *drambalet* in this period, and *The Limpid Stream* was one of several efforts to explore the Romantic genre as an alternative, or at least companion, to *drambalet*. Repertoire decisions, theatre protocols, and contemporary critical discourse all pointed to the Romantic genre as a potential model for Soviet ballet. The Leningrad State Academic Theatre staged many Romantic productions, as it always had, of course, but it also added more Romantic ballets to its repertoire in the early 1930s both through revivals and through new productions of the nineteenth-century repertoire. Moreover, critical discussion drew attention to Romantic works for their potential to achieve "choreographic drama" and "psychologically real" portrayals. The terms would soon become synonymous with *drambalet*, but in the early 1930s they were not yet exclusive to that genre. Of course, Romantic ballet had never been lost from the repertoire, and decisions to program it were also pragmatic: the dancers knew the ballets.

But the role of Romantic ballet grew in importance in the early 1930s as the genre became new testing ground for expressing ideology in dance.

This renewed interest in Romantic ballet initially arose in connection with a shift in repertoire policy at the Leningrad State Academic Theatre. Following the failure of *The Bolt*, the Theatre's Artistic Council noted its dissatisfaction with "frivolous experiments" on the stage and its desire for "more serious content" in future productions.[40] Classical literature, historical stories, and the old balletic repertoire were potential sources of such content and were promoted as part of a shift toward "realism." While productions like *The Flames of Paris* and *The Fountain of Bakhchisarai* responded to these emphases, discussions of new content also specifically took up the possibility of new Soviet treatments of Romantic ballet. Work on "Sovietizing" Romantic ballet ran in tandem with the development of *drambalet*. In fact, the two paths were often pursued by the same collaborators.[41]

Six months after *The Bolt*'s disastrous premiere, productions of the Leningrad State Academic Theatre reflected the renewed conservatism. The Theatre drew heavily from the Petipa repertoire (*Swan Lake, Esmeralda, Sleeping Beauty, Raymonda, Corsaire*), while including a handful of Soviet works (*The Red Poppy* and *The Ice Maiden*) and pre-Revolutionary productions from Gorsky's choreography (*The Little Humpbacked Horse* and *Don Quixote*).[42] Repertoire lists also featured *Chopiniana* (as *Les sylphides* was known in Russia), Fokine's meditation on the Romantic ballet, which returned to the stage together with his *Egyptian Nights* and *Carnaval*. In many ways, this repertoire mirrored productions of the late 1910s and early 1920s, when the ballets of Petipa, Fokine, and Gorksy shared the stage in Leningrad. The continuity also highlighted the scarcity of new Soviet works that could aspire to the permanent repertoire.

In 1931, Agrippina Vaganova took over from Lopukhov as artistic director of the Leningrad State Academic Theatre, and the early years of her tenure coincided with new explorations of Romantic ballet.[43] Vaganova led revivals of nineteenth-century productions and, in her most significant contributions, mounted her own productions of the Romantic repertoire. Reviving *Giselle* and *La Bayadère* in 1932, Vaganova preserved elements of the nineteenth-century stagings, including scenarios, dances, and *mise-en-scène*, where possible. But her choreographies of *Swan Lake* (1933) and *Esmeralda* (1935) aimed to extend the Romantic legacy with new dramatic and psychological "realism." *Swan Lake*, in particular, was Vaganova's own production, with a new libretto, setting, and designs; new danced scenes that replaced pantomime episodes; split roles for Odette and Odile; a happy ending; and other changes aimed at increasing "realism" and "heroism."[44] Odette, for example, was not a swan maiden under the curse of enchantment but an extension of Siegfried's overwrought imagination. Odile was not a force of evil as Odette's malevolent double, but a local noblewoman and Siegfried's betrothed. Vaganova's *Swan Lake* was ultimately superseded by choreographies that restored much of the Petipa/Ivanov version, with its dualism between fantastical and real worlds.[45] But her production was important in the early 1930s for its attempt to Sovietize Romantic ballet and to marry the Romantic genre to contemporary discussions of Soviet "realism."

Soviet ballet of the 1930s increasingly hinged on the notion of "realism." Yet the concept presented a thorny problem for Soviet balletic efforts in general and for Sovietized Romantic ballet in particular. Politically, "realism" in the Soviet 1930s meant socialist realism. As Ezhari explains, construing socialist realism in classical ballet was complicated by the genre's "highly formalized" vocabulary, its roots in "aristocratic court culture," and its lack of models for depicting "real life" and "social problems."[46] Historically, however, "realism" had another, quite different meaning in ballet, a meaning that reached back to early nineteenth-century French Romantic ballet, the genre that had most deeply examined, critiqued, and tested the concept of "realism" in dance. Romantic ballet turned on the dualism between real world settings (ordered realities represented by town, city, or village life) and fantastical settings (locations outside ordered life, like the forest at night, that served as a catalyst for encounters with the supernatural). Romantic realism was thus in opposition to, yet also the corollary of, Romantic fantasy.

When the practitioners of Soviet ballet took up the genre of Romantic ballet in the 1930s, they faced a conundrum: a tension between the political meanings of Soviet realism, aimed at a socialist utopia, and the historical meanings of balletic realism, aimed at a dualism designed to explore ballet's narrative and poetic possibilities. Two productions that looked to Romantic ballet as a model—but took entirely different approaches to addressing this tension—were Vaganova's *Swan Lake* and Lopukhov's *The Limpid Stream*. Whereas Vaganova sought to adapt *Swan Lake* seriously to Soviet priorities (for example, a swan-maiden who is "not real" because she is imagined), Lopukhov in *The Limpid Stream* engaged in lighted-hearted parody of the conventions of Romantic ballet itself. In doing so, he turned away from the resources of *drambalet* and "choreographic drama," and even from his own earlier experiments in mixing media (like the acrobatics and classical dance in *The Ice Maiden* or the "machine dances" in *The Bolt*). He turned instead to the history of ballet and insisted on classical dance as an avenue to realism. Ultimately, in *The Limpid Stream*, Lopukhov made the conventions of ballet the subject of the work and sought in them a source of renewal for Soviet dance.

Professional Collaborations

When *The Limpid Stream* premiered in 1935, however, few would have expected the evolution of dance to emerge at the Maly Opera Theatre. The Maly was known for its experimental approach to Soviet opera, but it had never been a ballet theatre. It had no independent balletic repertoire or dance tradition, and its troupe by 1935 was little more than a decade old. Through the 1920s, the Maly had occasionally cultivated new approaches to dance in evenings of experimental choreographies. The most important of these were performed by the Young Ballet, founded in 1922, which included—most famously—George Balanchine until his departure for Paris in 1924. More traditional opportunities occurred when dancers were needed in Maly operas or dance concerts, which were choreographed by aspiring young talents who remained under the oversight of the Leningrad State Academic Theatre. Before Lopukhov took a job at the Maly in 1931, the theatre had never mounted a full-length ballet.

Lopukhov was the Maly's first artistic director of ballet and its first major choreographer employed directly by the theatre. He arrived in his new position experienced yet bruised from events at the Leningrad State Academic Theatre, where his work had become increasingly divisive and contentious. When *The Bolt* failed after a single performance at the Academic Theatre, the debacle proved to be the final straw for a directorate weary of the talented but headstrong choreographer. Lopukhov lost his position at the city's premiere ballet stage and moved to the Maly across town. The Maly was Leningrad's youngest official ballet stage, and producing ballets for it involved Lopukhov—and ultimately Shostakovich too—not only in a fresh professional and theatrical context but also in a host of practical challenges.

With limitations on repertoire and opportunity, Maly dancers were inexperienced and technique varied wildly. The Maly had no ballet school of its own and therefore drew its dancers from various venues. Some had graduated from the Choreographic Institute, but those who ended up at the

Maly were typically weaker performers who had not been offered positions at the Leningrad State Academic Theatre.[47] Other dancers had little, if any, formal training. (Internal reports claimed virtuously that these aspirants had "discovered their talents" in factories.[48]) The result of such mixed backgrounds was a weak *corps de ballet*. To inspire his troupe (and his audiences), Lopukhov engaged excellent soloists, sometimes drawing from the ranks of the Leningrad State Academic Theatre. Gusev and Vasilieva, who danced the roles of "Pyotr" and "Zina" in *The Limpid Stream*, were two such hires.

Lopukhov's first job as artistic director was to train his troupe and produce ballets that they could perform. Choosing repertoire to develop their skills and hide their flaws, he mounted *Harlequinade* to Riccardo Drigo's music in 1933 for the Maly's first full-length ballet, and *Coppélia* to Delibes' music in 1934.[49] *The Limpid Stream* in 1935 was the Maly's third ballet, but its first new—contemporary—ballet and its first ballet on a Soviet topic. It was both a practical choice for an inexperienced troupe and an artistic statement for a demoted but determined impresario. Lopukhov characterized *The Limpid Stream* as an alternative model of dance: "[The ballet] differs significantly from all the ballets in the repertoire of the State Academic Theatre of Opera and Ballet, which are built on dance and pantomime. The dominating theme [of *The Limpid Stream*] is dance."[50] *The Limpid Stream*'s light-hearted spoof on Romantic ballet became a vehicle for Lopukhov's advocacy of classical dance over drama as "the basis of ballet."[51]

As a work for the Maly Theatre, *The Limpid Stream* accomplished several goals. It allowed the company to continue training classical technique, and it confirmed comedy as a mark of the Maly repertoire as well as an alternative to the serious, "heroic" repertoire of the Leningrad State Academic Theatre. The ballet also established the Maly's interest in commissioning new works and its aspiration to contribute to the development of Soviet ballet as the theatre already did to Soviet opera. Significantly, it extended Romantic ballet into contemporary Soviet repertoire and attempted to internationalize Soviet balletic models. *Harlequinade* explored Italian models, and *Coppélia*, Franco-Russian ones. *The Limpid Stream* turned to French and Danish Romanticism (for example, in the references to *La Sylphide*), filtered through the Russian tradition.

While Lopukhov was negotiating the challenges of founding a ballet troupe and running the city's second stage, Shostakovich was enjoying fame and popularity. Amid the artistic triumph of *Lady Macbeth*, he accepted the commission for *The Limpid Stream* possibly at Lopukhov's encouragement. Laurel Fay suggests that the invitation to work on the ballet came from Lopukhov himself and that financial considerations might have prompted Shostakovich to accept the offer if he was otherwise unenthusiastic about the creative constraints of another balletic collaboration.[52] Regardless of his personal motivations, Shostakovich seems to have become reasonably interested as the work went on, writing that he was "very satisfied" with the libretto and deeply admired Lopukhov's "brilliantly successful" creation of "dance comedies" at the Maly.[53] Their collaboration was mutually respectful and apparently rewarding, and it was undoubtedly a relief to Shostakovich that his third ballet was not beset by the factionalism and in-fighting that had marred his experiences at the Leningrad State Academic Theatre. In describing *The Limpid Stream*, Shostakovich articulated a creative concept that hewed closely to Lopukhov's—a marriage of "classical dance" and "realistic ballet," conveyed through "danceable" music.[54] Whatever his assessments were privately, Shostakovich supported *The Limpid Stream* publicly.

The Limpid Stream was Shostakovich and Lopukhov's closest collaboration, and this had a profound impact on the way Shostakovich's music supported and was deployed in the ballet. Shostakovich submitted individual dances to Lopukhov, discussed requirements, and responded quickly and in detail to the choreographer's requests. Lopukhov offered both specific and general guidance, sometimes showing Shostakovich the choreography and at other times describing the mood or character of a passage.[55] The closeness of the collaboration resulted in Shostakovich's least unified ballet score from a musical perspective, but his most coherent ballet in the way the work consistently integrated musical and visual components. This integration reached its most compelling form in Act II, where the evocation of the Romantic genre occurred in the stage situation and was confirmed, elaborated, and deepened by the music. The synthesis also enriched the interpolation from *Sylvia* in Act III, which was treated on one level as Romantic borrowing and on another as a meditation on *The Limpid Stream*'s place in the lineage of Russian dance.

Shostakovich described his music for *The Limpid Stream* as "happy [merry], light, entertaining, and, most important, danceable."[56] Indeed, the work's musical charms were many, and after the ballet was withdrawn, several of its dances enjoyed a robust concert life in the composer's suites and in numerous arrangements and transcriptions made by his contemporaries. The ballet's music employs a variety of techniques familiar to the ballet composer—folk dance (invented or otherwise), musical borrowing (from the composer himself and from Delibes), interpolation (the allusion to *Sylvia*), and strictly narrative music (or music to accompany gesture). In these functions, the music confirms setting, characterizes roles, contributes to mood and atmosphere, and shapes dramatic and poetic scenes. The music is touching in moments—as in Zina and Pyotr's dance in the forest—but not profound. Most fundamentally, the score reflects the composer's grasp of choreographic requirements and stage conditions, that is, the qualities of composition familiar in Romantic ballet and suited to a new ballet that reinterpreted the Romantic genre.

Shostakovich and Lopukhov's earlier collaboration on *The Bolt* was also a point of reference musically. Mining expressive resources from that ballet, Shostakovich reused nine dances, in part or in full, for *The Limpid Stream*. When *Pravda* condemned *The Limpid Stream*, it cited this recycled music as evidence of Shostakovich's "indifferent attitude" to his task (a conclusion with which subsequent scholarship has never disagreed). But this was hardly the whole story; it certainly took no account of how the recycled music was used or how the use of pre-existing music fit into balletic practice. Recycled material in *The Limpid Stream* tends to support mood and get through choreography—for example, the "Dressing-up Scene" in Act II, in which Zina, the Ballerina, and the *Danseur* change their costumes ahead of their assignations in the forest. The music serves as a colorful *entr'acte* that accompanies a great deal of activity on the stage (and off it) in preparation for the continuation of the narrative. In *The Bolt*, the same music accompanies the "Entry of the Komsomol Members and Pioneers" for an amateur concert in a factory—in other words, a parallel situation in which not much is happening in the story, though a great deal of busyness is happening on the stage, and the music accounts for the general stage conditions. Shostakovich's recycled music from a ballet that no one would see was one solution to a familiar balletic problem: the sheer amount of choreography necessitated certain lengths of music that fit the purpose. His reuse of his own work responded to practical demands of the genre; it also allowed new theatrical applications for music that he might have liked or at the very least did not wish to discard.

Shostakovich's music for *The Limpid Stream* emerged as a series of musical "sketches" (as contemporaries called them).[57] These largely self-contained units of expression gently parodied the sounds, scenes, characters, and moods that *The Limpid Stream* called up. The music eschewed large-scale unity, a fact noted by its earliest reviewers. Sollertinsky berated it for this deficiency. But the musicologist Mikhail Druskin suggested that Shostakovich had created a kind of *"singspiel"* in ballet; in other words, in Druskin's view, *The Limpid Stream* was a popular form of ballet whose musical elements avoided sophisticated ("lofty") forms in favor of comic and vernacular ("everyday") idioms.[58] Yet at certain moments, Shostakovich's score invested the narrative material with lyrical and emotional depth, as well as allusions to past balletic repertoire, in ways that heightened the dramatic import of scenes. The music also demonstrated Shostakovich's command of a range of approaches to ballet music and his literacy in advancing this specific collaboration. While *The Limpid Stream* succeeded as an individual work, however—with Shostakovich's music being credited for much of its achievement—its position within the national enterprise of Soviet ballet, and even the composer's own view of it, proved to be less secure.

The Limpid Stream in the National Enterprise

The Limpid Stream's creators and many of its critics were at pains to explain how the ballet's aesthetic goals responded to the practical and ideological requirements of Soviet ballet. In an article for the libretto booklet, Shostakovich characterized *The Limpid Stream* as a "search for principles of a new Soviet ballet"—a search that not only took account of "ballet specifics" (the demands of dancing) but also responded to "socialist reality" (the narratives of Soviet life).[59] The composer continued provocatively, "I think the attempts to replace genuine ballet with a surrogate of dramatized pantomime are fundamentally wrong."[60] In embracing "genuine ballet" and snubbing "dramatized pantomime," Shostakovich distinguished *The Limpid Stream* from its contemporaries, especially the heavily dramatized ballets of the Leningrad State Academic Theatre. Lopukhov, in turn, explained that *The Limpid Stream* was rooted in classical dance and argued that this emphasis aligned with Soviet demands for realism: "We strove to ensure that our ballet was a danced ballet ... This requirement by no means contradicts searches for a realistic style. But the fact of the matter is that *realism in ballet must be realized with its own specific means, that is, first of all, with the means of dance and, in particular, classical dance.*"[61] This emphasis on "classical dance" and ballet's "own specific means" was a direct response to *drambalet* and "choreographic drama," which called for balletic realism derived from non-balletic genres, like literature and dramatic theatre. Both Shostakovich and Lopukhov made every effort to distinguish *The Limpid Stream* from such works and to highlight its unique contributions to a narrowing field of balletic endeavor.

The Limpid Stream was also distinctive for what contemporaries dubbed its "choreographic comedy."[62] In another article in the program booklet, the critic Yuri Slonimsky described French comic ballet, explaining the genre as a descendent of Jean Dauberval's eighteenth-century productions (*La fille mal gardée* and other works), which drew from both ballet and popular theatres.[63] For Slonimsky, Dauberval's efforts were models of "choreographic comedy" for their socially relevant topics, true-to-life portrayals, dance arising from narrative, and close association with other forms of theatre.[64] While these were the values of Soviet ballet critics in general, Slonimsky's analysis implied several ideas that helped to contextualize *The Limpid Stream* specifically. First, his article called for comic ballet as an avenue to realism. Second, he legitimated balletic efforts in the comic genre and aimed to show how they fulfilled the goals of Soviet dance. Third, his argument tacitly situated *The Limpid Stream* along a continuum of history and linked it to French ballet. The implication was that the genre's international history conferred cultural and balletic legitimacy. In this view, *The Limpid Stream* did not simply create Soviet ballet, though it certainly did that. It stood in a line of balletic endeavor, offering continuity from a French past to a Soviet future.

Ultimately, despite the rationales and explanations, Shostakovich distanced himself from his work, writing to Sollertinsky during the Moscow production that "*The Limpid Stream* is my shameful failure . . . [and] I have felt this way from the very beginning."[65] Sollertinsky had sharply criticized *The Limpid Stream* in reviews of the Leningrad performance and had even characterized Shostakovich's music as derivative and mediocre, in no way of the same standard as *The Golden Age* (a favorite with Sollertinsky) and "mostly put together from pieces from *The Bolt*" (a wild exaggeration).[66] When Shostakovich criticized *The Limpid Stream* in his letter, he asked Sollertinsky "to believe," "to understand," and "to forgive" him—surprisingly intense and personal language about a light-hearted ballet. A few weeks later, while preparing for the Bolshoi premiere, the composer expressed renewed uncertainty about his ballet. If it failed to reach the stage in Moscow, he wrote, he himself felt calm but his regrets would be for Lopukhov: "I will be painfully sorry for him if this whole enterprise collapses. He is a good man and I sincerely love him."[67]

If Shostakovich had concluded that *The Limpid Stream* was a creative betrayal, however, he had already decided on a new endeavor: a ballet to be created in collaboration with Sollertinsky himself. This was to be a new Soviet "Don Quixote" (a ballet that would inevitably have drawn comparisons with Petipa's renowned *Don Quixote* of 1869 and Gorsky's revival of 1900). Sollertinsky was to write the libretto and Shostakovich the music. Both the Maly and the Leningrad State Academic Theatre considered commissioning the work, although Sollertinsky warned the latter that Shostakovich was still disillusioned from its handling of his first two ballets and believed the Maly was more willing to support his efforts.[68] If neither Shostakovich nor Sollertinsky saw *The Limpid Stream* as a viable answer to Soviet ballet's still-pressing problems, both remained ready to create new ballets.

A week after Shostakovich's apology, Sollertinsky saw *The Limpid Stream* in Moscow and softened his opinion. He approved of the Bolshoi's leaner libretto—which removed "the most tasteless and absurd episodes," he noted with a touch of his earlier acerbity—and found brilliance and cohesion in the music.[69] Under Yuri Fayer's baton, "the score of *The Limpid Stream* glistened for the first time," he wrote; "its lack of coherence disappeared ... and [Fayer] managed to feel out the nodes of symphonic development."[70] In any event, the view of most Moscow critics, not to mention the attitude of the Bolshoi itself, more than made up for Sollertinsky's grudging acceptance. *The Limpid Stream* was immensely popular with critics, public, and dancers, and its performance on Stalin's birthday sealed its place in the pantheon of Soviet cultural products. Whatever Sollertinsky (or even Shostakovich) thought of the ballet, it had won a starring role in the national enterprise of creating Soviet dance. *The Limpid Stream*'s success positioned the ballet as a major contribution to an emerging Soviet repertoire.

But when *Pravda* published "Balletic Falsity" in February 1936, it abruptly accused the ballet of "puppetry" and a "fake attitude toward life."[71] To represent a collective farm, the article averred, the creators of the ballet should have gone to a collective farm in the Caucasus to study lifestyle, dances, dress, and customs. Having failed to do that, they had betrayed their indifference to the demands of Soviet art and had offered up stylized characters ("doll-like '*kolkhozniki*'"), inauthentic costumes ("clothes that have nothing in common with the clothes of the Kuban Cossacks"), aberrant behaviors ("jumping" and "raving" on stage), bizarre choreography ("an unnatural mixture of false-folk dances with numbers of dancers in tutus"), and "characterless" music (having "absolutely nothing in common with either the collective farms or the Kuban"). In sum, the article judged, "ballet nonsense in the foulest sense of the word reigns on stage." *The Limpid Stream* was withdrawn and even its production components were deemed unfit for reuse.[72] The ballet on Stalin's birthday became the pariah of Soviet dance.

Because *Pravda*'s assault on *The Limpid Stream* came days after its denunciation of *Lady Macbeth*, the attacks united two criticisms—of the models of Soviet ballet and of Soviet opera—in one person, making the denunciation of Shostakovich both convenient and devastating. The condemnation of *The Limpid Stream* also signaled an important message about Soviet ballet by defining through a negative model what Soviet ballet would *not* be. Ezrahi suggests that *Pravda*'s call for "realism" excluded "classical dance" and "'inauthentic' character dance" and required "productions [based] on a conscientious observation of reality adapted for the stage."[73] In fact, *Pravda* demanded not realism but literalism, not a distillation of ideals either culturally or balletically but a reenactment of Soviet life, or at least myths about that life. Historical and literary stories, like those used for *drambalet*, offered one source of new mythologies—like *The Flames of Paris*, set during the French Revolution but offering a mythologized image of revolutionary ideals that could be deemed "Soviet." Yet a contemporary story like *The Limpid Stream* could not reflect literally what happened on a collective farm or anywhere else. Recognizing that, the creators of *The Limpid Stream* had used the topic of Soviet life to engage the codes of ballet itself. The shift had been successful for the ballet, but *Pravda* judged it untenable for Soviet art.

* * *

The Limpid Stream showed how a Soviet ballet might reconcile specific balletic conventions with contemporary artistic and political priorities. In taking up Romantic ballet, it situated Soviet requirements—for contemporary topics and ideologically correct content—within ballet's perennial questions of realism and narrative. At the same time, it addressed the dualism at the heart of the genre: the tension between narrative and poetry, epitomized in Romantic ballet's "real world" and "otherworldly" components, and reimagined by Shostakovich and Lopukhov through the prism of Soviet ideals. *The Limpid Stream* did not represent Soviet life. Rather, it used an everyday setting as a means of exploring the conventions of ballet itself and of creating new myths about its subjects. In doing so, the ballet, like its Romantic models, imagined or aspired to a world that exists only in the imagination. This strange kinship, humorously explored, between *The Limpid Stream* and Romantic ballet emerged as Shostakovich and Lopukhov's most captivating, coherent, yet ill-fated, solution to the problem of Soviet dance.

Despite its many successes, *The Limpid Stream* faltered in its balletic milieu as it ran up against the artistic and ideological challenges of creating ballet in the 1930s. The emergence of *drambalet* in 1932 promised to resolve some controversies about Soviet ballet, but it would also, in conjunction with state pressures, suffocate other ideas. Meanwhile, Romantic ballet and comedy persisted alongside *drambalet* for a time, and Lopukhov's ballets at the Maly Opera Theatre explored these topics as alternatives to the productions of the Leningrad State Academic Theatre. Created amid shifting artistic and political requirements, *The Limpid Stream* both acknowledged and departed from some of the main emphases of Soviet ballet production. Like ballets of its time, it aimed at "Sovietizing" the repertoire, but unlike many of its contemporaries, it rejected heavily dramatized productions. Turning away from both the experimentation of the 1920s and the monumental heroism emerging in the 1930s, *The Limpid Stream* offered a simple Romantic comedy.

Many practical challenges also emerged in the production of *The Limpid Stream* at the Maly Theatre. The balletic setting and professional situation were wholly different from those at the Leningrad State Academic Theatre where both Shostakovich and Lopukhov had enjoyed (and suffered) their formative experiences in ballet. Lopukhov faced all the difficulties involved in founding a new ballet troupe while placing his artistic stamp on the repertoire—a negotiation that required a careful balance of classical technique and new choreographies. After two productions of "old" ballets, he encouraged the Maly to commission a new Soviet ballet and, for this, he was keen to collaborate again with Shostakovich. His enthusiasm might have been buoyed by Shostakovich's success with *Lady Macbeth*, but it was also stimulated by their previous work together on *The Bolt*. Composer and choreographer took up *The Limpid Stream* in what proved to be their closest partnership.

Ultimately, however, *The Limpid Stream* failed in the national enterprise of creating Soviet culture. *Pravda*'s judgment cast the ballet from the summit of cultural acceptance into the chasm of cultural repudiation. The condemnation also brought an end to Shostakovich and Lopukhov's collaborations. Having lost his position at the Maly and a job offer from the Bolshoi, Lopukhov took a job at the Leningrad Choreographic Institute, where he and Slonimsky organized a department of choreography. (Piotrovsky, who had co-authored the libretto with Lopukhov, was arrested in 1937, a victim of the political purges that swept Soviet institutions in the late 1930s.) Shostakovich continued to review ballet libretti and sometimes contemplated new collaborations, yet he wrote no more ballets or operas and instead channeled his most serious creative efforts into his concert works. The larger story of political repression, and particularly of the fall of *Lady Macbeth*, tended to overshadow *The Limpid Stream*'s role in his output. But the ballet held an important place in Shostakovich's artistic collaborations and illuminated his most successful approach to the genre. In its engagement with the Romantic genre, it completed his examination of the dominant models of Russian ballet and staged a final scene in Soviet ballet's transitional period.

5
Shostakovich and Ballet: Lives and Afterlives

The idea that Shostakovich's music could find expression in ballet did not perish with *The Limpid Stream* but continued to be held by choreographers and continued to be important. Reengagement with Shostakovich's music in ballet began in the 1930s not long after *The Limpid Stream* was condemned. The interest was not in Russia (and would not be for many years), but it marked an attention to Shostakovich that has persisted among choreographers to the present. As early as the 1930s, Léonide Massine in France choreographed Shostakovich's symphonic music in *Rouge et noir*, an abstract ballet based on the composer's *First Symphony*. Massine's achievement was, in the estimation of contemporaries, "a visual symphony of forms and colors in movement."[1] In the 1960s, the Soviet choreographer Igor Belsky also turned to Shostakovich's symphonies in an effort to express their poetry in dance. Belsky's *Leningrad Symphony*, after Shostakovich's eponymous work, asserted the primacy of music and drew on Lopukhov's ideas about interpreting symphonic structures through movement. Twenty years later, Yuri Grigorovich restaged *The Golden Age* at the Bolshoi Theatre, albeit in a production that altered most elements of the work, including music, dance, design, scenario, and stage action. In the early 2000s, undeterred by the Soviet topics of Shostakovich's ballets, Alexei Ratmansky revived *The Bright Stream* (as it is known in his production) and *The Bolt* in new choreographies and returned them to the stage after seventy years. Ratmansky has since taken up Shostakovich's concert music in choreographies that explore the danceable qualities of that repertoire.

This chapter is about these lives and afterlives of Shostakovich's music in the work of Massine, Belsky, Grigorovich, and Ratmansky, four choreographers who worked in very different traditions and milieus. The ways in which these choreographers interacted with Shostakovich's music illuminated the composer's significance to ballet and intersected with developments in the genre over nearly a century. Moreover, the successful

Shostakovich's Ballets and the Search for Soviet Dance. Laura E. Kennedy, Oxford University Press.
© Oxford University Press 2025. DOI: 10.1093/9780197698082.003.0006

return of Shostakovich's ballets in Ratmansky's choreographies and the ongoing exploration of the composer's concert music opened new possibilities for the evolution of dance in the twenty-first century. In the work of these choreographers, Shostakovich, the Russian composer who did not produce a lasting Russian ballet, remained vital to the advancement of the art form. The afterlives of his ballets emblematized the dramatic potential of these works—potential, which, in the face of artistic repression, remained unrealized by Shostakovich himself.

"Symphonic Ballets"

Massine's *Rouge et noir*

Rouge et noir (later titled *L'Etrange farandole*) was created in 1939 for the Ballet Russe de Monte Carlo in a collaboration between Massine as choreographer and Henri Matisse as designer. A successful work, it was staged across Europe and twice at the Metropolitan Opera House in New York City (1939 and 1948). *Rouge et noir* was one of Massine's five "symphonic ballets," a repertory of the late 1930s that drew mostly on nineteenth-century symphonic music—with the exception of *Rouge et noir* to Shostakovich's *First Symphony*—to explore modernist movement and gesture while conveying personal and allegorical meaning.[2] Lynn Garafola explains that in the period in which he worked on *Rouge et noir*, Massine expressed despair and questioned the value of his art in the face of political turmoil in Europe.[3] The ballet marked Massine's "deepening pessimism" as war loomed and fascist and communist movements consolidated totalitarian regimes.[4] The choreographer could not have known, of course, the poignancy of selecting Shostakovich's music for a ballet in which he wrestled with these matters.

Rouge et noir had an abstract program around the idea of metaphysical struggle explored through color and gesture. Massine explained that the ballet dealt with "the conflict between the spiritual and the material world"—a conflict played out in the ballet's yellows, blues, reds, and blacks, which stood, respectively, for wickedness, nature, materialism, and violence.[5] Dressed in white, the ballet's lead pair represented Man and Woman. According to one French reviewer, the scenario posed a struggle between these two: "Man, who represents the poetic spirits, is pursued by brute forces. He is separated from the Woman, tries to join her and is finally overwhelmed by his fate."[6] Massine also linked color to political meaning, telling one of his dancers that "white stood for Russia, black for fascism, and red for communism."[7] European critics in 1939 were quick to pursue political interpretation, finding in the ballet a metaphor for the "crushing of helpless nations."[8] To them, the work reflected the existential longings of artists separated from their homelands, like Massine cut off from the Russia of his birth. The use of Shostakovich's music—a Russian artist in that homeland to which Massine could not return—probably enhanced these readings of political and existential crisis. The overt political themes in *Rouge et noir* might even have helped to suggest that the composer's music too possessed political meaning.

Photographs and some surviving footage from the Met's production of *Rouge et noir* in 1948 give some sense of the experimental form and movement through which Massine interpreted Shostakovich's music.[9] Color photographs show a back curtain in three panels of solid colors (yellow, red, and blue), against which the ballerina Alicia Markova is captured in different poses—*en pointe*, on her knees, and even lying across the floor with arms outspread.[10] She is dressed in a white leotard, which is overlaid with white shapes edged in black, in a manner reminiscent of Matisse's cut-out method. The video from 1948 has no sound, making it impossible to establish moment-to-moment relationships between music and movement, but the footage leaves an impression of volatility and ambiguity, as though the dancers dance at the edge of control. Sudden and explosive movements from the principals emphasize extreme athleticism while the *corps de ballet* dances in a seemingly disordered environment. One excerpt shows a *pas de deux* for the principals. The male dancer lifts and dips the ballerina in all directions while she holds her body straight. He drops her into a backbend over his knee and they balance—his arms in a rigid L-shape, her arms dangling while her knees are bent and her feet remain *en pointe* despite her recumbent position. Toward the end of their sequence, the ballerina extends one leg backward as the male dancer lowers her to a kneeling position. Her forward leg remains *en pointe* as he spins her body—her backward leg describing a circle (rather like a figure skater) while she remains balanced on her supporting leg. The male dancer then kneels with one hand extending back. The ballerina grabs this hand and jumps onto his back with her right knee. Throughout the footage, the *corps de ballet* dance classical and vernacular steps, often with familiar Massine gestures (such as the forward foot on the heel and the arms extended). Several shots show the *corps* arranged with a kind of architectural asymmetry in which bodies, heads, and *port de bras* are organized in various groupings or tableaux. Small groups dance and arrange themselves into different positions, making the effect visually chaotic. Even within groups, dancers do not execute the same movements.

At its premiere in Monte Carlo, *Rouge et noir* was performed between *Swan Lake* in Petipa's choreography and *Le Tricorne* in Massine's choreography.[11] The two established ballets were not only staples of Ballet Russe de Monte Carlo's repertoire but also representatives, respectively, of Russian Imperial ballet and of the innovations of the Ballets Russes. Sandwiched between them, *Rouge et noir* drew on artistic directions forged both within and outside Russia. Its position affirmed its place within the Russian balletic tradition and aligned the work with modernism. Moreover, the use of music by Shostakovich, a contemporary Russian composer, cemented associations with Russian artistic accomplishments.

Massine must have encountered Shostakovich's music in Europe under conditions in which the composer was recognized as one of Soviet Russia's most prolific and innovative artists. European audiences knew Shostakovich's music well in the 1930s through Russian artistic developments that reached into Europe, albeit sometimes in a fragmented way. Bruno Walter had led the European premiere of Shostakovich's *First Symphony* in 1928 with the Berlin Philharmonic, an event that initiated the symphony's Western reception and brought Shostakovich to international recognition. Other high-profile performances quickly followed (Leopold Stokowski with the Philadelphia Orchestra in 1928 for the US premiere, Arturo Toscanini with New York Philharmonic in 1931, Stokowski with the first recording in 1933). The symphony captivated orchestras, audiences, and critics and was hailed as a work of "genius" in the press. It was also published in multiple editions in Europe, including scores by Sikorski (Hamburg), Boosey and Hawkes (London), and Universal Editions (Vienna). In the 1930s, European audiences saw Shostakovich's opera *Lady Macbeth*, heard his piano music, and encountered his next two symphonies—and they also knew that Shostakovich composed ballets. In September 1935, French radio carried a Soviet broadcast of "a ballet by Shostakovich" from "le Grand Théâtre" of Russia.[12] This must have been *The Limpid Stream*, which was in rehearsal at the Bolshoi Theatre that autumn. In 1938, Radio Brussels broadcast *The Golden Age* in a program that included music by Milhaud, Berg, Debussy, and Prokofiev.[13] In these conditions, Massine's ballet *Rouge et noir* illuminated for European and

American audiences how Shostakovich's music could be used in ballet and how the dramatic possibilities of his scores might be explored.

Like many of Massine's works in this period, reimagining Shostakovich's music also became part of his company's attempts to reanimate the Ballets Russes in the decade after Diaghilev's death. After the Ballets Russes collapsed, several new ballet companies had formed, each vying for a piece of the legacy, and a rivalry had emerged between Massine and Balanchine over which choreographer would be seen as the heir to Diaghilev. Massine was the more successful choreographer for a time, although his popularity was forgotten after the consolidation of Balanchine's legacy.[14] Another rivalry, never acknowledged by either Massine or Balanchine but equally important, was over Russian ballet after Diaghilev. Would it continue to exist, and, if so, in what form and what artistic resources would it take up? In turning to Shostakovich, Massine followed the approach pioneered by Diaghilev, namely, taking up ballet music of young and rising Russian composers (like Stravinsky and Prokofiev) as well as reinventing for ballet the concert music of other Russian composers (like Rimsky-Korsakov). Massine used Shostakovich's symphonic music twice—first for *Rouge et noir* and later for the ballet *Leningrad Symphony* (1945) to the first movement of Shostakovich's *Seventh Symphony*.[15] The reiterative use of Shostakovich's music suggested just how much the choreographer continued to find Russian artistic developments important to an experimental aesthetic in dance.

Belsky's *Leningrad Symphony*

Belsky also adopted Shostakovich's *Seventh Symphony* for his symphonic ballet, *Leningrad Symphony*, created in 1961.[16] There is no evidence that Belsky knew of Massine's Shostakovich ballets, although Soviet dance professionals certainly knew about the Western practice of choreographing concert music (and generally disapproved of it). Rather, Belsky's models were Soviet, particularly the ideas of Lopukhov. Belsky created his *Leningrad Symphony* in a period of experimental choreography early in his choreographic career when he studied with Lopukhov and was part of the Kirov Theatre's "young choreographers," a group of Lopukhov's pupils who were known to experiment with choreographic methods.[17] *Leningrad Symphony* was Belsky's second ballet but his first symphonic ballet—or "ballet symphony," as Belsky and contemporary Soviet critics called it. Shostakovich expressed interest in Belsky's concepts (advising the young choreographer, however, that a "ballet symphony" should have a choreographic score akin to a musical score), but while he consented to the use of his music, he did not participate in the production.[18] Belsky's *Leningrad Symphony* returned music by Shostakovich (albeit not the composer's ballet music) to the Soviet ballet stage for the first time since the condemnation of *The Limpid Stream* in 1936. The event paid homage to Shostakovich's music and to the composer's seminal place in Soviet cultural life. It also marked the beginning of renewed Soviet interest in Shostakovich's music as a resource for ballet.

Leningrad Symphony premiered at the Kirov Theatre on April 14, 1961, on a double bill with Leonid Yakobson's ballet *Choreographic Miniatures*.[19] Konstantin Sergeyev, the theatre's chief choreographer, was skeptical of Belsky's work but agreed to program it on an evening of "youthful, unscheduled performance," a designation that indicated just how different these works would be from the Theatre's usual fare.[20] Both ballets that evening were experimental, but each drew on a different strand of the modernist tradition. *Leningrad Symphony* extended the ideas that Lopukhov had pioneered in *Dance Symphony: Magnificence of the Universe* of 1924. Lopukhov had created "dance symphonism," which aimed at a direct correspondence between music and dance, that is, at choreographic structures capable of expressing the music's preexisting structures. It was this concept that Belsky elaborated as he sought a similar intimacy between music and dance. Lopukhov himself recognized the relationship in *Leningrad Symphony* and applauded Belsky's achievement.[21] Meanwhile, Yakobson's *Choreographic Miniatures* evoked the methods of the Ballets Russes in featuring a potpourri of short ballets to original choreographies based on contemporary scores, including piano pieces by French and Russian composers like Debussy, Ravel, and Scriabin, as well as excerpts from Russian ballets and operas like those by Rimsky-Korsakov, Stravinsky, Prokofiev, and contemporary Soviet composers.[22] The evening of ballets skipped over Soviet *drambalet*, which had dominated the Kirov's repertoire for almost three decades, to reach for models in pre-Revolutionary and Soviet avant-garde ballet. Shostakovich's music was a central feature in this experiment.

Symphony No. 7 ("Leningrad") was Shostakovich's most famous and celebrated work of the Great Patriotic War (as World War II is known in Russia). It had an uncontested place in the "canon" of Shostakovich's output and enjoyed international fame as well as near-mythological resonance in Soviet Russia. Written in 1941 as the Germans invaded Russia and laid siege to Leningrad, the symphony was a programmatic work dedicated to the heroism of the people of that city. Its premiere in March 1942 had been an event of national importance. As Laurel Fay writes in her assessment of the work's extraordinary effect: "The resonance of [the symphony's] reception and the immediacy and universality of its morale-boosting effect turned it almost overnight into a potent national—even international—symbol of just cause and steely resolve in the war against fascism. It anchored itself in the popular consciousness as an instantaneous cultural icon, something totally unprecedented for a serious symphonic work."[23]

A few months later, on August 9, 1942, the Leningrad premiere took place on the date that Hitler had nominated for celebrating the city's fall. The story of this event became legendary—a tale of defiance, resilience, and moral courage that emblematized the patriotism of the Soviet people. Combined military and civilian operations were required to ensure the performance. The score was flown into the besieged city by night. The musicians were given special rations to strengthen them for the performance. Some were even brought back from the front since too few were left in the city. Rehearsals were disrupted by air-raid sirens. Concert halls were damaged. Yet the premiere took place and was broadcast throughout the city and over loudspeakers to the German lines that had been unable to breach the city's defenses. With its story of heroism and triumph, the *Seventh Symphony* had unprecedented emotional and psychological impact in Soviet Russia. It became (and remains) one of Russia's most beloved cultural monuments of the Great Patriotic War.

Belsky dealt with Shostakovich's music by extending its program through visual images, scenarios, and nameless characters that generalized themes of conflict, suffering, and heroism. In a review of the premiere, the critic and dance historian Galina Dobrovolskaya described the events of *Leningrad Symphony* (the ballet) as "images and episodes" arising from the music to portray the conflict between the Soviets and the Germans.[24] "Belsky does not [merely] illustrate the music," she wrote; "it is as if the dance is born from the music and develops inseparably from it."[25] In Dobrovolskaya's account, the principals represented the Soviet hero and heroine. At the beginning, they danced alongside other pairs from the *corps de ballet*, blending classical steps with some sports elements.[26] Each pair of dancers performed individual dances that gradually coalesced, illustrating the idea of lives merging in common purpose. The Germans' theme (or the "invasion theme" in other reviews) interrupted the Soviet couples. Men and women bade each other goodbye as the men departed for the front. Germans appeared, giving way to wanton destruction and tormenting the Soviet women, who "walk[ed], barely moving their legs, helping each other, while others rush[ed] swiftly driven by fear, despair, and pain."[27] The Soviet men entered, and although many fell into German hands, the stream of Soviet fighters continued seemingly unabated. Dobrovolskaya commented that victory was not portrayed because the ballet presented only the first movement of the symphony; but she expressed the views of her contemporaries in interpreting the ballet, as they interpreted the symphony, as a picture of "the inexhaustible strength of the Soviet people, their free and proud spirit."[28]

Mikhail Gordon created the costumes and décor for this scenario. His background as an artist lay in graphic posters, and elements of that genre's two-dimensional forms, simple images, negative spaces, and select color schemes can be seen in his designs for *Leningrad Symphony*.[29] Gordon's stage had no props, only changing projections as backdrops and a color scheme limited to white, black, red, and blue.[30] At the opening of the ballet, a leaf from Shostakovich's autograph score of the *Seventh Symphony* (in the composer's distinctive handwriting) was projected onto the wall.[31] Another image sketched an outline of the Spire of the Admiralty Building, and yet another image projected a huge hand reaching toward the city of Leningrad. The projections were highly effective according to contemporaries—and they have been retained in the annual performance of the ballet at the Mariinsky Theatre—but Gordon's costumes were considered less distinctive.[32] Photographs showed traditional outfits. In one, the prima ballerina wore pointe shoes and a simple dress falling to the knee, while her partner appeared in a white top, dark tights, and ballet slippers. Costumes for the Soviet women ranged from soft dresses to light-colored tunics with matching headscarves. The Germans wore brown clothing and Teutonic helmets with horns.[33]

Soviet critics were enthusiastic about Belsky's ballet, but they were also puzzled about how to explain it, both for the presence of Shostakovich's music and for the use of symphonic music. "Shostakovich has not turned to ballet music [since 1935]," wrote Dobrovolskaya, acknowledging a fraught legacy for Shostakovich's ballets, yet "Soviet ballet feels a huge need for [his music]."[34] *Leningrad Symphony* was an answer to that need in the eyes of many critics for the way it restored Shostakovich's music to the ballet stage and generated new forms and content for the genre.[35] Some Soviet critics explained Belsky's work as experimental. They recognized Lopukhov's ideas of "dance symphonism" and invoked the precedent of Isadora

Duncan's performances to concert music in the first part of the century.[36] These reviewers acknowledged that the use of concert music for ballet was common in the Western repertoire (although this practice was typically labeled "formalism" in a Soviet context, not a term that anyone wanted to associate with Shostakovich's beloved *"Leningrad" Symphony*).[37] Deflecting any potential reproach, however, the same critics affirmed that Belsky avoided formalism by adopting program music. Meanwhile—and somewhat astonishingly—other reviewers justified Belsky's ballet as a contribution to the pantheon of Soviet *drambalet* and linked it to ballets like *Spartacus* and *The Stone Flower*.[38] *Leningrad Symphony* was clearly not a *drambalet*, but such comments reflected a desire to assert a Soviet "canon" of dance and to mark a place for Shostakovich's music within that. The reception of *Leningrad Symphony* in Russia suggested a shared belief among Soviet ballet specialists that Shostakovich the composer belonged on the ballet stage even if his ballets (of the 1930s) did not.

Outside Russia, *Leningrad Symphony* won attention in the United States and Europe for its uniqueness in the Soviet repertoire as a non-narrative ballet to concert music. Despite his initial reservations about the work, Sergeyev must have been won over quickly. He added the ballet to the Kirov's repertoire for a US tour in 1961, only months after the premiere in Russia, and programmed it alongside Fokine's *Chopiniana* and scenes from *Don Quixote* and *Taras Bulba*.[39] Balanchine saw *Leningrad Symphony* in New York City and immediately recognized Lopukhov's influence.[40] He had, of course, danced in the single performance of *Dance Symphony* in 1924. In the late 1960s, *Leningrad Symphony* was programmed on the Kirov's European tour. On that occasion, European critics compared it to Massine's "symphonic ballets" of the 1930s, probably because those were the models known in Europe.[41]

Within Russia, Belsky's *Leningrad Symphony* heralded the beginning of a reengagement with Shostakovich's music by Soviet choreographers. In 1962, a year after the ballet's premiere, the Maly Opera Theatre produced the one-act ballet *The Young Lady and the Hooligan* to a medley of Shostakovich's music, including numbers from *The Bolt*, *The Limpid Stream*, and film scores as well as a passage from the Cello Sonata.[42] Around the same time, Shostakovich's concert music began to attract further attention from Soviet choreographers. In 1966, Belsky extended his ideas of a "ballet symphony" to the *Eleventh Symphony*, based on the music of Shostakovich's eponymous work, and produced this at the Maly Theatre in Leningrad.[43] In 1970,

Yakobson choreographed Shostakovich's *Piano Trio No. 2* (Op. 67) for an original ballet titled *Jewish Wedding*, with décor by Valery Levanthal after Marc Chagall's surrealist paintings (which were officially banned but privately accessible to some in Russia).[44] Around the same time, discussions about reviving Shostakovich's ballets of the 1930s began to reemerge, but the prospect raised many questions. How might these works be rehabilitated? What scores would be used since none had been published? What was the relation between music and dance in the ballets? Did the original scenarios have relevance, and how should the political elements be treated? The relationship between Shostakovich and ballet continued to be vexed. In the struggle to reconcile it, all three of the composer's ballets from the 1930s would return to the stage in some form.

The Revival of Shostakovich's Ballets

Grigorovich's *The Golden Age*

In the early 1970s, Grigorovich approached Shostakovich about reviving *The Golden Age* for the Bolshoi Theatre.[45] In the Bolshoi's telling of this story, Shostakovich was dubious because he did not have his manuscripts or scores and "had no idea as to their archive condition."[46] But he opened his personal records to the Bolshoi's musicians, inviting them to find what they could. They found that the manuscripts were in Leningrad, dispersed across different archives and the Music Library of the Kirov (Mariinsky) Theatre and "in such a chaotic condition" that it took five years to sort through them. Shostakovich died before the work was finished, but *The Golden Age* was then re-created for the stage with the consent of his widow Irina Shostakovich. The ballet was a collaboration between Grigorovich as choreographer, Isaak Glikman as librettist, Simon Virsaladze as designer, and the team of musicians who had been sent to the archives.[47]

The Golden Age by Grigorovich was a very different work from the ballet of 1930. The libretto and choreography were entirely new, and much of the music was altered. Only a setting in the 1920s and the outlines of class conflict remained: that is, "good" Soviets vs. "bad" capitalists. The new *Golden Age* premiered in the 1982–83 season at the Bolshoi Theatre and quickly became part of the company's repertoire. In 1986, the Bolshoi took the ballet on tour, performing it in London, Paris, New York City, and Los Angeles.

Alongside performances of the full ballet, Grigorovich regularly excerpted the Adagio *pas de deux* from Act I, based on music from Shostakovich's Piano Concerto No. 1. (This became the best-known scene from *The Golden Age*, although it was not part of the original work of 1930.) Critics in Russia and abroad hailed Grigorovich's *Golden Age* as a "modern" achievement, "a brilliant adaptation," a "super-production," and a "milestone" in Soviet ballet.[48]

The new libretto for Grigorovich's *Golden Age* retained the setting in the 1920s during the NEP but changed the narrative, events, and stage action. In this new story, characters had names (thus personalizing them), the scenario took place in the Soviet Union rather than abroad, and a romance lay at the heart of the story. The ballet is set in an unnamed Soviet port where encounters between capitalist villains and Soviet fishermen play out in a restaurant-cabaret called "The Golden Age." Crooks and lovers carouse, profiteer, and quite literally rob guests at the restaurant, while upstanding fishermen and workers at the propaganda theatre offer a foil to the scurrilous antics. Rita (a dancer at "The Golden Age") and Boris (a fisherman) fall in love. This makes Rita's dance partner Yashka furious. An unsavory character, Yashka is not only a cabaret dancer but also the leader of a band of thieves. He and his fellow hooligans are eventually overcome by Boris and the fishermen. As Rita is drawn into Boris's world by her love for him, she is saved from the sordid NEP world and welcomed into the communion of Soviet comrades.

Whatever the merits of a new libretto, there was one obvious problem: Shostakovich had written his music for an entirely different scenario. A new scenario altered relationships between music and stage action and necessitated music suitable to these changes. The Bolshoi's account of reconstructing Shostakovich's music for *The Golden Age* implied a coherent outcome in which Shostakovich's ballet score was restored. But this was hardly the case. Rather, a new sequence of music was created, some of which came from Shostakovich's music for *The Golden Age* (of 1930) and some of which came from other works he had written. This was partly a practical decision because the sources were partial and complex, but it was also an artistic decision to select music that evoked a time and place (the Soviet 1920s) in the manner of Shostakovich's original ballet but that supported a different set of events. To this end, passages from the original ballet were present, albeit reordered and re-purposed, alongside music written for entirely different purposes but interpolated into the ballet, sometimes for the sake of the story and sometimes for the sake of the setting. At the same time, a significant amount of Shostakovich's original music for the ballet was not present. The most striking absence was Diva's *Adagio* from Act I of the original ballet. This was the music that had most impressed critics in 1930 and had led Sollertinsky to place Shostakovich in the pantheon of Russian ballet composers alongside Tchaikovsky and Stravinsky. The result of the recreations, additions, and omissions was a pastiche: the new *Golden Age* consisted entirely of Shostakovich's music, but only partly of the composer's music for *The Golden Age* itself.

Musically, the most significant additions came in the love scenes—the *pas de deux* between Rita and Boris, which had not existed in the original scenario but were the centerpiece of the new version. These used Shostakovich's non-ballet music. The *pas de deux* in Acts I and III were danced to the slow movements from the Piano Concertos, and the *pas de deux* in Act II featured "Elegy" from Shostakovich's incidental music for *The Human Comedy*. The added music implied an expressive outpouring that was not in the original ballet. This approach to musical borrowing evoked, perhaps inadvertently, the early nineteenth-century Parisian practice of interpolating non-ballet music into ballets to help elaborate the stage action.[49] Audiences often recognized the interpolated music and were able to make associations between what they heard and what was happening on the stage.[50] In *The Golden Age*, the music from Shostakovich's piano concertos conveyed emotion and atmosphere in the love scenes. At the same time, the use of concerto music suggested virtuosity, a quality that was on full display in the classical *pas de deux* of the principals.

What the new *Golden Age* preserved musically from Shostakovich's original concept was the use of sonority and style to mark "good" and "bad" characters. NEP villains danced to popular and ballroom styles (tango, foxtrot, cancan) while "good" Soviets did not. Meanwhile, the band of thieves danced to music that featured strong dissonance, harmonic ambiguity, and metrical disruption. The *pas* for the various performers followed the same divisions. As Grigorovich explained, "bad" characters performed "everyday dance" (implying less class, technique, and refinement), but "good" characters performed steps based on classical dance fused with movements from folk dance, *fizkultura*, and work routines like fishing.[51] (Or as one British reviewer put it more caustically, "The crooks and suckers have better music, better steps, better costumes."[52]) For a scene in "The Golden Age" restaurant in Act III, for example, the "Foxtrot" from *Jazz Suite No. 1* was inserted for Rita and Yashka's performance as professional dancers. Immediately after this, "No. 19: Foxtrot ... Foxtrot ... Foxtrot ... " from

Shostakovich's score for *The Golden Age* featured the restaurant's clientele dancing with one another. The sonority of the numbers was similar—both evoked dance music of the 1920s—and there was a strong correspondence between music and stage action as popular dance music accompanied a scene of social dancing.

At times, mixed musical styles suggested a conflict between "good" and "bad" elements. This was particularly true of Rita's music. Although she danced the role of a cabaret dancer, her first variation—that is, the moment she was first presented to the audience—featured music that was "pure" or free from popular elements. The variation was assembled from Shostakovich's music for "No. 24: The Dance of the Western Komsomol Girl and Four Sportsmen" in Act II of the 1930 ballet.[53] The sonority of this number placed Rita in the sound world of the "good" Soviet fishermen, even though she would also have to perform ballroom dances at the cabaret with the villainous Yashka. In other instances, Rita danced some of Diva's music from the 1930 ballet—like "Diva's Despair," which accompanied Rita's desperate attempts to escape from the abusive Yashka.[54] The music's dissonance, polytonal layers, use of 7ths and tritones, and metrical ambiguity conveyed confusion and anguish, emotions that were consonant with Rita's situation. By contrast, Rita's *pas de deux* with Boris to Shostakovich's "absolute" music evoked lyricism and virtuosity with no popular elements in music or choreography. Rita's costumes reinforced the complexity of her position. She wore red in her first variation, aligning her with the Soviets. Then she wore white in her *pas de deux* with Boris and black in her ballroom dances with Yashka. Her conflict was played out musically and visually as she was drawn to the "good" Soviets but trapped in the vicious world of the NEP.

Was Shostakovich's music for *The Golden Age* malleable to this approach that reordered and re-characterized parts of the score and interpolated new elements into it? We will recall that *The Golden Age* was Shostakovich's most independently written ballet score and that he completed most of the music ahead of the choreography. His music had internal coherence, sharp characterization, and distinct sonic divisions. Shostakovich's disappointment in *The Golden Age* of 1930 had been in the choreographic realization, which, unlike his music, was inconsistent in concept and quality. Grigorovich aimed to right what had gone wrong in that production, that is, to unify choreography with music and stage action, and he achieved this in many instances. But by rejecting Shostakovich's score for *The Golden Age*, or at least taking it piecemeal, Grigorovich helped to emphasize the perception of the original ballet as a "failure," a work in need of redemption. Implicit in his staging was the notion that even "great" choreography could not save Shostakovich's ballet music.

Grigorovich's *Golden Age* was important, however, for returning a Shostakovich ballet to the stage (albeit in significantly altered form) and for exploring how the Soviet topic could be treated. His revival gave impetus to the idea that Shostakovich's ballets played a meaningful role in the development of early Soviet dance and deserved a place on the stage, despite their topics and their troubled histories. The next revivals, by Ratmansky in the early 2000s, would continue to explore the complexity and contributions of these ballets, their political elements, and their relevance in a modern context. Most significantly, Ratmansky would revive Shostakovich's ballets solely to the composer's ballet music.

Ratmansky's *The Bright Stream* and *The Bolt*

In 2003, Ratmansky choreographed *The Bright Stream* for the Bolshoi Theatre, a seminal revival that enjoyed huge and enduring acclaim. Two years after the premiere, the Bolshoi performed the ballet in New York City, where critics lauded the work's sophistication and nuance, its trenchant characterization and witty comedy, and the freshness and modernity of its choreography.[55] "It was as if every idea Shostakovich had developed in the music had found its equivalent in the steps Ratmansky devised for the dancers," wrote Marina Harss, recalling the surprise and delight of seeing *The Bright Stream* for the first time.[56] In 2009, American Ballet Theatre mounted its own production of *The Bright Stream* under Ratmansky's direction and took the ballet into its repertoire, making this the only Shostakovich ballet to enter the repertoire of a Western company. Two years after *The Bright Stream*, Ratmansky revived *The Bolt* at the Bolshoi, but to less success, partly due to the ballet's strange mixture of artistic resources and its awkward relationships. To complete the trilogy of Shostakovich ballets, he also considered a new choreography of *The Golden Age* but decided (perhaps diplomatically) to re-stage Grigorovich's version instead. All three of Shostakovich's ballets were performed during the Bolshoi's centennial celebrations of the composer's birth. Since then, *The Bright Stream* continues to be performed at the Bolshoi, and a new production opened last season at the ballet's home theatre, the Mikhailovsky (formerly Maly) Theatre in St.

Petersburg.[57] *The Bright Stream* was "the great turning point" of Ratmansky's life, according his biographer.[58] Professionally, it propelled him to the highest echelons of ballet as he became artistic director of the Bolshoi Theatre and later artist in residence at American Ballet Theatre, and he continues to choreograph for the world's leading ballet companies. Artistically, *The Bright Stream* inaugurated Ratmansky's retrospective of early Soviet ballet and initiated ideas about the relationship between Shostakovich and ballet that would continue to unfold in the choreographer's subsequent ballets. The success of *The Bright Stream* brought international exposure to Shostakovich's ballet music and placed that music at the forefront of the modern ballet repertoire.

Ratmansky's revival of *The Bright Stream* and *The Bolt* completed the return of Shostakovich's ballets to the stage and allowed their artistic and political elements to be reassessed. The ballets raised persistent questions. Did they have artistic value? Was it possible to perceive and retrieve their aesthetic ideas despite their political contexts? What was the line between art and propaganda in the ballets? In *The Bright Stream*, the political element was muted and mostly limited to the setting on the collective farm. Witty artistic parody rather than political moralizing lay at the heart of the work. In *The Bolt*, however, the political element almost superseded the artistic one. Ratmansky's revival suggested that this was not in itself a deterrent to staging the ballet, but he exposed the difficulty of dealing with an artistic work that is ultimately a vehicle for the political needs of a specific setting. One scholar described the complexity in this confrontation of the past: "Ratmansky's work fascinates in how it choreographs a nuanced, reflective relationship to the past—a past that is not completely rejected but rather taken in hand, understood, and reimagined."[59] His cool detachment, gentle irony, and sometimes sympathy for unexpected characters softened the "Sovietness" of these ballets, exposed their artistic resources, and elevated their humor and power of characterization. As inventive as they were, however, the revivals of *The Bright Stream* and *The Bolt* were not equally successful with audiences. *The Bright Stream* delighted everywhere it was performed, while *The Bolt* was quickly dropped from the repertoire. The outcome mirrored the reception of the ballets in the 1930s and pointed again to *The Bright Stream* as the more enduring ballet, the work that elevated artistic elements over political concerns.

Ratmansky's revival of Shostakovich's ballets also inaugurated his larger project of reviving long-forgotten early Soviet ballets, including *The Flames of Paris* to Boris Asafiev's music (1932/2008) and *Lost Illusions* to Leonid Desyatnikov's score (1936/2011). Early Soviet ballets had earned the soubriquet "tractor ballets" because they featured topics dealing with Soviet agriculture and industry and were laden with moralizing lessons about Soviet life. Ratmansky was undeterred, however. "Why is everyone afraid of the milkmaid and the tractor driver?" he quipped ahead of the premiere of *The Bright Stream*.[60] If one difficulty lay in the topic, another lay in the form. These were story ballets, a form that had long been set aside as old-fashioned in ballet. In his revivals, Ratmansky challenged the precept that narrative ballet had nothing new to offer the art form. As Anne Searcy explains, he maintained that "there is no serious difference between abstract and narrative ballet."[61] The position was radical because the departure from narrative had been framed throughout the twentieth century as ballet's central innovation. Searcy writes that abstract and narrative ballet were "polar opposites" in Western discourse, a central difference lying in the approach to the music. Abstract ballet was deemed "musical" for its ability to reflect the musical score and musical forms, but narrative ballet required that music serve the story and the demands of dancing. During the Cold War, the opposition was cemented along ideological lines. Abstract ballet was associated with "progress" and Western balletic innovation, while narrative ballet was seen as "conservative," Soviet, and stuck in the past.[62]

Ratmansky's revivals, however, showed that early Soviet ballet, including Shostakovich's ballets, could demonstrate new form and content for the genre and could be musically responsive, even musically driven. As one enthralled reviewer wrote after seeing *The Bright Stream* and *Lost Illusions*:

> "Story ballets ... [have] been unfashionable with current, forward-thinking choreographers for years. But there has been a sea change recently, a new interest in the plot-driven narrative ballet, and no one has been more important to that renaissance than Alexei Ratmansky ... [His revivals were] the first full-length ballets in decades to show new possibilities within the form, and this had much to do with Mr. Ratmansky's ability to present a historical context while brilliantly deploying a ballet vocabulary to tell stories and display character."[63]

The reviewer touched on a central element of Ratmansky's work: narrative ballet that was progressive. The fact that this progressive quality lay in Soviet ballet also challenged the perception of that genre, especially of its early period. Ratmansky underscored the innovations and possibilities of that period and of Shostakovich's contributions to it. In doing so, he did not just retrieve the artifacts of a past time but demonstrated their relevance to the present and found in them sources of renewal for the genre.

Most significantly, Ratmansky treated Shostakovich's ballets as legitimate artistic endeavors. Rather than trying to make them what they "should have been" (an approach that underlay Grigorovich's revival of *The Golden Age*), he re-created what they were and allowed the music to articulate this identity. "Everything Shostakovich wanted to say about the subject, he said in the music. Why don't we let the audience figure it out?" Ratmansky responded when told that Shostakovich's ballets were "too Soviet."[64] His revivals preserved the artistic concept of the ballets while searching for a way in which these works might be relevant and appealing to audiences today. The approach was very different from reconceiving or reworking the ballets altogether on the assumption that they were not good enough in the first place. Ratmansky showed that Shostakovich's ballets were not foolish but funny. They were not "too Soviet"; they were musical.

Shostakovich's music has remained a motivating force in Ratmansky's career, and the choreographer has continued to explore it in three important ways: as music for dance, as a conscious interaction with Shostakovich's biography, and—with the revival of Shostakovich's ballets—as a way of coming to terms with Shostakovich's own interaction with genre. Before *The Bright Stream*, Ratmansky made five short ballets to Shostakovich's music: namely, to the last movement of the *Sixth Symphony* (*Duet Bouffe 1*), the *Scherzo for Orchestra in F# Minor* (*Duet Bouffe 2*), an excerpt from *Dances of the Dolls* (*Gavotte*), the second movement of the *First Symphony* (*La Sylphide-88*), and the finale of the *First Piano Concerto* (*Pas de Graham*).[65] In recent years, Ratmansky has pioneered choreographic explorations of Shostakovich's concert music in danced interpretations that attempt to intersect with the creative biography of the composer and to offer literate, albeit imaginative, readings of the themes of Shostakovich's oeuvre (such as love, creativity, or oppression). His most acclaimed works in this regard have been *Concerto DSCH* to Shostakovich's Second Piano Concerto (created for New York City Ballet) and *Shostakovich Trilogy* to the Ninth Symphony, the Chamber Symphony, and the First Piano Concerto (created for American Ballet Theatre). Ratmansky's influence on present-day reception of Shostakovich's music in dance is immense. His revivals of *The Bright Stream* and *The Bolt* have offered fresh assessments of Shostakovich's ballet music, while his choreographies of Shostakovich's concert music have placed the composer's "absolute" music in the modern tradition of dance. In reviving Shostakovich's ballets and mining the "canon" of his creative output, Ratmansky has linked the composer to the most contemporary artistic innovation.

Epilogue

In the early Soviet period, the future of ballet as a genre and Shostakovich's future as a composer had both been uncertain. Ballet was a contested art form. Its right to exist was in question, and its contributions to Soviet culture remained unclear. In the same period, Shostakovich emerged as a musician of immense talent, but he was a young composer seeking his place in the Soviet musical milieu where he aimed to establish himself as a composer for the stage. His dramatic compositions in these years took shape amid the experimentation of the 1920s and the abrupt regulation, but vague definition, of Soviet aesthetic doctrine in the early 1930s. With the condemnation of *Lady Macbeth* and *The Limpid Stream* in 1936, a year that inaugurated the most traumatic period of political repression, his future as a composer was anything but assured. By the late Soviet and post-Soviet periods, however, both ballet as a genre and Shostakovich as a composer held uncontested positions in Russian culture. They had transcended their tenuous positions of the early period to become immensely successful representatives of Soviet achievement. Yet the fact remained that Russia's most celebrated Soviet composer had not written an enduring work in that country's most iconic genre. In the assembly of Russian composers, including most obviously Tchaikovsky, Stravinsky, and Prokofiev, Shostakovich's lack of success in ballet was conspicuous.

The choreographers of this chapter—Massine, Belsky, Grigorovich, and Ratmansky—offered four perspectives on this gap in ballet's history and Shostakovich's output. Their approaches suggested that Shostakovich's music belonged on the ballet stage, or at the very least that it could find a home there, yet there was continued uncertainty about how or in what form that relationship might exist. Massine treated Shostakovich's music within the modernist tradition that used absolute music in ballet and that drew on Diaghilev's approach of mining Russian artistic developments as a resource for modernism. Belsky inclined toward the modernist approach too when he selected Shostakovich's concert music for choreography, but his roots lay in the early Soviet experiments of Lopukhov who had pioneered choreographic expression of musical form. For both choreographers, the desire to choreograph Shostakovich's symphonies aligned with the notion that concert music, especially that of Russian composers, could be reimagined for the ballet stage and that balletic innovation could be expressed in music that was released from or only loosely connected to narrative. In the late Soviet and post-Soviet periods, Grigorovich and Ratmansky looked back to Shostakovich's ballets to rehabilitate them. Grigorovich revived *The Golden Age* by selecting music from across Shostakovich's oeuvre and using unrelated excerpts for a new scenario and new choreography. His ballet was a kind of retrospective drama that evoked the spirit of the 1920s and imagined a ballet that might have been. Ratmansky rehabilitated Shostakovich's ballets themselves, staying close to the composer's scores and creating an intimate link between music and dance. His approach differed from that of the other choreographers examined in this chapter in that he dealt unflinchingly with Shostakovich's ballet music. Ratmansky explored how Shostakovich's ballets could be staged, how their political elements could be treated, and how the relationship between music and dance could develop.

The work of these choreographers offered a series of prisms on what might have been. What work might Shostakovich have written had his circumstances been different—had he been a more mature composer in the early 1930s, for example, or had better collaborators, or enjoyed a freer artistic context? The question is speculative, of course, but the choreographers addressed it repeatedly and imaginatively both by reconstructing the ballets that Shostakovich wrote and by exploring the balletic potential of music he never intended for the stage. Their approaches suggested at least two potential speculations: either that Shostakovich's original ballets could transcend their initial reception and re-enter the balletic canon, or that a new ballet could be made out of the music that proved to be appropriately significant (however that might be judged). Both speculations turned out to be tenuous, but they implied the pursuit of some kind of ideal form for Shostakovich's music in ballet—a form that would adhere to the conventions of the genre, allow for appealing innovations, and support Shostakovich's own place within the Russian pantheon. Ratmansky's revivals, in particular, suggested how the artistic collaboration between Shostakovich and Lopukhov—or even Shostakovich's own interest in ballet—might have developed. As one expert has commented, "[Ratmansky] has appealed to a counterfactual past in which Lopukhov collaborated with Shostakovich far beyond *Bright Stream*... Ratmansky is this history's alternate heir."[66]

In the real past, however, there was no tolerance for Shostakovich and Lopukhov to continue their collaborations, and ideological pressures on early Soviet ballet continued to insist on things that the genre could not accomplish. At a crossroads of aesthetic and political demands, the makers of Soviet ballet produced and tested a range of ideas for dance in the early 1930s. Shostakovich's ballets illuminated some of those ideas, to mixed results, and subsequent historiography was quick to erase their "failures." Yet the less-than-perfect works illuminated as much, if not more, than the polished products that ultimately emerged as exemplars of the Soviet period—exemplars of Soviet ballet on the one hand or of Shostakovich's musical maturity on the other. Shostakovich's ballets return us to a time before those exemplars were codified and before the achievements of the composer and the genre were firmly separated. In that liminal period, Shostakovich's ballets proved formative for Soviet ballet and formative for the composer himself.

APPENDIX A

Chart 1. *The Golden Age*, Act I, Scene 1: Different scenarios for Scene 1, as traced in two scores.

The left-hand column shows the titles of the dances according to the *New Collected Works* edition of *The Golden Age*. The right-hand column gives the titles as they appear in the manuscript orchestral score from 1930. Shostakovich's music did not change, but the scenario did and his music was recycled to new purposes. For a full comparison of dance titles in the two scores, see Daniil Petrov's chart in the *New Collected Works*, vol. 61:284–86 (Russian) or 296–98 (English).

Titles of Dances in the *New Collected Works* edition (correlating with the published libretto)	Titles of dances in the orchestral score preserved in the St. Petersburg State Museum of Theatre and Dance
Act I, Scene 1	
No. 1: "Overture"	
No. 2: "Procession of the Guests of Honor"	
No. 3: "Inspection of Display Windows"	"Sportsmen's training session"
No. 4: "Demonstration of 'Important' Exhibits. Appearance of the Soviet Football Team"	"Entrance of the maître d' of the hotel, the Aristocrats, and the Soviet football team"
No. 5: "Magician-Advertising Agent. Dance of the 'Indian'"	"Dance of the tennis players and training session for the Soviet football team"
No. 6: "Boxing as an Advertising Stunt"	"The maître d' of the hotel reports on Diva's arrival" ["Diva" is also written at the head of this dance]
No. 7: "Scandal during the Boxing Match. Entrance of the Police"	"Preparations for meeting Diva" "Diva's Arrival"

APPENDIX B

Librettos

These translations are kindly provided by Mark Sutcliffe (Fontanka Press) and are made from the original libretto booklets published for *The Golden Age* (*Zolotoi vek*, Leningrad, 1931), *The Bolt* (*Bolt*, Leningrad, 1931), and *The Limpid Stream* (*Svetlyi ruchei*, Leningrad, 1935).

The Golden Age

Act I

The raising of the curtain is preceded by a short orchestral introduction in the form of a fugue[1] on a chorale-like theme in a fast tempo.

The Industrial Exhibition

> The industrial exhibition "The Golden Age" in a large capitalist city in the West. Advertising displays.
>
> **Procession of the guests of honor.** A group of fascists is received with great ceremony, with a carpet rolled out for them. A team of Soviet footballers appear more discreetly, invited to the exhibition by local worker organizations.
>
> **Tour of the displays.** The bourgeois public is delighted with the exhibits. The fascists, as especially honored guests, are taken around the exhibition in chairs [carried aloft]. This scene is accompanied by scherzo-type (playful) music with very light orchestration.
>
> **Demonstration of the most "significant" exhibit.** The exhibition director and the city's chief of police show the group of fascists a newly invented type of cannon.
>
> The Soviet football team's appearance at the exhibition is not received positively by the fascists.
>
> **Magician-advertising agent.** A boxing-glove company has put on an eye-catching form of advertising. A boxing-match referee is dressed as an "Indian," whose unusual movements and incantations capture the public's attention. His unexpected transformation (the "Indian" quickly divesting himself of his theatrical costume to reveal a tailcoat) shows the real intention of the advertisement. Musically the "Indian's" dance is a virtuoso etude for orchestra at a fast tempo.
>
> **Boxing as an advertising stunt.** The public rushes over to the boxing. For promotional purposes, the boxing-glove company is putting on a match between a black man and a white man (a fascist). An agent of the fascists bribes the referee. The police are called just in case. The match gets underway. With an illegal punch, to which the referee turns a blind eye, the white boxer delivers a decisive blow to his black counterpart, who was on the verge of defeating his opponent. The referee hastily calculates the tally of punches and declares the white man, who is almost losing consciousness from the rigors of the fight, to be the winner.

Scandal. Local workers are incensed by what has happened. They surge to the ringside intending to beat up the referee. At a sign from their chief, the police intervene. The police drive the workers back. The bourgeoisie, in a wild frenzy, brandish their umbrellas, sticks and canes with threatening intent. A local female Komsomol member suddenly breaks away from the crowd and slaps the referee in the face. This whole scene takes place against a continuation of the orchestral etude that accompanied the dance of the "Indian." The music expands in movement and power, reaching (as a brass band strikes up) a dramatic conclusion.

A Hall at the Exhibition

Dance of "the golden youth." A Music-Hall venue. Fascist "golden youth" dance the foxtrot between the tables (saxophones are introduced to the orchestration for this number). Serving boys perform their tasks at a dynamic pace.

Appearance of the exhibition director and Diva. The exhibition director enters, accompanied by the chief of police and assistants. Everyone is in high anticipation for the appearance of the great favorite, the famous dancer (and fascist) Diva. At last Diva enters the hall to universal delight. In the breaks the men kiss her hands, the women swoon over her attire. Musically, the scene is an introduction in recitative style to the subsequent adagio.

Adagio. Diva performs a dance which is received ecstatically due to the Western bourgeoisie's admiration for strong women who use their charms to further political intrigue and blackmail (Diva is a weapon in the hands of the fascist group). The music for this dance is formed from an alternating series of instrumental solos: saxophone, violin, baritone horn, clarinet, and flute. The moment of crescendo is the baritone horn solo.

Appearance of the Soviet football team. The Soviet football team arrives to look around the exhibition areas, accompanied by local workers. The leader of the team attracts Diva's attention.

Variation. To show off her appeal, Diva performs a sophisticated and impassioned dance. The music for the variation is in recitative style with sudden changes in tempo.

Soviet folk dance. In stark contrast to the music-salon dance of Diva, the Soviet team perform a folk dance that is full of life and vivacious energy (accordions are used in the orchestration of this piece which is fast-paced in its musical movement). Diva becomes even more drawn to the leader of the Soviet team. She asks her partner (a fascist) to invite him to dance with them. The team leader politely turns down this "honor"—even when Diva asks him herself. This rejection of Diva causes outrage amongst the bourgeois public that idolizes her.

Dance of Diva and a fascist. Diva makes a show of dancing an erotic dance with her fascist partner. The music for this piece is a slow movement with a slightly quicker tempo in the middle part. The mood of the music is exalted [ecstatic].

Dance of the black man and two Soviet footballers. The black man, warmly received by the workers after the boxing match scandal, performs a "dance of solidarity" with two of the Soviet footballers. Musically, this is a broadly developed piece with a lyrical middle part (where the saxophone and banjo are introduced) and more lively beginning and end parts. At the dance's conclusion, the theme of the first part is in counterpoint with the melody of the middle part.

APPENDIX B

The supposed terrorist ("The Hand of Moscow"). Waltz. The Soviet team leader, a fine dancer, is noticed by the head of the fascists—the exhibition's director—and the chief of police. The director decides to invite the Soviet team leader to take part in a special dance at the propaganda advertising party in the Music Hall in order to demonstrate the "peaceful union of the classes." A poster is brought out announcing the forthcoming joint dance of the worker and the fascist Diva. Diva offers the Soviet team leader a glass, asking him to drink the health of the fascists. Completely befuddled by all that is happening, the Soviet team leader refuses the toast. The fascists are enraged and are on the verge of beating up the leader of the Soviet team, who instinctively lifts up a football to defend himself. Thinking it is a bomb (the Hand of Moscow!), the fascists throw themselves onto the ground expecting an explosion. The team leader leaves the ball (as factual proof of their mistake) by the head of the exhibition director, who is stretched out on the ground, and goes off with his comrades. This entire scene is accompanied by a salon-type waltz ending in a great crescendo.

The fascists' embarrassment. The terrified fascists gradually recover their equilibrium and realize their mistake (a rare case of mass hysteria). This leaves them shamefaced. The director summons the chief of police. The police appear. The musical arrangement for this scene is based on alternating instrumental duets: oboe and bass clarinet, piccolo clarinet and bassoon. At the end, a solo English horn, playing a scherzo-like melody, is heard against a more muted brass section, followed by a virtuosic recitative by the first violins.

Foxtrot ... foxtrot ... foxtrot ... Calm resumes. The unrest just experienced is dissipated in a general foxtrot. The exhibition foxtrots. The bacchanalia foxtrots. A fugue forms part of this number, played by a military orchestra.

Act II

A Street in the Same City

Pantomime of agents provocateurs, set-up, and arrest. The black man, the leader of the football team, and the female Soviet Komsomol member are walking through the city, taking in the sights. They are being followed by agents provocateurs. The chief of police and a police detachment are involved in the planned set-up. After several failed attempts, the secret agents manage to slip some forged documents into the football leader's pocket. They then accost and arrest him, along with the black man and the Komsomol member. The three under arrest are led through the city. The black man decides to escape. With the punch of a skilled boxer, he manages to grab the Komsomol member from the police's clutches and carries her away. The leader of the football team does not take part in the escape and remains in the hands of the police. The police detachment chases after the fleeing black man. The chief of police is furious about the black man's escape and delivers a slap in the face to the police who let him go. Musically, this whole scene is an extended introduction to the next scene in the workers' stadium. The music of this scene has a tragic air.

The Workers' Stadium

Procession of the workers to the stadium. Dance of the Pioneers. Worker-sportsmen arrive in organized formation at the competition. The Pioneers perform a game, its purpose revealed toward the end when an "outed" Fascist is exposed (one of the Pioneers plays the role of the "Fascist"). Musically, the procession and Pioneers' dance form a single piece; the musical content of the dance is also slightly reminiscent of the tune of the famous Pioneer song "Bang-bang, and then there's nothing."

Sporting games—dances of the worker-sportsmen. A series of sporting activities (boxing, discus throwing, tennis, fencing, volleyball, basketball, javelin throwing, shot put and so forth) are musically combined in one big dance number in a lively, dynamic tempo.

Meeting of the Soviet Football Team. A triumphal march, sonorously played in an extremely cheerful and uplifting way.

Football. An ambitious symphonic scene with the brass and percussion instruments predominating. It concludes with a fugue, played by a brass band accompanied by percussion.

Interlude. "Each to his own." Like the cinematic technique known as "dissolve," the previous scene becomes a scene of the fascists spending their time gambling at cards, provoking exploitative passions. The accompanying music—the rhythm of a minuet and instrumentation of chamber music—contrasts with the action.

Sporting dance of the female Komsomol member and four sportsmen. Back at the stadium. The Komsomol member dances with four sportsmen. The music is in alternating tempos, slow then livelier. The formal style of this number (with a big clarinet solo at the beginning) takes its lead from classical symphonic music.

General sporting dance. This is written in the style of big orchestral concerts (so-called *concerti grossi*).

Red Front. A dissolve, showing the police chasing the black man and Komsomol member through the workers' stadium. The workers organize themselves into a Red Front. The police are forced to give up the chase. The music for this scene is dramatic and energetic.

Act III

The Music Hall

Prelude. The orchestral music preceding the beginning of the act is an adapted variation (displaying remarkable ingenuity in the selection of orchestral tones) of the famous dance "Tahiti Trot" (which has been performed on several occasions by symphony orchestras in Leningrad, Moscow, and Kiev).

"The Golden Age" celebration. A series of divertissements ensue.

Chechotka (tap dance) "Shoeshine of the best quality." Advertising dance. Intermittent music with many pauses (fermata).

Polka "Once upon a time in Geneva..." (Angel of Peace). A dance illustrative of the nonsense spoken by the Western bourgeoisie about the peace of nations, disarmament and other wonderful things.

The touching union of the classes, slightly falsified. The partner of Diva (a fascist) has dressed up as the leader of the football team and performs a dance called "the peaceful collaboration of the classes." The dance is rapturously received by the bourgeois public in the Music Hall. Musically, the number is written in the style of a *pas d'action* (dance of action) with an intense and passionate melody. A solo for two saxophones comes in the middle part (a languorous waltz).

Can-can. Large-scale dance at a quick tempo, like a bacchanalia, evoking the rapture of the bourgeoisie for the number just performed.

Scene of the prisoners being freed. General unmasking. A dissolve. The Prison. Political prisoners. The Red Front frees them and surrounds the Music Hall. The female Western Komsomol member exposes the fascist disguised as the leader of the Soviet football team. The bourgeoisie are panic-stricken. The scene is accompanied by a four-voice fugue with the full orchestra at a high tempo.

Final dance of solidarity with the Western workers and Soviet team. This dance is essentially a dance of the working professions, a dance that celebrates work. The music ends in upbeat fashion, with the brass section predominating.

The Bolt

Act I

The workers are heading in to work after morning exercises. Lyonka Gulba, a worker at the factory, turns up in the aftermath of a drinking session. He is moving sluggishly. His head hurts. He does not want to go to work.

The factory director is carrying out a final inspection of the new workshop, along with the chief engineer and shock workers; even in the factory the clerk Kozelkov dreams of the foxtrot.

A meeting is taking place outside the factory about the opening of the new workshop.

The women cleaning the workshop listen in to what is being said at the meeting.

Columns of workers march into the new workshop to music. Here, in the workshop itself, the trainees are putting on a concert for the workers. The Komsomol members and Young Pioneers, doing their best to keep up, perform their factory marching dance.

Work in the factory begins.

Lyonka Gulba and his friends quietly sidle off from work. They get drunk and fall asleep. The machinery is stopped. Shockworker Boris finds the sleeping men, and he summons them back to work. The drunkards refuse. The workers are incensed by their behavior. They dismiss the inebriated men from the workshop, which is now in full swing.

Act I Dances and Scenes

Overture

Scene 1—In the locker room

1. On the way to work with exercise routine. Radio-rhythmical scene.
2. On the way to work after drinking session—mime scene.

Scene 2—In the workshop

1. Checking the machine installation—mime scene.
2. Cleaners—radio-mime-dance.
3. Scene filling the workshop—march.
4. Workshop concert:
    a) Saboteurs: poster-interlude.

b) Bureaucrat: poster-dance.
   c) Blacksmith: poster-dance.
   d) Factory march—dance of Komsomol members and Pioneers.
5. Workshop starts up.

Scene 3—In the locker room

1. Drinking session: mime dance.
2. Workers' indignation: mime scene.

Scene 4—In the workshop

1. Workers of the workshop: rhythmical scenes.

Act II

The Pioneers, under the command of Komsomol branch secretary Olga, are going on a demonstration. They have with them a dummy of a *kulak* and a poster reading, "Down with the Kulaks!" The beggar women ask for the priest's blessing. It is hot. The priest settles down by the tavern entrance. Sounds coming from somewhere disturb the priest's "peace." Unable to contain himself, the priest starts to dance. The Pioneers observe him surreptitiously. The toll of the bell brings the priest back to his senses. He heads to the church, followed by worshippers. The Komsomol members bring the procession to a halt. The Komsomol members dance—joyfully and energetically. Among them are several people from national minorities. The Komsomol dance develops and reaches its apogee. Kozelkov the clerk appears in his bathing costume. For a joke, the Komsomol members ask him to dance. Kozelkov agrees, not realizing that they are making fun of him. The two beggar women, harking back to their youth, dance the "chaconne." The young lad also shows off his dancing prowess. The church sexton, unable to resist, launches into a [folk] dance. He dances with the *kulak* puppet. The priest sees all of this. He sternly stops the dancing sexton and invites the worshippers into church. The Komsomol members organize a comic procession. A drunken gang, led by Lyonka Gulba, roll out of the tavern. Gulba wants revenge for being thrown out of the factory. Gulba suggests inserting a bolt [into the factory machinery]. Boris, who happens to be walking past, hoping to catch the conspirators, is knocked out by a blow to the head with the bolt. The priest, emerging from the church, blesses the drunken gang. Kozelkov and his cronies approach the tavern. They are full of good cheer and they dance. Olga appears and Kozelkov pesters her. Boris regains consciousness. He staggers around, seemingly drunk. The factory security on its rounds also think he is drunk. Kozelkov and his friends make fun of Olga. The bartender appears with beer for Kozelkov. Kozelkov and companions dance (the "Kozelkovshchina'").

Act II Dances and Scenes

Village in front of the factory

1. Musical prelude. Scene with the sexton, young lad, beggar women, priest and Pioneers.

2. Priest's mime dance.
3. Worshippers: scene.
4. Komsomol circle: [folk] dance.
5. Kozelkov's dance.
6. Beggar women's dance.
7. Young lad's dance.
8. Komsomol members' quadrille and sexton's folk dance.
9. Scene with priest and sexton. Entrance of the worshippers.
10. Coming out of the tavern—dancing pantomime.
11. "Vodka and Sabotage"—scene.
12. Kozelkov and cronies—scene and dances.
13. "Kozelkovshchina"—[folk] dance.

Act III

Work is over, the workers are leaving the workshop. Lyonka Gulba and his friends appear along with the young boy. Lyonka instructs the lad how to insert the bolt. The boy goes off to do so. Boris, recalling the plot he overheard earlier, goes to the workshop. He sees the boy at the far end of the workshop inserting the bolt. Boris rushes into the workshop. The boy runs out and warns Lyonka Gulba, who locks the workshop, trapping Boris inside. The jammed-in bolt creates a short circuit. The factory security come running. Lyonka Gulba tells them he has caught Boris inserting the bolt. Remembering his strange "drunken" behavior of the day before, the factory security arrest Boris. Lyonka Gulba and his gang maliciously taunt Olga. The young lad is unable to accept this turn of events and decides to tell the truth. He calls everyone back and tells them what happened. Lyonka Gulba cannot control himself and gives himself away. Boris is freed, Lyonka is arrested. Olga asks Boris to forgive her for doubting him. Under Olga's and Boris's leadership, the young boy can become a Pioneer. A meeting with the Red Army takes place in the factory club. A concert is put on. Afterward the Red Army soldiers, bearing all types of arms, initiate a dance-game involving all those present.

Act III Dances and Scenes

Part 1—By the workshop entrance

1. Musical prelude and scene of the workers leaving.
2. Scene with the bolt: pantomime and [folk] dance.
3. The set-up exposed: scene.
4. Musical entr'acte.

Part 2—The club

1. Red Army: march
2. Performance of the club company.

3. "Naval conference".   }
4. "Sophisticated young lady".   }
5. "Sycophant".   }
6. "Textile workers".   } choreographic performances
7. "Drayman".   }
8. "Female Colonial worker".   }

9. Paramilitary dance: male and female Komsomol members.

10. Red Army: dance-game:
    a) Infantry and artillery.
    b) Osoviakhim (Society for the Promotion of Aviation and Chemical Defense).
    c) Bicyclists.
    d) Red Army soldier and Red Navy sailor.
    e) Airmen.
    f) Budyonny soldiers.

The Limpid Stream

Act I

Scene 1

A small station deep in the steppes on one of the branches of the Northern Caucasus railway. Early autumn. The local *kolkhozy* (collective farms) have harvested the cereal crops and completed their autumn sowing.

A group of performers from the city theatre are about to arrive in time for the harvest festival that marks the end of this work in the fields; their arrival is eagerly anticipated. People from the nearby Limpid Stream *kolkhoz* have come to the waystation to meet the guests. Here is Gavrilych, the *kolkhoz* activist, getting on in years but full of life and bonhomie, loved by everyone; here too is the young Galya, with her friends, who has made a colorful bouquet for the guests. And here is the young agronomist and student worker Pyotr, with his wife Zina, the local entertainments officer. The last to arrive are the dacha dwellers—an elderly man and a woman who looks like mutton dressed as lamb: husband and wife. Both of them, disintegrating from boredom, have come to have a good gawp at the performers as they arrive. Zina, pensive and rather wistful, awaits their arrival with her head in a book. Her husband Pyotr, as happy and cheerful as a lark, tries his best to distract Zina, embroiling others in this endeavor too. Eventually everyone, except Zina, heads onto the platform.

A lively crowd of greeters and newly arrived performers is heading back. The performing group is made up of an accordion player, a classical dancer and her partner.

Entertainments officer Zina calls out to the dancer, who stops. They are left alone. What an unexpected meeting! After all, they have known each other well for a long time. They once studied together at ballet school. Since then, Zina has married the agronomist and gone off with him to work in the *kolkhoz*. And now in fact nobody knows that she used to be a dancer. The two friends take a good look at each other.

"Have you forgotten your dances?" the ballerina asks, as if by chance pulling out some ballet shoes. No, while working in the countryside Zina has not forgotten her artistic talent and immediately shows that this is so. The friends put on the ballet shoes and happily start to rehearse their old dance lessons, competing with each other. But coming up behind them are old Gavrilych and Zina's husband. Zina introduces her husband to the dancer. Gavrilych and Zina go on. Pyotr is smitten by the newly arrived artiste. She seems so wonderful to him, so unique, so dazzling. He starts to flirt with the dancer. Gavrilych and Zina return and they see this. Zina feels the first twinge of jealousy.

Scene 2

Day starts to turn into evening. The pattern of the harvested *kolkhoz* fields looks somehow unreal. Between the golden stacks of wheat is the camp of one of the field-working teams of the Limpid Stream *kolkhoz*.

The team has gathered every last ear of wheat from its plot. Tomorrow is the joint *kolkhoz* festival marking the end of the summer's harvesting work—the harvest festival—and so everyone is in a good mood. And now here is the team of performers. Pyotr introduces them to the *kolkhoz* field-working team.

The *kolkhozniki* and the performers greet each other. A spontaneous ceremony takes place. The performers have brought presents for the best shock workers in the *kolkhoz*. Here is a gramophone, which they award to Gavrilych himself. Here is an elegant silk dress which is given to the best milkmaid.

The recipients of the awards are cheerfully congratulated. The merriment naturally and unwittingly turns into dancing. The first to "sow the seeds" of the dancing are the grey-haired, bearded "quality inspectors" with their Gavrilych.

The dacha dwellers arrive late. They are urged to do a dance. To general mocking the dacha residents do an old-fashioned *chaconne*. Then some young girls dance—these are members of Zina's amateur group, which she has formed as entertainments officer. However, everyone's attention has already moved on, for the milkmaid must perform a dance in the elegant new dress she has been given. The milkmaid dances with a sprightly tractor driver. The company becomes increasingly merry. An old quality inspector winds up the gramophone; he asks the newly arrived performers if they in turn would perform a dance.

The artistes are a little uneasy at the idea of dancing in their ordinary clothes, but they do not want to say no to the *kolkhozniki*, who have given them such a warm welcome, nor do they wish to spoil the comradely merriment. They perform an improvised dance amongst the wheat stacks. Their dance evokes a mixture of reactions. The *kolkhozniki* watch them in friendly admiration. The dacha residents admire the artistes themselves (the husband admires the female classical dancer, the wife—the male dancer). Zina feels jealous of her husband.

The young agronomist Pyotr is becoming increasingly infatuated with the ballerina. He feels that his wife, the shy country-girl Zina, is so unremarkable and unattractive compared with this dazzling visitor. Zina even tries to break in to the guests' dance. The accordion player, too, is asked to dance with the young girl Galya.

But now some young crop growers from the Kuban region and the Caucasus perform an exhilarating folk dance. Everyone is enthralled by their lively, combative dance. The merriment reaches a crescendo.

At last they are all invited to go and eat. As everyone heads off, the old dacha dweller manages to whisper to the guest ballerina that he would like to meet up with her. His wife conveys the same message to the ballerina's partner. Pyotr, meanwhile, simply goes off with the ballerina. Zina is now utterly distraught. She even starts to cry. The young people and old Gavrilych comfort Zina. But now the ballerina returns. She tries to make Zina understand that she has no intention of responding to her husband's flirtation. The ballerina suggests to Zina that she disclose to the young people her former profession.

Zina agrees and again they both dance. There is great astonishment. The ballerina comes up with the idea of making fun of Pyotr and the others by turning up to their rendezvous, but in disguise. She suggests changing into her partner's clothes and going along to meet the mutton-dressed-as-lamb dacha resident. Her male partner will change into her clothes and go to the rendezvous with the old dacha resident. Zina, meanwhile, will go to meet her husband wearing the ballerina's performing costume. The plan is agreed.

Act II

Scene 3

A warm southern evening. A meadow, surrounded by hedges and trees, where the young people have gathered. The dacha owners arrive late. They are given a neighborly welcome. The accordion player has taken a shine to the young Galya. She danced with him so merrily earlier in the day. The accordion player whispers to Galya that he will come back and that she should wait for him. The girl is taken aback. The old dacha resident, his wife and Pyotr remind their "sweethearts" about their respective rendezvous. The young people are even more determined to teach them a lesson. The cross-dressing quickly takes place: the ballerina into her partner's clothes, he into hers, and Zina into the ballerina's performing outfit. As a joke the tractor driver dresses up in a dog's pelt. Everyone is ready. But now Galya mentions that she, too, has been invited to a rendezvous—with the accordion player. This unexpected development seems to present a problem, but the tractor driver comes to the rescue. He offers to accompany Galya to the meeting with the accordion player, but, disguised as a dog, he will prevent the accordion player from getting near her. This is agreed. Galya stands there waiting, with "Kolka" the dog alongside. The accordion player appears. He is perplexed. The dog seems an unnecessary addition. It turns out to be aggressive and lunges at the accordion player. In the end the accordion player realizes that he has been fooled. He is not the least offended and joins forces with the remaining conspirators.

The old dacha resident approaches the meeting place with his bicycle. He wishes to appear handsome and brave. He has a gun, cartridge belt and field glasses. He has put on everything he thinks makes him look good. The ancient old man is nervous about the imminent rendezvous. His wife, too, is approaching the same spot. She has even put on dress shoes to impress the male dancer. It is time to act. Suddenly he sees his wonderful dancer, his Sylphide, in the trees. This is the ballerina's male partner in female attire. The old man does not notice the change. But his prying wife is not pleased and she chases her husband with a stick. However, she is then given a fright by the tractor driver in canine disguise, all the more so as he is riding a bicycle. The ballerina appears in her partner's apparel and pokes fun at her. In the end they run off. The young agronomist turns up. He is expecting to meet the city-dwelling dancer but instead it is his own wife, dressed up as the ballerina, who greets him. He does not recognize his shy, humdrum Zina in this wonderful dancer. Zina jokes with him and teases him; she hides in the bushes. The lyrics again give way to buffoonery. The grizzled old dacha resident and cross-dressing dancer are running all over the place. The farce increases. The "romances" reach their height of passionate intensity. The ballerina in her male outfit emerges from the bushes and plays the betrayed lover, demanding satisfaction from the seducer. There is a farcical duel. The "male" ballerina fires first. A disappointing miss. The old dacha resident is given the pistol. Although terrified, he takes aim. Instead of a gunshot, Gavrilych bangs a bucket which the old man assumes is his shot and that it has hit the dancer's partner. The amorous dacha resident is horrified. He has no more thoughts of romantic escapades, but runs off stricken with terror. As soon as he is gone, the "killed one" is back on her feet and merrily dancing to the general hilarity of the "conspirators."

The practical joke is coming to an end. The young pranksters finish off this night of hijinks by all joining in folk dances.

Act III

Scene 4

It is the morning of the next day, the day of the harvest festival. In the meadow swings and a stage have been set up, decorated for the festival. The area in front of the stage is thronged with people. Now is the time for the performers to begin their show.

The agronomist breathlessly awaits the start of the performance. He is waiting for the ballerina, whom he saw (or so he believes) in the wood the night before, to dance.

But to his astonishment there appears not one dancer but a pair of identical dancers. Their faces are hidden by veils [masks]. The dance finishes. The agronomist cannot restrain himself. He rushes up to the artistes. All this is interrupted by the appearance of the old dacha residents. The old man falls heavily to his knees and asks forgiveness for his nocturnal crime, but brought before him is not just one "killed" by him, but two. He feels he has been made a fool of.

But now the female dancers remove their veils. The secret is revealed. The shame-faced agronomist, realizing how he has been hoodwinked, meekly begs his wife's forgiveness. They are finally reconciled. The agronomist sees that his shy wife is in fact both a wonderful worker and a remarkable, brilliant dancer. Everyone at the festival is caught up in a folk dance. The young *kolkhozniki* and the old residents, along with their guests, the artistes, celebrate the harvest festival.

Translations by Mark Sutcliffe

Notes

Introduction

1. "Baletnaya fal'sh': Balet 'Svetlyi ruchei,'" *Pravda* (February 6, 1936); "Sumbur vmesto muzyki: ob opere 'Ledi Makbet Mtsenskogo uyezda,'" *Pravda* (January 28, 1936).
2. Scholl, *"Sleeping Beauty"*, 72. Lunacharsky was the first Soviet commissar of education (or cultural minister), a position he held until 1929.
3. Ezrahi, *Swans of the Kremlin*, 22.
4. Souritz, *Soviet Choreographers*, 317–18.
5. Garafola, in the forward to Ross, *Like a Bomb*, ix.
6. Wiley, *Tchaikovsky's Ballets*, "Introduction," 1–10; Garafola, "Diaghilev's Musical Legacy," 46–47.
7. Asafyev's essay on *Sleeping Beauty* (1922) introduced the term "symphonism" and was originally published in *Yezhenedel'nik petrogradskikh gosudarstvesnnykh teatrov* [Weekly of the Petrograd State Theatres] (vol. 5: 28–36) and later republished in Asaf'yev, *Akademik B. V. Asaf'yev*. The term *symphonism* or *symphonic* in relation to ballet was also used extensively in Sollertinskiy, *Istoriya sovetskogo teatra*, vol. 1. (1933), and Krasovskaya, *Russkii baletnyi teatr vtoroi poloviny 19 veka* (1963). See Scholl's excellent discussion of *symphonism* in *"Sleeping Beauty"*, chapter 3 ("Achieving Symphonism"), 64–100.
8. Scholl, *"Sleeping Beauty"*, 76, 83.
9. Asaf'yev, *Akademik B. V. Asaf'yev*, 175–76, quoted in Scholl, *"Sleeping Beauty"*, 85.
10. Lopukhov, *Puti baletmeistera* and *Writings on Ballet and Music* (the latter of which reproduces parts of *Puti balemeistera* and other writings by Lopukhov). See also Scholl, *"Sleeping Beauty"*, 91–92.
11. Titus, *The Early Film Music*, 4; Scholl, *"Sleeping Beauty"*, 82–84.
12. Scholl, *"Sleeping Beauty"*, 85.
13. Sollertinskii, "Novyi balet 'Dinamiada,'" 14.
14. Since Russia's invasion of Ukraine, Ratmansky has requested that the Bolshoi and the Mariinsky Theatres suspend his choreographies.
15. For example, see Chernova, Chepalov, Ross, and Souritz on Soviet choreographers; Scholl and Morrison on the theory and politics of early Soviet ballet; Morrison and Stern on ballet institutions; Ezrahi, Gayevsky, Homans, Katonova, Morrison, Ross, Scholl, and Stern on *drambalet*; Croft and Searcy on ballet as cultural-political exchange; and Carr, Cross, Garafola, Homans, Scheijen, and Steichen (to name a few) on Russian ballet in the West. The relevant works of these scholars appear in the bibliography.
16. For example, see Haas, Edmunds, Frolova-Walker, and Fairclough—among others.
17. Barsova, Bobrik, Fortunova, and Vlasova have made some of the most recent contributions in this area.

Chapter 1

1. Shostakovich, letter to Glivenko, quoted in Kovnatskaya, *Letopis'*, 1:120–21. Shostakovich's letters to Glivenko are preserved in Maxim Shostakovich's personal archives with excerpts reproduced in several sources, including Kovnatskaya, *Letopis'*, *T. 1* (drawing on Sapozhnikov,

Moi Shostakovich), and the Sotheby's catalogue, "Autograph Manuscripts," in *Fine Printed and Manuscript Music* (1991).
2. Shostakovich, letter to Glivenko, quoted in Kovnatskaya, *Letopis'*, 1:114, 121.
3. Shostakovich, letter to Glivenko, quoted in the Sotheby's catalog, 150.
4. Fay, *Shostakovich*, 49.
5. For material on Shostakovich's biography, I rely on the meticulous work of Olga Dombrovskaya and Olga Digonskaya, chief archivists at the Dmitri Shostakovich Archive, and on the scholarship of Fay, Fairclough, and Wilson. The Shostakovich apartment on Marat Street is held privately by the Rostropovich family.
6. Katzenellenbaum, *Russian Currency and Banking*, 77.
7. Bogdanov-Berezovskii, *Vstrechi*, 16, as quoted in Fay, *Shostakovich*, 15.
8. Shostakovich was disappointed to earn only honorable mention and not one of the prizes at the competition. Around 1930, he stopped concertizing for more than two years. His mother later attributed this fallow period to his disappointment in Warsaw. The First Piano Concerto (1933) was a vehicle for his own performance and helped to rekindle his concertizing career. Fay, *Shostakovich*, 35, 73.
9. Beumer, "Post-Revolutionary Russian Theatre," in *The Routledge Companion to Russian Literature*, 210.
10. Titus, *The Early Film Music*, 1–2.
11. TRAM turned "professional" in 1929. Although the theatre was based in Leningrad, some of its plays were simultaneously staged by Meyerhold in Moscow, including *The Shot*, for which Shostakovich wrote the music.
12. Fay, *Shostakovich*, 58.
13. Fay, *Shostakovich*, 71. In 1937, Shostakovich joined the faculty of the Leningrad Conservatory. His faculty positions, first in Leningrad and later in Moscow, offered professional and financial stability.
14. Fay, *Shostakovich*, 61.
15. Fay, *Shostakovich*, 49.
16. Shostakovich, "Deklaratsiya obyazannostei kompozitora"; see also Fay's summary in *Shostakovich*, 63–64.
17. Souritz, *Soviet Choreographers*, 315.
18. Souritz, *Soviet Choreographers*, 315; Garafola, "Russian Ballet in the Age of Petipa," in *The Cambridge Companion to Ballet*, 151.
19. Ezrahi, *Swans of the Kremlin*, 15.
20. Lopukhov, *Shest'desyat let*, 193, as quoted in Ezrahi, *Swans of the Kremlin*, 16.
21. Pierre Michaut (from Paris) and Igor Glebov (Boris Asafyev), as quoted in Souritz, *Soviet Choreographers*, 44.
22. Clark explains that *Glaviskusstvo* (the artistic division of *Narkompros*) had to "set up courses" to educate the hundreds of workers that it appointed to the boards of Leningrad's cultural institutions. Clark, *Petersburg*, 266.
23. Morrison, *Bolshoi Confidential*, 262; Stern, "Politics in Pointe Shoes," 52–53, citing Morrison.
24. Pleshcheyev, "O balete, ego demokratizatsii, fokinizatsii i pr."
25. I am grateful to the late Elizabeth Souritz for sharing her invaluable insights into this period. My discussion of the Soviet ballet theatre is indebted to our conversation as well as to her meticulous scholarship in *Soviet Choreographers of the 1920s*.
26. Souritz, *Soviet Choreographers*, 31.
27. Ibid., 24–30.
28. Romanov, Leontiev, and Zhukov had also danced in Diaghilev's Ballets Russes in the pre-Revolutionary period.
29. Ezrahi, *Swans of the Kremlin*, 50.
30. Quoted in Souritz, *Soviet Choreographers*, 167; Chernova, "Kasian Goleizovsky," 369.
31. Chepalov, "Nikolai Foregger," 367.
32. Nepomnashchy, "Dance as Metaphor," 202; Tyerman, "Resignifying *The Red Poppy*," 445.
33. Souritz, *Soviet Choreographers*, 236–37.
34. Ibid., 253.
35. The ballet's Constructivist aesthetic is elaborated in Sayers, "Re-Discovering Diaghilev's 'Pas d'Acier'"; and in Sayers and Morrison, "Prokofiev's *Le Pas d'Acier*."
36. Sayers and Morrison, "Prokofiev's *Le Pas d'Acier*," 101; Morrison, *The People's Artist*, 8–13.

37. Performance lists from the Leningrad State Academic Theatre, 1918–26, can be found in TsGALI f. 337, op. 1, d. 7.
38. Sheremetyevskaya, *Tanets na estrade*, 158.
39. Several scholars have charted these aesthetic questions and the way they were framed in the early Soviet period. Souritz focuses on choreographic ideas, Ezrahi on the development of genre, Scholl on reception history, and Stern on theoretical debates.
40. Ezrahi, *Swans of the Kremlin*, 37.
41. Gvozdez, "O reforme baleta," and Sollertinskii, "Kakoi zhe balet." A number of different terms were used in the 1920s to try to describe this new type of ballet. See also Ezrahi, *Swans of the Kremlin*, 41–46, for a discussion of the "dramatization of ballet."
42. Dobrovolskaya, *Tanets, pantomima, balet*, 80.
43. Ezrahi, *Swans of the Kremlin*, 33.
44. Ezrahi, *Swans of the Kremlin*, 44; Stern, "Politics in Pointe Shoes," 44.
45. The announcement was published in *Zhizn' iskusstva*, no. 2 (January 6, 1929) and is referenced by several scholars, including Dobrovolskaya, Ezrahi, Morrison, Ross, Stern, and Swift.
46. Khentova, *Shostakovich: Zhizn' i tvorchestvo*, 113.
47. Ibid. See also Hulme, *Dmitri Shostakovich Catalogue*, 9.
48. Souritz, *Soviet Choreographers*, 313; Moshevich, *Dmitri Shostakovich, Pianist*, 33.
49. Iving, "Tanets v 'Krivom zerkale'" (1927), quoted in Sheremetyevskaya, *Tanets na estrade*, 157.
50. Quoted in Khentova, *Shostakovich: Zhizn' i tvorchestvo*, 103–4.
51. Fay, *Shostakovich*, 23.
52. Recollections of D. A. Popov, as recorded in Khentova, *V mire Shostakovicha*, 63.
53. Sheremetyevskaya, *Tanets na estrade*, 157, 161.
54. It is not entirely clear who choreographed Ponna's performance of the *Fantastic Dances*. Popov attributed the choreography to Goleizovsky (Khentova, *V mire Shostakovicha*, 63). Fay attributes it to Ponna herself (Fay, *Shostakovich*, 23), while Sheremetyevskaya notes that most of Ponna's choreographies were created by Kaverzin (Sheremetyevskaya, *Tanets na estrade*, 157).
55. Kopytova, "Yunyi baletoman," in *Shostakovich v Leningradskoi konservatorii 1919–1930*, comp. Kovnatskaya, 3:61. See also Shostakovich's letters to Bogdanov-Berezovsky as reproduced in Kovnatskaya, "'Khochu c toboi,'" in *Dmitrii Shostakovich*, ed. Digonskaya and Kovnatskaya.
56. Ibid.; also, Bogdanov-Berezovsky's reminiscences, as recorded in Kovnatskaya, *Letopis'*, 1:107.
57. Shostakovich, as quoted in Kovnatskaya, *Letopis'*, 1:123, based on Sapozhnikov, 62–63.
58. Shostakovich, letter to Bogdanov-Berezovsky, as reproduced in Kovnatskaya, "'Khochu c toboi,'" 71; Kopytova, "Yunyi baletoman," 70.
59. V. Prokopenko, "Za obnavleniye baleta," *Rabis*, no. 42 (October 16, 1928): 11; also quoted in Kovnatskaya, *Letopis'*, 1:351.
60. Sollertinskii, *Istoriya sovetskogo teatra*.
61. Katonova, *Muzyka sovetskogo baleta*, 375.
62. Fay, *Shostakovich*, 51; Ezrahi, *Swans of the Kremlin*, 43. See also Slonimskii, *Chudesnoye bylo ryadom*, chapter 1, for a discussion of Sollertinsky's activities and influence on ballet in this period. The Choreographic Institute was known as the Choreographic College (Tekhnikum) from 1929 until 1937. For a chronology of the Vaganova Ballet Academy, including the names by which it was known in different periods, see *Vestnik Akademii Russkogo baleta im. A.Y. Vaganovoi* no. 7 (1999): 64–69.
63. Garafola, Foreword to Ross, *Like a Bomb*, ix.
64. Garafola, "Diaghilev's Musical Legacy," 46–47; Wiley, *Tchaikovsky's Ballets*, 1–10.
65. Lopukhov, *Puti baletmeistera*, especially the first and second sections.
66. Scholl, *"Sleeping Beauty"*, 91.
67. *Stenka Razin* was choreographed by Fokine to Glazunov's music in 1915 and presented in a new choreography by Gorsky in 1918 for the first anniversary of the October Revolution. Gorsky's work was not successful and fell out of the repertory after three performances (Souritz, *Soviet Choreographers*, 97–103). The proposed collaboration between Goleizovsky and Shostakovich would have offered a new ballet on this popular topic.
68. Quoted in Chepalov, "Nikolai Foregger," 360.
69. Ibid.
70. Shostakovich, in *Zolotoi vek*, libretto, 4–5; Sollertinskii, "Novyi balet 'Dinamiada,'" 14.

Chapter 2

1. The premiere on October 26 was a private performance for Red Army officials. The ballet opened the next day to the general public.
2. Positive critiques included Sollertinskii, "Novyi balet 'Dinamiada'" (1929) (which documented Sollertinsky's enthusiastic response to the music for Act I); Gres, "Simfonicheskiye novinki" (1930) (which hailed *The Golden Age* as a positive turn away from the musical "excesses and exaggerations of *The Nose*"); Yakobson, "Zolotoi vek," *Spartak* (Leningrad) (1930), as quoted in Armashevskaya, *Vainonen*, 67 (which described audiences' enthusiastic responses to the ballet)—among others.
3. Broderson, "Legalizatsiya prisposoblenchestva," 9.
4. Sollertinskii, "Kakoi zhe balet?" (1929) and "Za novyi khoreograficheskii teatr," (1928).
5. Clark, *Moscow, the Fourth Rome*, 44.
6. Stern, "Politics in Pointe Shoes," 86–101. For other accounts of the competition, see Ezrahi, *Swans of the Kremlin*, 45–46; Ross, *Like a Bomb*, 105–8; Swift, *The Art of the Dance*, 85–88—to name a few.
7. Quoted in Stern, "Politics in Pointe Shoes," 95–97, 100. Although the libretto submissions are not preserved in Theatre records, transcripts of the Council's discussions in March and April of 1929 offer insights into the proposed libretti.
8. Shostakovich, letter to Lyubinsky, July 1, 1929, quoted in V. Kiseleva, "Iz pisem 30-kh godov," 85. For Goleizovsky's work on *Joseph the Beautiful* with the Moscow Chamber Ballet, see Souritz, *Soviet Choreographers*, 185–96.
9. Shostakovich, letter to Lyubinsky, July 1, 1929.
10. Souritz, *Soviet Choreographers*, 65.
11. Shostakovich's complaints about the production of *The Golden Age* appear in letters, notes, minutes, and protocols preserved in the *fond* of the Mariinsky Theatre, TsGALI f. 337.
12. *Rabochii i teatr* reported on theatrical and artistic life in Leningrad, announced upcoming performances, and (in relation to ballets) listed choreographers, performers, composers, and other contributors. In cases of collective choreography, announcements indicated the part or parts of a ballet for which each choreographer was responsible.
13. "Leningrad: K postanovke 'Dinamiady,'" 15.
14. For example, Alexei Ermolayev and Leonid Lavrovsky appeared on published lists of the choreographic team well into 1930.
15. Broderson, "Legalizatsiya prisposoblenchestva," 9.
16. Shostakovich, letter to Lyubinsky, February 26, 1930, in GTsTM, f. 629, no. 61; also reproduced in Kiseleva, "Iz pis'em 1930-kh godov," 87–88.
17. Kaplan had no experience in ballet. He had graduated from the Conservatory as a tenor, and his ideas about stage production had been shaped by Meyerhold's plays (Gauk, *Aleksandr Vasil'yevich Gauk*, 124). The practice of involving opera directors in ballet productions increased in the late 1920s. The hope was that practitioners from more "dramatic" genres (so perceived), like operas or stage plays, would help to enhance "drama" (that is, dramatic rationale) in ballets. Contemporaries like Aleksandr Gauk as well as scholars like Ezrahi, Krasovskaya, Morrison, Ross, and Stern document these practices.
18. The complaints were recorded during meetings of the special commission of the director of State Theatres and of the Artistic Council in May 1930. TsGALI f. 337, op. 1, d. 63, l. 42–46ob.; and TsGALI f. 337, op. 1, d. 71, l. 8.
19. Stern, "Politics in Pointe Shoes," 114–15.
20. TsGALI f. 337, op. 1, d. 71, l. 16 ob., recorded May 26, 1930. Shostakovich's statement is also quoted in part in Kovnatskaya, *Letopis'*, 1:472 (in Russian), and in full in Stern, "Politics in Pointe Shoes," 116–17, n. 226 (in Russian and English).
21. TsGALI f. 337, op. 1, d. 71, l. 16 ob.
22. Ibid.
23. Petrov, in Shostakovich, *New Collected Works* (hereinafter: NCW) 61:303.
24. Shostakovich, letter to Lyubinsky, February 26, 1930.
25. The costume might have been part of a window display for the set of Act I. Some of Khodasevich's surviving sketches show enormous shop windows filled with lacey lingerie, high-heeled shoes, jewelry, and fashion accessories.

26. In her study of Soviet fashion, Anne Gorsuch explains that the kerchief tied behind the head was part of the "revolutionary iconography" of 1920s styles and symbolized "Sovietness." Gorsuch, "Dance Class," 182.
27. Shostakovich, "Avtor—o muzyke baleta," in *Zolotoi vek*, libretto, 4–5.
28. *Zolotoi vek*, libretto, 11.
29. For ease of reference, I follow the titles of the dances in the *New Collected Works* edition of the ballet. Some of the titles are different in the manuscript score for *The Golden Age*, which is preserved in the Mariinsky Music Library and in the archives of the St. Petersburg State Museum of Theatre and Music. The content of the scene, however, is the same across the sources: it centers on Diva.
30. Wells, "'The New Woman,'" 172; Stites, *Russian Popular Culture*, 73.
31. Stites, *Russian Popular Culture*, 73.
32. *Zolotoi vek*, libretto, 7; Armashevskaya, *Baletmeister Vainonen*, 66.
33. Sollertinskii, "Novyi balet 'Dinamiada,'" 14.
34. Armashevskaya, *Baletmeister Vainonen*, 66.
35. Compare mm. 49–50 of Diva's Variation with mm. 175–76 of "No. 8: Dance of the 'Golden Youth.'"
36. Shostakovich, as quoted in NCW 61:271.
37. Garafola, *Diaghilev's Ballets Russes*, 108.
38. Ibid., 110.
39. Ibid., 98.
40. Souritz, *Soviet Choreographers*, 280, 291.
41. Ibid., 210, 280, 291, 313.
42. See Robert Leach's discussion of Meyerhold's system in chapter 4 ("Revolutionary Theatres 1921–1924") of *Revolutionary Theatre*, 104–61.
43. O'Mahony, *Sport in the USSR*, 29.
44. Ibid., 15, 22–23.
45. Ibid., 69.
46. Ibid., 9.
47. O'Mahony notes that Soviet youth were among the first young people anywhere to wear the soccer jersey as an article of daily dress. Ibid., 8.
48. Quoted by Messerer, *Tanets, mysl', vremya*, 129.
49. *Futbolist*, libretto, 1930. *Futbolist* won a prize at the libretto competition of 1929. It was not considered for production in Leningrad, however, but was produced at the Bolshoi in Moscow. Braginsky, *Shostakovich and Football*, 34, and Stern, "Politics in Pointe Shoes," 100, n. 177.
50. Braginsky, *Shostakovich and Football*, 38. Braginsky also notes that the Dinamo Moscow club had widely known connections to the Cheka, its first chairman being Felix Dzerzhinsky (*Shostakovich and Football*, 42).
51. O'Mahony, *Sport in the USSR*, 34. For an extended analysis of the first Spartakiad and its promotion in Soviet visual culture, see pp. 30–37 of O'Mahony's discussion.
52. Ibid., 30, 37.
53. *Zolotoi vek*, libretto, 14.
54. Messerer, *Tanets, mysl', vremya*, 129; Meleikina, "Neizvestnyi Igor' Moiseyev: balet 'Futbolist,'" 33–35.
55. According to notes in the rehearsal score, Yakobson also choreographed a few numbers in Act I, Scene 2 (No. 8: "Dance of the Golden Youth"; No. 15: "The Supposed Terrorist," also called "Waltz"; No. 16: "General Confusion"; and No. 19: "Foxtrot . . . Foxtrot . . . Foxtrot"). *Zolotoi vek—Klavier*, GMTMI (SPb), TTsK 16903/2.
56. Broderson, "Legalizatsiya prisposoblenchestva," 9.
57. The photographs are preserved in the St. Petersburg State Museum of Theatre and Music and in the Dmitri Shostakovich Archive. Some are reproduced in Dobrovolskaya, *Baletmeister Leonid Yakobson*.
58. Dobrovolskaya, *Baletmeister Leonid Yakobson*, 13.
59. Ross, *Like a Bomb*, 114–15.
60. I am grateful to Natalya Zozulina and the Vaganova Ballet Academy for sharing this material with me. Lopukhov and Gusev, nar., *Iskusstvo russkogo baleta—peredacha sed'maya*, aired 1965 on Leningradskoye televideniye. A brief excerpt of the forty-five-minute broadcast can be seen at https://www.youtube.com/watch?v = I2Vr2X58aqQ (last accessed June 4, 2021); the "Sports Quintet" occurs at 1:33–4:00.

168   NOTES

61. Shostakovich, as quoted in Vol'fson, *Leonid Yakobson*, 11; see also Yakubov, quoting Shostakovich, in "*The Golden Age*," 196, and NCW 61:271.
62. Yakubov, quoting Shostakovich, in "*The Golden Age*," 196, and NCW 61:271.
63. Ibid.
64. Curtis, "Down with the Foxtrot," 223, 226–27.
65. Ibid., 230.
66. Ibid., 226. For the role of jazz in Meyerhold's plays, see Fitzpatrick, *The Cultural Front*, 191.
67. Vladimir Slepkov, "Rytsari skorbi i pechali" (1928), as quoted by Gorsuch, "The Dance Class," 176.
68. See, for example, Rubin, "Vybory v strane sporta," 11 (*Smena*), where the young conservatives (Tories) of Britain are described as that country's "golden youth." Shostakovich read *Smena* and followed its critiques (expressing his annoyance, for example, with its coverage of *The Nose*); he would have been aware of the kind of contemporary discourse that filled its pages.
69. Stepanov, *Zhan-Pol' Marat*, 36.
70. Petrov speculates that instructions for this act may have been changing as Shostakovich wrote, leaving the composer uncertain of how and where dances were to be deployed. NCW 61:299.
71. Smith, "The Orchestra as Translator," in *The Cambridge Companion to Ballet*, 143.
72. Titus, "Modernism, Socialist Realism, and Identity," 201.
73. Broderson, "Legalizatsiya prisposoblenchestva," 9.
74. Shostakovich, *Pis'ma I.I. Sollertinskomu*, 53; and Minutes of the Artistic Council's meetings, TsGALI f. 337, op. 1, d. 71, l. 2–3 ob.

Chapter 3

1. Slonimskii, *Sovetskii balet*, 90.
2. Shostakovich, letter to Sollertinsky, February 10, 1931, in *Pis'ma I.I. Sollertinskomu*, 53–54.
3. Brodersen, "Neudavsheyesya perevooruzheniye baleta"; Gauk, *Aleksandr Vasil'yevich Gauk*, 126 (reminiscing in 1975); Sollertinskii, "*Bolt* i problema sovetskogo baleta"; Yankovskii, "*Bolt*"; and a range of contemporary critics in *Smena*, *Rabochii i teatr*, *Bytovaya gazeta*, *Leningradskaya Pravda*, and other journals.
4. Morrison, *Bolshoi Confidential*, 267; Ross, *Like a Bomb*, 121; Stern, "Politics in Pointe Shoes," 108.
5. Fitzpatrick, *The Cultural Front*, 116.
6. Nelson, "The Struggle for Proletarian Music," 110.
7. Fitzpatrick, *The Cultural Front*, 112, 118.
8. Ibid., 115.
9. A. I. Kritnitsky, head of the Agitation and Propaganda (agitprop) section of the Central Committee, quoted in Fitzpatrick, *The Cultural Front*, 117.
10. Chepalov, "Nikolai Foregger," 363; Souritz, "Constructivism and Dance," 137. In 1991, sixty years after *The Bolt*, Bruni recalled that the "machine dances" had not been staged because the Artistic Council withdrew them at the first dress rehearsal. However, her designs representing machines on stage remained. Bruni, "O balete s neprekhodyashchei lyubov'yu," 36.
11. Sitsky, *Music of the Repressed Russian Avant-Garde*, 173.
12. Sayers and Morrison observe a similarity between the final bar of *Zavod* and the final bar of Prokofiev's *Le Pas d'acier*. Sayers and Morrison, "Prokofiev's *Le Pas d'Acier*," 89.
13. Sitsky, *Music of the Repressed Russian Avant-Garde*, 62–63.
14. "Usloviya konkursa libretto sovetskogo baleta," *Zhizn' iskusstva*.
15. Quoted in Stern, "Politics in Pointe Shoes," 97.
16. Souritz, "Constructivism and Dance," 129.
17. Ibid., 130.
18. Sayers, "Rediscovering Diaghilev's 'Pas d'Acier,'" 163.
19. Morrison, "Shostakovich as Industrial Saboteur," 120; Sayers, Rediscovering Diaghilev's 'Pas d'Acier,'" 183.
20. Bruni's sketch is reproduced in several places, including in Souritz, "Constructivism and Dance," 140, and in Morrison, "Shostakovich as Industrial Saboteur," 124. See also Levitin, *Tat'yana Georgiyevna Bruni*, 34–35, for a discussion of Bruni's designs for *The Bolt*.

21. Fay, *Shostakovich*, 62; Morrison, "Shostakovich as Industrial Saboteur," 118, 155; Ilichova, "Shostakovich's Ballets," 205.
22. Mally, *Revolutionary Acts*, 1–2. Mally offers an excellent discussion of amateur theatre's "small forms" in Chapter 2 ("Small Forms on Small Stages") of *Revolutionary Acts*, 47–80.
23. Ibid., 56–57.
24. Ibid., 73.
25. For an extended description of "living newspapers" and their cultural significance, see Mally, *Revolutionary Acts*, 65–73.
26. Ibid., 116–17.
27. Ibid., 126.
28. Ibid., 117–20, based on Piotrovskii and Sokolovskii, eds., *Teatr rabochei molodezhi* (1928). Incidentally, Adrian Piotrovsky, one of TRAM's early organizers and the co-editor of its collection of plays, later co-authored the libretto for *The Limpid Stream*.
29. Bonnell, *Iconography of Power*, 187.
30. Ibid., 191, 193.
31. Garafola, "The Making of Ballet Modernism," 31.
32. Compare *The Bolt*, R176 (No. 15: The Hooligan's Mime Dance—Carousing) with *Petrushka*, R5.
33. Photographs and costume sketches for *The Bolt* are preserved in the St. Petersburg State Museum of Theatre and Music. Some of Bruni's costume sketches are original and date from 1931; others date from 1979 when Bruni re-sketched several items because her original sketches were not in her possession.
34. "'Bolt' i BOLTlivyye formalisty"; also quoted in Ilichova, "Shostakovich's Ballets," 207; and in NCW 62v: 575.
35. Hooligan attire on the amateur stage was often a crooked cap, a sailor's shirt, and a pair of bell-bottom trousers. Mally, *Revolutionary Acts*, 114.
36. *The Young Lady and the Hooligan* was composed of recycled numbers from Shostakovich's earlier music (from Opp. 27, 39, 40, 50a, 95, and 97). Hulme, *Shostakovich Catalogue*, 78–79.
37. Yankovsky, as quoted in Morrison, "Shostakovich as Industrial Saboteur," 118; original reference Yankovskii, "Bolt," 11.
38. This is the order of events according to the 1931 libretto: sabotage, confession, arrest, club concert. In the *New Collected Works* edition, however, Goshka's confession and Lyonka Gulba's arrest occur in the middle of the "club concert," that is, between the dances of the Club brigade and those of the Red Army men. This ordering reflects the autograph piano and autograph orchestral scores of the ballet (NCW 63:342–45). Morrison rightly suggests that placing Goshka's confession between parts of the concert may reflect a misreading of sources and that the interruption "decreases, rather than increases, the dramatic effect of the ballet" (Morrison, "Shostakovich as Industrial Saboteur," 135). In any case, the final scene emphasizes *divertissement* over narrative.
39. *Bolt*, libretto, 16.
40. There is some evidence that the Act III concert was, at one point, the only amateur concert planned for the ballet. Some of Shostakovich musical manuscripts as well as Smirnov's drafts of the libretto support this idea. See Shostakovich's piano score draft of *The Bolt*, preserved as *Chernovyye nabroski*, RGALI, f. 2041, op. 2, yed. khr. 41; Smirnov's drafts of the libretto, preserved in TsGALI, f. 337, op. 1, yed. khr. 73, l. 7–10, 23–36. See also NCW 63: 343–44; and Morrison, summarizing Smirnov via Fay, in "Shostakovich as Industrial Saboteur," 132–33 and n. 41.
41. Spence, *A History of the Royal Navy*, 136. See Asada, *From Mahan to Pearl Harbor*, 69–95, for an extensive discussion of "The Washington Conference."
42. "The USSR and Disarmament," 1, 7.
43. Ibid., 1, 8.
44. Quoted in Grant, *Between Depression and Disarmament*, 144.
45. Photographs of the puppets are preserved in the archives of the St. Petersburg State Museum of Theatre and Music. Additional information on the costumes can be found in Bruni's costume sketches for the American and Japanese "fleets" (preserved in the St. Petersburg State Museum of Theatre and Music); from certain costumes reconstructed by E. P. Koptyayeva in 2005 (for Ratmansky's revival of *The Bolt*); from Kuznetsova, "Etikh pa ne smolknet slava" (which describes the French and English "fleets"); and from Morrison, "Shostakovich as Industrial Saboteur," 126 (which suggests that the "fleets" might have appeared as "sandwich boards").
46. Bonnell, *Iconography of Power*, 200–1.
47. Clayton, *Three Republics, One Navy*, 90.

48. Parkinson, *Dreadnought*, xiii–xiv.
49. Japan was the leading naval power in developing the heavy cruiser as a substitute for the battleship, the latter being forbidden under the Five-Power Treaty of 1922. Asada, *From Mahan to Pearl Harbor*, 106.
50. Morrison, "Shostakovich as Industrial Saboteur," 147–48.
51. Dobrovolskaya, *Fyodor Lopukhov*, 199; Souritz, "Constructivism and Dance," 140.
52. Souritz, "Constructivism and Dance," 136, fig. 3.
53. Mussorgsky's "Bydlo" in *Pictures at an Exhibition* was another famous musical portrait of a hauler of goods. In Mussorgsky's rendering, low timbres, oscillating thirds in the bass, and a folk-like modal melody depict the ponderous progress of a cart and its burden. Shostakovich certainly knew Mussorgsky's depiction but made his own carter quite different.
54. Luckyj and O'Leary, *The Politics of Female Alliance*, 131.
55. Hodson, "Nijinsky's Choreographic Method," 11; Garafola, "Russian Ballet in the Age of Petipa," in *The Cambridge Companion to Ballet*, 159. The convention of apotheosis was so much a part of the genre by the end of the nineteenth century that it appeared even in works aimed only at popular entertainment, such as the music hall ballets of Paris. Sarah Gutsche-Miller, *Parisian Music-Hall Ballet*, 102.
56. Garafola, "Russian Ballet in the Age of Petipa," in *The Cambridge Companion to Ballet*, 158.
57. Levitin, *T. G. Bruni*, 34–35, as quoted in Morrison, "Shostakovich as Industrial Saboteur," 122.
58. Ibid.
59. NCW 62v:547, n. 31; Morrison, "Shostakovich as Industrial Saboteur, 145.
60. Minutes of the production meeting of the ballet troupe of the Leningrad State Academic Theatre, as recorded on November 22, 1935, in TsGALI, f. 337, op. 1, d. 107, and quoted in Serdyuk, "Balet Mikhailovskogo teatra—MALEGOTa," 54.

Chapter 4

1. Lopukhov, *Shest'desyat let v balete*, 273.
2. Ibid. See also Manashir Iakubov, NCW 64b: 298, n. 29.
3. In order of quotations: Bogdanov-Berezovskii, "Pervaya repetitsiya"; Kriger, "Novyi baletnyi sezon"; Erlikh, "*Svetlyi ruchei* v Bol'shom teatre"; Potapov, "Vozvrashcheniye k tantsu"; Polyanovskii, "Novyi balet D.D. Shostakovicha"; Yermolayev, "*Svetlyi ruchei* v Bol'shom teatre."
4. Kriger, "Novyi baletnyi sezon"; Potapov, "Vozvrashcheniye k tantsu."
5. For example: Dolgopolov, "Spektakl' sverkayushchei molodosti"; Erlikh, "*Svetlyi ruchei* v Bol'shom teatre"; Sollertinskii, "Tvorcheskiye profili muzykal'nykh teatrov Leningrada."
6. The opera's other two Soviet productions were at the Maly Opera Theatre (Leningrad) and the Stanislavsky-Nemirovich-Danchenko Musical Theatre (Moscow).
7. Vlasova, "Stalin smotrit 'Svetlyi ruchei,'" 161. The premiere on November 30 featured principal dancers from the Maly Opera Theatre in Leningrad.
8. Ibid.
9. Clark, *Moscow, the Fourth Rome*, 5; Clark and Dobrenko, eds., *Soviet Culture and Power*, 139.
10. Clark, "Socialist Realism in Soviet Literature," 176.
11. Shostakovich's contract with the Maly Theatre listed the ballet as "The Two Sylphs." Other working titles for the ballet were "Kuban" and "Whimsies," and eventually "The Limpid Stream." The Maly's internal records, "Priyomo—sdatochinii akt-direktirov teatra 1 noyabrya 1934," TsGALI f. 290, op. 1, d. 33, l. 18.
12. The terms "national" and "character" dance are used interchangeably in relation to Romantic ballet. See Arkin and Smith, "National Dance in the Romantic Ballet," 13.
13. The placement of these dances was somewhat fluid; dances could be rearranged, renamed, added, or even excluded in a given performance. In the Bolshoi production, for example, the whole *divertissement* was shifted to the opening of the ballet, a position in which it offered little narrative motivation, only an occasion for visual display.
14. Recycled from *The Bolt*, where it was No. 23: Dance of the Beggar Women.
15. Recycled from *The Bolt*, where it was No. 11: Dance of the Textile Workers.

16. See NCW 65, Appendix I: No. 3 for the original music for this number. It includes a sixteen-bar strophic tune in chordal setting with the melody in the trumpet. The melodic profile is evocative of singing in its tuneful line, homophonic texture, regular phrasing, range within the octave, and strophic recurrence.
17. Lopukhov, Shiryayev, and Bocharov, *Osnovy kharakternogo tantsa*, trans. Lawson, *Character Dance*, 54. *Osnovy kharakternogo tantsa* was one of the period's standard textbooks on character dancing. Incidentally, one of its authors, Andrei Lopukhov, danced the role of a "Cossack" in *The Limpid Stream*.
18. Morrison, *The People's Artist*, 87. Frolova-Walker discusses *narodnost'*—the evocation of "national classical and folk legacies"—in Soviet opera of the period. Frolova-Walker, "The Soviet Opera Project," 194.
19. "Rukopisi V.I. Ivinga," RGALI, f. 2694, op. 1, yed. khr. 56, l. 54–55.
20. Ibid., 54–56.
21. Garafola, *Rethinking the Sylph*, 3; Arkin and Smith, "National Dance in the Romantic Ballet," 36.
22. Arkin and Smith, "National Dance in the Romantic Ballet," 23.
23. Ibid., 24.
24. Ibid., 34, 36.
25. Ibid., 26.
26. *Pravda*, "Baletnaya fal'sh."
27. Romantic *travesty* dancing was typically done by a ballerina dressed as a man, but this trope was inverted in *The Limpid Stream* where the man dressed as a ballerina. In the Bolshoi production, the *travesty* sylph was excised from the "forest scene," a decision that might have streamlined some of the fussiness of the narrative but surely diluted the Romantic model. Moscow critics credited the *regisseur*, Boris Mordvinov, with this change. Without the *travesty* sylph, however, the Romantic dualism of the scene must have been lost.
28. Bobyshev's sketches and set models, as well as production photographs from 1935, are preserved in the Mikhailovsky Theatre Archives.
29. Lopukhov had toured with the Imperial Theatre in Copenhagen in 1908. In that same year, the Danish ballet was dancing Petipa's *Harlequinade*, Bournonville's *Napoli*, and their own *Coppélia*. We do not know what repertoire Lopukhov saw in Copenhagen, but points of contact certainly existed between the Royal Danish Theatre and the Russian Imperial Theatre in the period in which Lopukhov was a soloist at the latter.
30. Christensen, "Deadly Sylphs and Decent Mermaids," in *Cambridge Companion to Ballet*, 129.
31. Column 1 gives the titles of the dances as they appear in the *New Collected Works* edition of the ballet (NCW 64–65). These titles are not always identical to those in the autograph scores preserved in the Mikhailovsky Theatre Archives, though differences are usually small. The *New Collected Works* edition tends to use titles that slightly elaborate the stage action. (For example, Pyotr and Zina's *Adagio* is titled simply "Adagio" in the autograph piano and orchestral scores, but it is called "Adagio. Pyotr and Zina in Ballerina's Costume" in the *New Collected Works*.)
32. Potapov, "Vozvrashcheniye k tantsu."
33. Libretto for *Sylvia*, as published in *Yezhegodnik imperatorskikh teatrov, Sezon 1901–1902*, 183.
34. *Svetlyi ruchei*, libretto, 40.
35. Wiley, *The Life and Ballets of Lev Ivanov*, 208; Krasovskaya, *Russkii baletnyi teatr*, vol. 1, 612–13. Karsavina danced the title role when *Sylvia* was revived in 1916 as a one-act ballet with new choreography by Samuil Andrianov. Diary entry May 14, 1916, in Maurice Paléologue, *An Ambassador's Memoirs*, vol. 2.
36. Scheijen, *Diaghilev*, 137.
37. Smith, "Borrowings and Original Music," 4; Smith, "*La sylphide* and *Les sylphides*," 262.
38. The development, promotion, and functions of *drambalet* have received extensive treatment in the scholarship of Dobrovolskaya, Ezrahi, Gayevsky, Homans, Katonova, Morrison, Ross, Scholl, Searcy, and Stern—to name a few.
39. Sollertinsky, as quoted in Scholl, "*Sleeping Beauty*," 78.
40. Krasovskaya, *Vaganova*, 165.
41. *The Flames of Paris* (1932) and *Swan Lake* (1933), five months apart, offered one example of an overlap in creative teams. Stern, "Politics in Pointe Shoes," 135.
42. Leningrad's *Yezhenedel'niki* ("Weeklies") documented all performances in the city's theatres and is an invaluable source on the ballet repertoire of the early 1930s. For the numbers of performances that each ballet received, see Degen and Stupnikov, *Leningradskii balet: 1917–1987* (original edition).

43. The theatre and opera director Sergei Radlov was also appointed to the artistic leadership and shared responsibility with Vaganova.
44. Igor Glebov [Boris Asafyev], "K novoi postanovke baleta 'Lebedinoye ozero,'" in *Lebedinoye ozero*, libretto. See also Krasovskaya and Stern for discussions of Vaganova's changes to *Swan Lake*. Krasovskaya details the ballet's narrative progression and the achievements of individual scenes (Krasovskaya, *Vaganova*, 169–81) while Stern illuminates how realism was developed through the "literaturization" of the work (Stern, "Politics in Pointe Shoes," 139).
45. Lopukhov's choreography in the 1940s and Sergeyev's in the 1950s.
46. Ezrahi, *Swans of the Kremlin*, 31.
47. The ballerina Natalya Sheremetyevskaya recalled in her memoirs that the Maly was "considered less prestigious among ballet dancers." She lamented being the only one of her graduating class to end up there while her friends got jobs at the Leningrad State Academic Theatre. Sheremet'yevskaya, *Dlinnyye teni*, 58.
48. Serdyuk, "Balet Mikhailovskogo teatra—MALEGOTa," 21 and 35, n. 92–93.
49. Lopukhov later claimed that he had chosen comedies partly at the suggestion of Sergei Kirov, who had taken an interest in the Maly's fledgling ballet program, and partly because he had been instructed not to duplicate the repertoire of the Leningrad State Academic Theatre. Lopukhov, *Shest'desyat let*, 258–59.
50. *Teatralnaya dekada*, "Balet 'Svetlyi ruchei' v Bolshom teatre SSSR," 10.
51. Lopukhov and Piotrovskii, "Balet 'Svetlyi ruchei,'" in *Svetlyi ruchei*, libretto, 6.
52. Fay, *Shostakovich*, 81–82.
53. Shostakovich, "God posle 'Ledi Makbet'"; and Shostakovich, "Moi tretii balet," *Svetlyi ruchei*, libretto, 15.
54. Shostakovich, "Moi tretii balet," *Svetlyi ruchei*, libretto, 15.
55. Notes in the margins of the musical manuscripts trace some of this interaction. Lopukhov also recalled their collaboration in *Khoreograficheskiye otkrovennosti*.
56. Shostakovich, "Moi tretii balet," *Svetlyi ruchei*, libretto, 15.
57. Druskin, "Baletnaya muzyka Dm. Shostakovicha," in *Svetlyi ruchei*, libretto, 31.
58. Ibid., 33–34.
59. Shostakovich, "Moi tretii balet," *Svetlyi ruchei*, libretto, 15.
60. Ibid.
61. Lopukhov and Piotrovskii, "Balet 'Svetlyi ruchei,'" in *Svetlyi ruchei*, libretto, 6. Emphasis added.
62. Slonimsky used the term "choreographic comedy" in the libretto booklet for *The Limpid Stream*, as did Shostakovich in "God posle 'Ledi Makbet'," *Vechernaya krasnaya gazeta*, January 14, 1935.
63. Lopukhov and Piotrovskii, "Balet 'Svetlyi ruchei,'" and Slonimsky, "Komicheskii zhanr v balete," in *Svetlyi ruchei*, libretto.
64. Slonimskii, "Komicheskii zhanr v balete," in *Svetlyi ruchei*, libretto, 20.
65. Shostakovich, letter of October 30–31, 1935, in Shostakovich, *Pis'ma I.I. Sollertinskomu*, 176; also quoted by Fay, *Shostakovich*, 83.
66. Sollertinskii, "*Svetlyi ruchei* v Gos. Malom opernom teatre," 15.
67. Shostakovich, letter of November 17, 1935, in Shostakovich, *Pis'ma I.I. Sollertinskomu*, 178.
68. "V leningradskom Malom opernom teatre," *Vechernaya Moskva*; "Protokol proizvodstvennogo soveshchaniya baletnoi truppy Teatra opery i baleta im. S. M. Kirova ot 22 noyabrya 1935 goda," TsGALI f. 337, op. 1 d. 107, l. 3–25. See also Fay, *Shostakovich*, 107, n. 2; and Serdyuk, "Balet Mikhailovskogo teatra—MALEGOTa," 53–54.
69. Sollertinskii, "*Svetlyi ruchei*: Baletnaya prem'yera v Bol'shom teatre."
70. Ibid.
71. *Pravda*, "Baletnaya fal'sh."
72. TsGALI (St. Petersburg), f. 290, op. 1, d. 49, l. 5; also reported in NCW 65: 249, n. 43.
73. Ezrahi, *Swans of the Kremlin*, 62.

Chapter 5

1. Garafola, "'Astonish me,'" 71, describing a review by the critic Pierre Michaut.
2. Garafola, "'Astonish me,'" 59–68.

3. Massine, *My Life*, 212.
4. Garafola, "'Astonish me,'" 70.
5. Massine, *My Life*, 212.
6. Bertrand, "La semaine musicale."
7. Garafola, "'Astonish me,'" 71.
8. Pierre Michaut, quoted in Garafola, "'Astonish me,'" 71.
9. *Rouge et noir* (videorecording). I am grateful to Lorca Massine, Theodore Massine, and Tatiana Massine Weinbaum for their kind permission to view this film and to ARS and DACS for copyright permissions from the Matisse estate. I am also indebted to Patricia Sasser for her insightful analysis of the dance, shared from her personal notes. (Although the film's title sequence incorrectly identifies Anton Dvorak as the composer, the music was, in fact, Shostakovich's *First Symphony*, as attested by Massine, Matisse, contemporary reviewers, and many surviving programs.)
10. Van Vechten, "Alicia Markova in 'Rouge et noir,'" New York Public Library. For reviews of the performances at the Met in 1939 and 1948, see, respectively, Martin, "Massine Presents Symphonic Ballet"; and Martin, "Massine Ballet Seen in Revival."
11. Bertrand, "La semaine musicale."
12. "Radio-Concerts: Qu'écouter aujourd'hui?," *L'Humanité*.
13. "Programmes de la journée," *Le Grand écho*.
14. Marcia Siegel, in Siegel and Hodson, "Restaging Works from the Ballets Russes," 349. Siegel suggests that Massine appealed to a sensibility that we no longer value or perhaps even understand, while Balanchine's ballets are more accessible to our modern notions.
15. By contrast, Balanchine considered Shostakovich "not right for dance." Jordan, *Moving Music*, 111.
16. The title of the ballet was originally *Seventh Symphony* but was adjusted to *Leningrad Symphony* after a handful of performances. I use the latter title in the discussion.
17. Abyzova, *Igor Bel'skii*, 149–50. Belsky had a distinguished career in dance. He trained in Leningrad in character dancing and acting and danced with the Kirov Ballet for twenty years. Upon retiring, he became chief choreographer at the Maly Theatre, then the Kirov Theatre, and later the Leningrad Music Hall. He also served as artistic director of the Vaganova Ballet Academy and professor of choreography at the Leningrad Conservatory.
18. Abyzova, *Igor Bel'skii*, 149–50; Dobrovolskaya, "Balet 'Sed'maya simfoniya'"; Lisochkin, "Rozhdeniye baleta."
19. First performance poster, Archives of the Mariinsky Theatre; also accessible via the digital exhibition "Shostakovich v Mariinskom," Mariinskii Teatr, https://www.mariinsky.ru/about/exhibitions/shostakovich111/leningradskaya/. *Choreographic Miniatures* had premiered a few years earlier, and a film of it had been released under the same title in 1958.
20. Abyzova, *Igor Bel'skii*, 150.
21. Lopukhov, *Shest'desyat let*, 342.
22. For a list of dances and composers in *Choreographic Miniatures*, see Ross, *Like a Bomb*, appendix, 447.
23. Fay, *Shostakovich: A Life*, 131.
24. Dobrovolskaya, "Balet 'Sed'maya simfoniya.'"
25. Ibid.
26. Ibid.; see also L. Entilis, "'Moguchii golos muz...'"
27. Dobrovolskaya, "Balet 'Sed'maya simfoniya.'"
28. Ibid.
29. In the post-war period, Gordon began to design theatrical productions in Leningrad and extended his collaborations to ballet in the 1960s. He created *Leningrad Symphony* and *The Little Humpbacked Horse* with Belsky. *Teatral'naya Leningrad* records the theatre and ballet productions for which Gordan designed sets and costumes in the late 1950s and 1960s.
30. Dobrovolskaya, "Balet 'Sed'maya simfoniya.'"
31. Photograph reproduced in the collection *Mariinskii Teatr*, 1961 (yanv–mai), 36.
32. Dobrovolskaya, "Balet 'Sed'maya simfoniya.'"
33. Photographs in the collection *Mariinskii Teatr*, 1961, (yanv–mai) and (iyun'–dek); see also the digital exhibition "Shostakovich v Mariinskom," *Mariinskii Teatr*; and Abyzova, *Igor Bel'skii*, 154.
34. Dobrovolskaya, "Balet 'Sed'maya simfoniya.'"
35. Krasovskaya, *Stat'i o balete*, 309.

36. Kremshevskaya, "Novatorskii balet."
37. Dobrovolskaya, "Balet 'Sed'maya simfoniya.'"
38. Zemlemerov, "Na muzyku Leningradskoi simfonii."
39. "Program Listed by Kirov Ballet" (1961); Abyzova, *Igor Bel'skii*, 164.
40. Abyzova, *Igor Bel'skii*, 164.
41. Barnes, "Dance: The Kirov Ballet" (1969).
42. The ballet was choreographed by Konstantin Boyarsky with designs by Valery Dorrer. The film music was drawn from Shostakovich's scores for *Maxim Trilogy, Song of the Great Rivers*, and *The Gadfly*. Hulme, *Shostakovich Catalogue*, 78–79.
43. Music from Shostakovich's Eleventh and Twelfth Symphonies was also used in a ballet based on Maksim Gorky's novel *Mother*. The ballet was created by Natalya Ryzhenko and Viktor Smirnov-Golovanov and premiered in Odessa. Hulme, *Shostakovich Catalogue*, 408.
44. Ross, *Like a Bomb*, 211, 214. Ross records that Yakobson saw some of Chagall's paintings thanks to his friendship with a curator at The Hermitage.
45. Grigorovich and Davlekamova, *The Authorized Bolshoi Ballet Book of* The Golden Age, 14; and Glikman, *Story of a Friendship*, 317–18, n. 25. Over the years, Grigorovich proposed several different ballet projects to Shostakovich's music. As early as 1962, for example, he told an interviewer that he was planning a ballet on Alexei Arbuzov's play *The Irkutsk Story* with music by Shostakovich. He also hoped to collaborate with Shostakovich on a ballet based on Nikolai Bulgakov's novel *The Master and Margarita*. Neither collaboration with Shostakovich came to fruition, and those ballets were eventually produced to music of other composers. See "1962–63, V teatrakh i kontsertnykh zalakh: Leningrad—Snova interesnyye zamysly," *Sovetskaya kul'tura* (September 4, 1962); Morrison, citing a personal interview with Grigorovich, in *Bolshoi Confidential*, 391 and 477, n. 139; and Anderson, "Baryshnikov Is Invited."
46. Grigorovich and Davlekamova, *The Authorized Bolshoi Ballet Book of* The Golden Age, 14.
47. Glikman was Shostakovich's close friend and a prominent theatre historian and dramaturg in Leningrad. His book *Story of a Friendship* (1993) charted his friendship with Shostakovich through more than three hundred of the composer's letters. Virsaladze had extensive experience in scene and costume design for opera and ballet; he worked exclusively with Grigorovich for over thirty years. The team tasked with reconstructing Shostakovich's music included Glikman, the composer Veniamin Basner, the violinist Sergei Sapozhnikov, and the conductors Yuri Simonov and Yuri Yurovsky. Grigorovich and Davlekamova, *The Authorized Bolshoi Ballet Book of* The Golden Age, 14–16; Hulme, *Shostakovich Catalogue*, 56.
48. Respectively: Askold Makarov, quoted in Inozemtseva, "Zolotoi vek" (2006); Crisp, "The Golden Age, London" (2006); Hersin, "'L'age d'or' vraiment?" (1986); Robinson, "A Shostakovich Ballet Returns from Limbo" (1983).
49. The practice is discussed at length in Smith, "Borrowings and Original Music."
50. Smith, "Borrowings and Original Music," 9.
51. Inozemtseva, "Zolotoi vek," 11.
52. Macauley, "Bolshoi Balletomania," 31.
53. This was the number for which Yakobson revived his "sports" choreography in 1965. See Chapter 2, n. 60.
54. The dance is "No. 17: A Rare Case of Mass Hysteria" in the *New Collected Works*, but it was originally titled "Diva's Despair" in Shostakovich's autograph manuscript. This was an instance in Act I where music written for one purpose (i.e., Diva) was recycled to another (i.e., a mass scene) in the production of 1930.
55. For a list of reviews of and reactions to Ratmansky's *The Bright Stream*, see Casey, "The Gesture of Memorial," 26, n. 4. For a description of the New York performance from a personal perspective, see Harss, *The Boy from Kyiv*, 3–6.
56. Harss, *The Boy from Kyiv*, 5.
57. The Bolshoi Theatre does not currently list Ratmansky as the choreographer on its website. The new production of *The Bright Stream* at the Mikhailovsky Theatre was choreographed by Aleksandr Omar, who trained at the Vaganova Ballet Academy and is now a soloist and choreographer at the Mikhailovsky Theatre.
58. Harss, *The Boy from Kyiv*, 12.
59. Casey, "The Gesture of Memorial," 25.
60. Ratmansky, interview with *Kul'tura* (3 April 2003), preserved at the Bolshoi Theatre Museum.
61. Searcy, "Alexei Ratmansky," 490.
62. Ibid., 490–91.

63. Sulcas, "In Nod to History."
64. Ratmansky, quoted in Harss, *The Boy from Kyiv*, 171.
65. Harss, *The Boy from Kyiv*, 413–14.
66. Scherr, *Ratmansky*, 653.

Appendix B

1. A fugue is a particular form of symphonic musical work, in which the main theme is carried through by several voices that gradually join and overlap with each other.

Select Bibliography

"1962–63, V teatrakh i kontsertnykh zalakh: Leningrad—Snova interesnyye zamysly." *Sovetskaya kul'tura*, no. 104 (September 4, 1962): 3.
Abyzova, Larisa. *Igor Bel'skii: simfoniya zhizn'*. St. Petersburg: Akademiya russkogo baleta im. A.Y. Vaganovoi, 2015.
Agranenko, Zakhar, dir. *Leningradskaya simfoniya*. 1957. Moscow: Krupnyi plan, 2002. Videocassette.
Akopyan, Levon. *Dmitrii Shostakovich: Opyt fenomenologii tvorchestva*. St. Petersburg: RAN, Ministerstvo kul'tury Rossiiskoi federatsii, Gos. in-t iskusstvoznaniya, 2004. Revised as *Fenomen Dmitriya Shostakovicha*. St. Petersburg: Russkaya khristianskaya gumanitarnaya akademiya, 2018.
Akopyan, Levon. *Music of the Soviet Era: 1917–1991*. New York: Routledge, 2017.
Anderson, Jack. "Baryshnikov Is Invited by Bolshoi to Dance Again in Soviet Union." *The New York Times*, January 20, 1987.
Aquilina, Stefan, ed. *Amateur and Proletarian Theatre in Post-Revolutionary Russia: Primary Sources*. London: Bloomsbury Methuen Drama, 2021.
Arkin, Lisa C., and Marian Smith. "National Dance in the Romantic Ballet." In *Rethinking the Sylph: New Perspectives on Romantic Ballet*, edited by Lynn Garafola, 11–68. Hanover, NH: University Press of New England, 1997.
Armashevskaya, Klavdiya. *Baletmeister Vainonen*. Moscow: Iskusstvo, 1971.
Asada, Sadao. *From Mahan to Pearl Harbor: The Imperial Japanese Navy and the United States*. Annapolis, MD: Naval Institute Press, 2012.
Asaf'yev, Boris. *Akademik B. V. Asaf'yev: Izbrannyye trudy*. Vol. 2. Moscow: Izdatelstvo, 1954.
Asaf'yev, Boris. *O balete: Stat'i, retsenzii, vospominaniya*. Leningrad: Muzyka, 1974.
Baer, Nancy Van Norman, and John E. Bowlt, eds. *Theatre in Revolution: Russian Avant-Garde Stage Design*. New York: Thames & Hudson, 1991.
Barnes, Clive. "Dance: The Kirov Ballet." *The New York Times*, June 8, 1969.
Barsova, Inna. "'Svetlyi ruchei' Dmitriya Shostakovicha: k istorii sozdaniya." In *Kontury stoletiya: iz istorii russkoi muzyki XX veka*, 122–36. St. Petersburg: Kompozitor, 2007.
Bel'skii, I. D. "1738–1998: Khronika 260 let—Vazhneishiye sobytiya v istorii Akademii Russkogo Baleta imeni A.Y. Vaganovoi." In *Vestnik Akademii Russkogo baleta im. A.Y. Vaganovoi*, no. 7 (1999): 64–69.
Bertrand, Denyse. "La semaine musicale." *Le Menestral*, June 16, 1939.
Beumer, Birgit. "Post-Revolutionary Russian Theatre." In *The Routledge Companion to Russian Literature*, edited by Neil Cornwell, 209–22. London: Routledge, 2001.
Bobrik, Oleysa. "Osushchestvlennyye i neosushchestvlennyye prem'yery sochinenii D. D. Shostakovicha v Bolshom teatre: konets 1920-kh–seredina 1940-kh godov." *Sovremennyye problemy muzykoznaniya*, no. 4 (2018): 101–65.
Bobykina, Irina, ed. *Dmitrii Shostakovich v pis'makh i dokumentakh*. Moscow: RIF Antikva, 2000.
Bogdanova, Alla. *Opery i balety Shostakovicha*. Moscow: Sovetskii kompozitor, 1979.
Bogdanov-Berezovskii, Valerian. "Pervaya repetitsiya." *Vechernaya krasnaya gazeta*, June 8, 1935.
Bogdanov-Berezovskii, Valerian. *Vstrechi*. Moscow: Iskusstvo, 1967.
Bolt. Balet v 3 deistviyakh. Libretto by Viktor Smirnov, with article by Ivan Sollertinskii, "Bolt i problema sovetskogo baleta." Leningrad: Gos. izdatel'stvo khudozhestvennoi literatury, 1931.

"'Bolt' i BOLTlivyye formalisty." *Bytovaya gazeta*, no. 20 (April 15, 1931): 2.
Bonnell, Victoria. *Iconography of Power: Soviet Political Posters under Lenin and Stalin*. Berkeley: University of California, 1997.
Braginskii, Dmitri. "Shostakovich's 'Football' Ballet." In *Shostakovich i futbol: territoriya svobody*. Moscow: DSCH, 2018. Translated by Alison Yermolova as *Shostakovich and Football: Escape to Freedom*. Moscow: DSCH, 2019.
Broderson, Yuri. "Legalizatsiya prisposoblenchestva." *Rabochii i teatr*, nos. 60–61 (November 6, 1930): 8–9.
Brodersen, Yuri. "Neudavsheyesya perevooruzheniye baleta ('Bolt' v Gosteatre opery i baleta)." *Krasnaya gazeta* (April 11, 1931): 4.
Brodersen, Yuri. "Sovetskaya tantseval'naya komediya." *Sovetskii teatr*, 1935.
Brodersen, Yuri. "*Svetlyi ruchei*." *Vechernaya Moskva*, June 15, 1935.
Bruni, Tatiana. "O balete s neprekhodyashchei lyubov'yu." *Sovetskii balet* 5, no. 59 (September–October 1991): 33–37.
Bulganov, "O balete *Svetlyi ruchei*." *Svarzovets*, December 5, 1935.
Bullock, Philip Ross. "Staging Stalinism: The Search for Soviet Opera in the 1930s." *Cambridge Opera Journal* 18, no. 1 (March 2006): 83–108.
Carr, Maureen. *After the Rite: Stravinsky's Path to Neoclassicism (1914–25)*. New York: Oxford University Press, 2014.
Carr, Maureen, ed. *Stravinsky's* Pulcinella: *A Facsimile of Sources and Sketches*. Middleton, WI: A-R Editions, 2010.
Carr, Maureen, Gretchen Horlacher, Severine Neff, and John Reef, eds. The Rite of Spring *at 100: Musical Meaning and Interpretation*. Bloomington: Indiana University Press, 2017.
Caute, David. *The Dancer Defects: The Struggle for Cultural Supremacy during the Cold War*. Oxford: Oxford University Press, 2003.
Casey, Carrie Gaiser. "The Gesture of Memorial: Ratmansky, Shostakovich, and the *Chamber Symphony*." *Dance Chronicle* 41, no. 1 (2018): 5–28.
Chepalov, Alexander. "Nikolai Foregger and the Dance of Revolution." *Experiment: A Journal of Russian Culture* 2, no. 1 (January 1996): 359–80.
Chernova, Natalia. "Kasian Goleizovsky and Eccentric Dance." *Experiment: A Journal of Russian Culture* 2, no. 1 (January 1996): 381–410.
Chiriac, Alexandra. "Fedor Lopukhov and *The Bolt*." *Studies in Theatre Performance* 36, no. 3 (2016): 242–56.
Clark, Katerina. "The Left *Avant-Garde* Theatre in the 1920s." In *New Directions in Soviet Literature: Selected Papers from the Fourth World Congress for Soviet and East European Studies, Harrogate, 1990*, edited by Sheelagh Duffin Graham, 18–35. New York: St. Martin's Press, 1992.
Clark, Katerina. *Moscow, The Fourth Rome: Stalinism, Cosmopolitanism, and the Evolution of Soviet Culture, 1931–1941*. Cambridge, MA: Harvard University Press, 2011.
Clark, Katerina. *Petersburg: Crucible of Cultural Revolution*. Cambridge, MA: Harvard University Press, 1995.
Clark, Katerina. "Socialist Realism in Soviet Literature." In *The Routledge Companion to Russian Literature*, edited by Neil Cornwell, 174–83. London: Routledge, 2001.
Clark, Katerina. *The Soviet Novel: History as Ritual*. 3rd ed. Bloomington: Indiana University Press, 2000.
Clark, Katerina, and Evgeny Dobrenko, eds. *Soviet Culture and Power: A History in Documents, 1917–1953*. New Haven, CT: Yale University Press, 2007.
Clayton, Anthony. *Three Republics, One Navy: A Naval History of France, 1870–1999*. Solihull, West Midlands: Helion, 2014.
Cogniat, Raymond. "Matisse et le Théatre." *Le point: revue artistique et littéraire* 21 (July 1939): 44–46.
Crisp, Clement. "The Golden Age, London." *Financial Times* (France), July 31, 2006.

Croft, Clare. *Dancers as Diplomats: American Choreography in Cultural Exchange.* New York: Oxford University Press, 2015.
Cross, Jonathan. *Igor Stravinsky.* London: Reaktion Books, 2015.
Cross, Jonathan, ed. *The Cambridge Companion to Stravinsky.* Cambridge: Cambridge University Press, 2003.
Curtis, J. A. E. "Down with the Foxtrot: Concepts of Satire in the Soviet Theatre of the 1920s." In *Russian Theatre in the Age of Modernism*, edited by Robert Russell and Andrew Barratt, 219-35. New York: Macmillan, 1990.
Danilov, A. "V Bol'shom teatre *Svetlyi ruchei*." *Za sovetskii podshipnik*, December 11, 1935.
Degen, A., and I. Stupnikov. *Leningradskii balet: 1917-1987: slovar'-spravochnik: solistki, solisty, baletmeistery, pedagogi, dirizhery.* Leningrad: Sovetskii kompozitor, 1988.
Digonskaya, Olga, and Galina Kopytova. *Dmitrii Shostakovich. Notograficheskii spravochnik, I: Ot rannikh sochinenii do Simfonii no. 4 op. 43 (1914-1936).* St. Petersburg: Kompozitor, 2016.
Digonskaya, Olga, and Lyudmila Kovnatskaya, eds. *Dmitrii Shostakovich—issledovaniya i materialy. Vypusk 3.* Moscow: DSCH, 2011.
Dobrovolskaya, Galina. "Balet 'Sed'maya simfoniya.'" *Vechernii Leningrad*, April 15, 1961.
Dobrovolskaya, Galina. *Baletmeister Leonid Yakobson.* Leningrad: Iskusstvo, 1968.
Dobrovolskaya, Galina. *Fyodor Lopukhov.* Leningrad: Iskusstvo, 1976.
Dobrovolskaya, Galina. *Tanets, pantomima, balet.* Leningrad: Iskusstvo, 1975.
Dolgopolov, Mikhail. "Spektakl' sverkayushchei molodosti: Balet *Svetlyi ruchei* v Bol'shom teatre." *Komsomol'skaya Pravda*, December 2, 1935.
Druskin, Mikhail. *Ocherki po istorii tantseval'noi muzyki.* Leningrad: Leningradskaya filarmoniya, 1936.
Edmunds, Neil. *The Soviet Proletarian Music Movement.* New York: Peter Lang, 2000.
Edmunds, Neil, ed. *Soviet Music and Society under Lenin and Stalin: The Baton and Sickle.* New York: Routledge, 2009.
Entilis, L. "'Moguchii golos muz . . .': Balet 'Sedmaya simfoniya' na stsenye Teatra imeni S. M. Kirova." *Leningradskaya Pravda*, April 25, 1961.
Erlikh, A. "*Svetlyi ruchei* v Bol'shom teatre." *Pravda*, December 2, 1935.
Ezrahi, Christina. *Swans of the Kremlin: Ballet and Power in Soviet Russia.* Pittsburgh, PA: University of Pittsburgh Press, 2012.
Fairclough, Pauline. *Classics for the Masses: Shaping Soviet Musical Identity under Lenin and Stalin.* New Haven, CT: Yale University Press, 2016.
Fairclough, Pauline. "From Enlightened to Sublime: Musical Life under Stalin, 1930-1948." In *Russian Music since 1917: Reappraisal and Rediscovery*, edited by Marina Frolova-Walker and Patrick Zuk, 148-63. Oxford: Oxford University Press, 2017.
Fairclough, Pauline. *Dmitry Shostakovich.* London: Reaktion, 2019.
Fairclough, Pauline. *A Soviet Credo: Shostakovich's Fourth Symphony.* Aldershot, UK: Ashgate, 2006.
Fairclough, Pauline, ed. *Shostakovich Studies 2.* Cambridge: Cambridge University Press, 2010.
Fairclough, Pauline, and David Fanning, eds. *The Cambridge Companion to Shostakovich.* Cambridge: Cambridge University Press, 2008.
Fanning, David. *The Breath of the Symphonist: Shostakovich's Tenth.* London: Royal Musical Association, 1988.
Fanning, David, ed. *Shostakovich Studies.* Cambridge: Cambridge University Press, 1995.
Fay, Laurel E. *Shostakovich: A Life.* Oxford: Oxford University Press, 2000.
Fay, Laurel E., ed. *Shostakovich and His World.* Princeton, NJ: Princeton University Press, 2004.
Fitzpatrick, Sheila. *The Cultural Front: Power and Culture in Revolutionary Russia.* Ithaca, NY: Cornell University Press, 2018.
Fortunova, Anna. "Balety D. D. Shostakovicha kak yavleniye otechestvennoi kul'tury 1920-kh—pervoi poloviny 1930-kh godov." PhD dissertation, Nizhegorodskaya Gosudarstvennaya konservatoriya imeni M.I. Glinki, 2007. Personal copy provided by the author.

Frolova-Walker, Marina, and Jonathan Walker. *Music and Soviet Power (1917–32)*. Woodbridge, UK: Boydell, 2012.
Frolova-Walker, Marina. "The Soviet Opera Project: Ivan Dzerzhinsky vs. *Ivan Susanin*." *Cambridge Opera Journal* 18, no. 2 (2006): 181–216.
Frolova-Walker, Marina, and Patrick Zuk, eds. *Russian Music since 1917: Reappraisal and Rediscovery*. Oxford: Oxford University Press, 2017.
Futbolist. Libretto, with article by Viktor Iving, "Futbolist." Moscow: Teakinopechat', 1930.
Gayevsky, Vadim. *Divertisment: Sud'by klassicheskogo baleta*. Moscow: Iskusstvo, 1981.
Gayevsky, Vadim. *Dom Petipa*. Moscow: Artist. Rezhisser. Teatr, 2000.
Gayevsky, Vadim, and Pavel Gershenzon. *Razgovory o russkom balete: kommentarii k noveishei istorii*. Moscow: Novoye izdatel'stvo, 2010.
Garafola, Lynn. "An Amazon of the Avant-Garde: Bronislava Nijinska in Revolutionary Russia." *Dance Research* 29, no. 2 (Winter 2011): 109–166.
Garafola, Lynn. "'Astonish me!': Diaghilev, Massine and the Experimentalist Tradition." In *The Ballets Russes in Australia and Beyond*, edited by Mark Carroll, 52–75. Kent Town: Wakefield Press, 2011.
Garafola, Lynn. "Dance, Film, and the Ballets Russes." *Dance Research* 16, no. 1 (Summer 1998): 3–25.
Garafola, Lynn. *Diaghilev's Ballets Russes*. New York: Oxford University Press, 1989.
Garafola, Lynn. "Diaghilev's Musical Legacy." In *Legacies of Twentieth-Century Dance*, 45–53. Hanover, NH: Wesleyan University Press, 2005.
Garafola, Lynn, "The Travesty Dancer in Nineteenth-Century Ballet." *Dance Research Journal* 17, no. 2, and 18, no. 1 (Autumn 1985/Spring 1986): 35–40.
Garafola, Lynn, ed. *Rethinking the Sylph: New Perspectives on Romantic Ballet*. Hanover, NH: University Press of New England, 1997.
Garafola, Lynn, ed. *Russian Movement Culture of the 1920s and 1930s: A Symposium Organized by Lynn Garafola and Catherine Theimer Nepomnyashchy, February 12–14, 2015*. New York: Columbia University, Harriman Institute, 2015. https://academiccommons.columbia.edu/doi/10.7916/d8-xanj-5740.
Gauk, Aleksandr. *Aleksandr Vasil'yevich Gauk: memuary, izbrannyye stat'i, vospominaniya sovremennikov*. Moscow: Sovetskii kompozitor, 1975.
George-Graves, Nadine, ed. *The Oxford Handbook of Dance and Theatre*. New York: Oxford University Press, 2015.
Glikman, Isaak. *Pis'ma k drugu: Dmitrii Shostakovich Isaaku Glikmanu*. Moscow: DSCH, 1993. Translated by Anthony Philips as *Story of a Friendship: The Letters of Dmitry Shostakovich to Isaak Glikman, 1941–1975*. Ithaca, NY: Cornell University Press, 2001.
Gonçalves, Stéphanie. "Ballet as a Tool for Cultural Diplomacy in the Cold War: Soviet Ballets in Paris and London, 1954–1968." In *Music, Art and Diplomacy: East-West Cultural Interactions and the Cold War*, edited by Simo Mikkonen and Pekka Suutari, 139–53. Farnham, UK: Ashgate 2016.
Gorchakov, N. "*Svetlyi ruchei* v Bol'shom teatre." *Rabochaya Moskva*, December 2, 1935.
Gorsuch, Anne E. "The Dance Class or the Working Class: The Soviet Modern Girl." In *The Modern Girl Around the World: Consumption, Modernity, and Globalization*, edited by Alys Eve Weinbaum, Lynn M. Thomas, Priti Ramamurthy, Uta G. Poiger, Madeleine Yue Dong, and Tani E. Barlow, 174–93. Durham, NC: Duke University Press, 2008.
Gorsuch, Anne E. "Flappers and Foxtrotters: Soviet Youth in the 'Roaring Twenties.'" *The Carl Beck Papers in Russian & East European Studies*, no. 1101 (March 1994): 1–33.
Grant, Jonathan A. *Between Depression and Disarmament: The International Armaments Business, 1919–1939*. Cambridge: Cambridge University Press, 2018.
Gres, S. "Simfonicheskiye novinki." *Rabochii i teatr*, no. 17 (1930): 9.
Grigorovich, Yuri, and Sania Davlekamova. *The Authorized Bolshoi Ballet Book of* The Golden Age. Translated by Tim Coey. Neptune City, NJ: T.F.H. Publications, 1989.

Gutsche-Miller, Sarah. *Parisian Music-Hall Ballet, 1871–1913*. Rochester, NY: University of Rochester Press, 2015.
Gvozdev, Aleksei. "O reforme baleta." *Zhizn' iskusstva*, no. 1 (3 January 1928): 5–6.
Haas, David. *Leningrad's Modernists: Studies in Composition and Musical Thought, 1917–1932*. New York: Peter Lang, 1998.
Haas, David, ed. *Symphonic Etudes: Portraits of Russian Operas and Ballets*. By Boris Asafyev. Lanham, MD: Scarecrow Press, 2008.
Harris, Andrea. *Making Ballet American: Modernism Before and Beyond Balanchine (Oxford Studies in Dance Theory)*. New York: Oxford University Press, 2018.
Harss, Marina. *The Boy from Kyiv: Alexei Ratmansky's Life in Ballet*. New York: Farrar, Straus and Giroux, 2023.
Harss, Marina. "Running Like Shadows." *The Nation* 297, no. 5–6 (August 5, 2013): 33–39.
Hersin, André Philippe. "'L'age d'or' vraiment?" *Les saisons de la danse* (Paris), no. 186 (October 1986): 8.
Hodson, Millicent. "Nijinksy's Choreographic Method: Visual Sources from Roerich for 'Le Sacre du printemps.'" *Dance Research Journal* 18, no. 2 (Winter 1986–87): 7–15.
Homans, Jennifer. *Apollo's Angels: A History of Ballet*. New York: Random House, 2010.
Homans, Jennifer. "Back in the USSR." *New Republic* 242, no. 4910 (September 28, 2011): 22–24.
Holzman, Franklyn D. "The Ruble Exchange Rate and Soviet Foreign Trade Pricing Policies, 1929–1961." *The American Economic Review* 58, no. 4 (September 1968): 803–25.
Hulme, Derek C. *Dmitri Shostakovich Catalogue: The First Hundred Years and Beyond*. 4th ed. Plymouth, UK: Scarecrow, 2010.
Ilichova, Marina. "Shostakovich's Ballets." In *The Cambridge Companion to Shostakovich*, edited by Pauline Fairclough and David Fanning, 198–212. Cambridge: Cambridge University Press, 2008.
Inozemtseva, Galina. "'Zolotoi vek' s pereryvom na dvadtsat' let." *Balet* 3, no. 139 (May–June 2006): 10–11.
Iving, Viktor. "Tanets v 'Krivom zerkale.'" *Program of State Academic Theatres* [subsequently renamed *Sovremennyi teatr*, 1927–29; *Rabochii i iskusstvo*, 1929–30; *Sovetskoye iskusstvo*, 1931–41, etc.], no. 20 (1927): 6.
Jordan, Stephanie. "Acts of Transformation: Strategies for Choreographic Intervention in Mark Morris's Settings of Existing Music." In *Music-Dance: Sound and Motion in Contemporary Discourse*, edited by Patrizia Veroli and Gianfranco Vinay, 76–90. Abingdon, UK: Routledge, 2018.
Jordan, Stephanie. *Moving Music: Dialogues with Music in Twentieth-Century Ballet*. London: Dance Books, 2000.
Kant, Marion, ed. *The Cambridge Companion to Ballet*. Cambridge: Cambridge University Press, 2007.
Katonova, Svetlana. *Muzyka sovetskogo baleta: ocherki istorii i teorii*. 2nd ed. Leningrad: Sovetskii kompozitor, 1990.
Katzenellenbaum, S. S. *Russian Currency and Banking, 1914–1924*. London: King & Son, 1925.
Kendall, Elizabeth. *Balanchine and the Lost Muse: Revolution and the Making of a Choreographer*. New York: Oxford University Press, 2015.
Kennedy, Laura. "'I begin writing, and then have second thoughts': Shostakovich and the Sketches for the Eighth Symphony." *Fontes Artis Musicae* 64, no. 1 (January–March 2017): 1–20. Published in Russian as "'Nachnyosh' pisat', a potom peredumayesh': Shostakovich i eskizy Vos'moi simfonii." Translated by Levon Hakopian. *Opera musicologica* (St. Petersburg) 30, no. 4 (2016): 18–45.
Kennedy, Laura. "Sketching the Symphonies: A Brief Report on Shostakovich's Manuscripts in Moscow." *Notes* 72, no. 2 (December 2016): 241–59.

Kennedy, Laura, and Patricia Sasser. "'Long-braided Lolitas,' or Teaching Undergraduate Music History in a Study Abroad Context." *Journal of Music History Pedagogy* 7, no. 2 (2017): 19–31.

Khentova, Sofia. *V mire Shostakovicha: zapis' besed s D.D. Shostakovichem.* Moscow: Kompozitor, 1996.

Khentova, Sofia. *Shostakovich: Zhizn' i tvorchestvo.* Leningrad: Sovetskii Kompozitor, 1985.

Kiseleva, V. "Iz pisem 1930-kh godov." *Sovetskaya muzyka* 51, no. 9 (1987): 85–91.

Kisselgoff, Anna. "Ballet: Bolshoi in Grigorovich's 'Golden Age.'" *The New York Times*, July 2, 1987.

Klapper, Melissa R. *Ballet Class: An American History.* New York: Oxford University Press, 2020.

Kovnatskaya, Lyudmila. "'Khochu c toboi koye o chyom pokalyakat' na bumage': neizvestnyye pis'ma Shostakovicha k Bogdanoi-Berezovskomu (1920-e rody)." In *Dmitrii Shostakovich—issledovaniya i materialy. Vypusk 3*, edited by Olga Digonskaya and Lyudmila Kovnatskaya, 46–123. Moscow: DSCH, 2011.

Kovnatskaya, Lyudmila, comp. *Shostakovich v Leningradskoi konservatorii, 1919–1930, v tryokh tomakh. T. 3, Gorod-teatr. GATOB. MALEGOT. TRAM, GOSTIM, Muzkomediya. Kinematograf. Kontserty. Bol'shoi zal.* St. Petersburg: Kompozitor, 2013.

Kovnatskaya, Lyudmila, ed. *Letopis' zhizni i tvorchestva Shostakovicha v 5 tomakh. T. 1, 1903–1930.* Moscow: DSCH, 2016.

Kovnatskaya, Lyudmila, ed. *Shostakovich: mezhdu mgnoveniyem i vechnost'yu.* St. Petersburg: Kompozitor, 2000.

Krasovskaya, Vera. "Balet simfoniya." *Sovetskaya kul'tura* 92, no. 1272 (5 August 1961): 3.

Krasovskaya, Vera. *Russkii baletnyi teatr nachala XX veka*, vol. 1, *Khoreografy*. Leningrad: Iskusstvo, 1971.

Krasovskaya, Vera. *Stat'i o balete.* Leningrad: Iskusstvo, 1967.

Krasovskaya, Vera. *Vaganova: A Dance Journey from Petersburg to Leningrad.* Translated by Vera M. Siegel. Gainesville: University of Florida Press, 2005.

Krasovskaya, Vera, ed. *Russkii baletnyi teatr vtoroi poloviny XIX veka.* Leningrad: Iskusstvo, 1963.

Krasovskaya, Vera, ed. *Sovetskii baletnyi teatr: 1917–1967.* Moscow: Iskusstvo, 1976.

Kremshevskaya, Galina. "Novatorskii balet," *Smena*, April 16, 1961.

Kriger, Viktorina. "Novyi baletnyi sezon." *Pravda* (Moscow), September 7, 1935.

Kuhn, Judith. *Shostakovich in Dialogue: Form, Imagery, and Ideas in String Quartets 1–7.* Farnham, UK: Ashgate, 2010.

Kuznetsova, Tat'yana. "Etikh pa ne smolknet slava." *Kommersant-Vlast*, February 21, 2005, https://www.kommersant.ru/doc/548973.

Leach, Robert. *Revolutionary Theatre.* London: Routledge, 1994.

Leach, Robert. *Vsevolod Meyerhold.* Cambridge: Cambridge University Press, 1989.

Leach, Robert, and Victor Borovsky, eds. *A History of Russian Theatre.* Cambridge: Cambridge University Press, 2000.

Lebedinoye ozero. Libretto, with article by Igor Glebov [Boris Asafyev], "K novoi postanovke baleta *Lebedinoye ozero*." Leningrad: Leningradskii Gosud. Teatr opery i baleta, 1933.

"Leningrad: K postanovke 'Dinamiady.'" *Zhizn' iskusstva*, no. 49 (December 8, 1929): 15.

Levitin, G[rigorii] M[ikhailovich]. *Tat'yana Georgiyevna Bruni.* Leningrad: Khudozhnik RSFSR, 1986.

Lisochkin, I. "Rozhdeniye baleta," *Smena* (March 14, 1961).

Lobenthal, Joel. *Alla Osipenko: Beauty and Resistance in Soviet Ballet.* New York: Oxford University Press, 2015.

Lopukhov, Andrei, Aleksandr Shiryayev, and Aleksandr Bocharov. *Osnovy kharakternogo tantsa.* Edited by Yuri Slonimskii. Leningrad: Iskusstvo, 1939. Translated by Joan Lawson as *Character Dance.* London: Dance Books, 1986.

Lopukhov, Fyodor. *Khoreograficheskiye otkrovennosti.* Moscow: Iskusstvo, 1972.

Lopukhov, Fyodor. *Puti baletmeistera.* Berlin: Petropolis, 1925.

SELECT BIBLIOGRAPHY   183

Lopukhov, Fyodor. *Shest'desyat let v balete: vospominaniya i zapiski baletmeistera*. Moscow: Iskusstvo, 1966.
Lopukhov, Fyodor. *Writings on Ballet and Music*. Edited by Stephanie Jordan. Translated by Dorinda Offord. Madison: University of Wisconsin Press, 2002.
Lopukhov, Fyodr, and Pyotr Gusev, nar. *Iskusstvo russkogo baleta—peredacha sed'maya. Rozhdeniye sovetskogo baleta*. Performed by Artists of the Kirov Ballet. Leningradskoye televideniye, 1965.
Luckyj, Christina, and Niamh J. O'Leary, eds. *The Politics of Female Alliance in Early Modern England*. Lincoln: University of Nebraska Press, 2017.
Lunarcharskii, Anatolii. "'Razvlekatel' pozolochennoi tolpy.'" 1927. Reprinted in *Sergei Diaghilev i russkoye iskusstvo*, vol. 2, 215–17. Moscow: Izobrazitel'noye iskusstvo, 1982.
Macauley, Alastair. "Bolshoi Balletomania." *Dancing Times* (October 1986): 28–31.
Mally, Lynn. *Revolutionary Acts: Amateur Theatre and the Soviet State, 1917–1938*. Ithaca, NY: Cornell University Press, 2000.
Mariinskii Teatr, 1961 (yanv–mai), k. Otdel'nyye stat'i (Vyrezki) (427), *m. khr*. Otdel spravochnoi i nauchno-bibliograficheskoi raboty, *sh*. Sankt-Peterburg, 1945–2019. Mariinskii teatr. 8 papka. 1961. http://lib.sptl.spb.ru/ru/nodes/7253-mariinskiy-teatr-1961-yanv-may.
Mariinskii Teatr, 1961 (iyun'–dek), k. Otdel'nyye stat'i (Vyrezki) (427), *m. khr*. Otdel spravochnoi i nauchno-bibliograficheskoi raboty, *sh*. Sankt-Peterburg, 1945–2019. Mariinskii teatr. 9 papka. 1961. http://lib.sptl.spb.ru/ru/nodes/7255-mariinskiy-teatr-1961-iyun-dek.
Mariinskii Teatr. "Shostakovich v Mariinskom: K 111-letyu so dnya rozhdeniya kompozitora." https://www.mariinsky.ru/about/exhibitions/shostakovich111/leningradskaya/.
Martin, John. "Ballet: Kirov's 'Gala Program No. 2.'" *The New York Times*, September 28, 1961.
Martin, John. "Massine Ballet Seen in Revival." *The New York Times*, September 29, 1948.
Martin, John. "Massine Presents Symphonic Ballet." *The New York Times*, October 29, 1939.
Massine, Leonid. *My Life in Ballet*. London: Macmillan, 1968.
Meisner, Nadine. *Marius Petipa: The Emperor's Ballet Master*. New York: Oxford University Press, 2019.
Meleikina, Kristina. "Neizvestnyi Igor' Moiseyev: balet 'Futbolist.'" *Balet*, no. 5 (2016): 33–35.
Messerer, Asaf. *Tanets, mysl', vremya*. Moscow: Iskusstvo, 1990.
Michaut, Pierre. *Le ballet contemporain, 1929–1950*. Paris: Libraire Plon, 1952.
Morrison, Simon. *Bolshoi Confidential: Secrets of the Russian Ballet from the Rule of the Tsars to Today*. New York: Liveright, 2016.
Morrison, Simon. *The People's Artist: Prokofiev's Soviet Years*. Oxford: Oxford University Press, 2009.
Morrison, Simon. "Shostakovich as Industrial Saboteur: Observations on *The Bolt*." In *Shostakovich and His World*, edited by Laurel E. Fay, 117–61. Princeton, NJ: Princeton University Press, 2004.
Moshevich, Sofia. *Dmitri Shostakovich, Pianist*. Montreal: McGill-Queen's University Press, 2004.
"Mukykanty i vreditel'stvo," *Proletarskii muzykant* 8, no. 16 (1930): 1.
Nelson, Amy. *Music for the Revolution: Musicians and Power in Early Soviet Russia*. University Park: Pennsylvania State University Press, 2004.
Nelson, Amy. "The Struggle for Proletarian Music: RAPM and the Cultural Revolution." *Slavic Review* 59, no. 1 (Spring 2000): 101–32.
Nepomnashchy, Catharine Theimer. "Dance as Metaphor: The Russian Ballerina and the Imperial Imagination." In *Mapping the Feminine: Russian Women and Cultural Difference*, edited by Hilde Hoogenboom, Catharine Theimer Nepomnyashchy, and Irina Reyfman, 185–208. Bloomington, IN: Slavica, 2008.
O'Mahony, Mike. *Sport in the USSR: Physical Culture—Visual Culture*. London: Reaktion Books, 2006.

Paléologue, Maurice. *An Ambassador's Memoirs*. Vol. 2. Translated by F. A. Holt. London: Hutchinson, 1924.
Parkinson, Roger. *Dreadnought: The Ship that Changed the World*. London: Tauris, 2015.
Percival, John. "Athletes or artists?" *Dance and Dancers* (October 1986): 10–16.
Piotrovskii, A[drian], and M[ikhail] Sokolovskii, eds. *Teatr rabochei molodezhi: Sbornik p'yes dlya komsomol'skogo teatra*. Moscow: Gosudarstvennoye izdatel'stvo, 1928.
Pleshcheyev, Aleksandr (A. P.). "O balete, ego demokratizatsii, fokinizatsii i pr.," *Vecherniye ogni*, no. 8 (March 29, 1918): 4.
Polyanovskii, Georgii. "Novii balet D.D. Shostakovicha." *Pravda*, June 6, 1935.
Potapov, Vladimir. "Yeshchyo o *Svetlom ruch'ye* v Bol'shom teatre." *Vechernaya Moskva*, December 5, 1935.
Potapov, Vladimir. "Vozvrashcheniye k tantsu: *Svetlyi ruchei* v Bol'shom teatre." *Vechernaya Moskva*, December 2, 1935.
Pravda. "Baletnaya fal'sh': Balet 'Svetlyi ruchei.'" February 6, 1936. Also in *Sovetskaya muzyka* 2 (1936): 6–8.
Pravda. "Sumbur vmesto muzyki: ob opere 'Ledi Makbet Mtsenskogo uyezda' D. Shostakovicha." January 28, 1936.
Pravda. "Svetlyi ruchei." September 7, 1935.
Press, Stephen D. *Prokofiev's Ballets for Diaghilev*. Aldershot, UK: Ashgate, 2006.
"Program Listed by Kirov Ballet: Leningrad Troupe Names Repertory for the Met." *The New York Times*, July 26, 1961.
"Programmes de la journée," *Le Grand écho du Nord de la France*, January 27, 1938.
Prokopenko, V. "Za obnavleniye baleta." *Rabis*, no. 42 (16 October 1928): 11.
"Radio-Concerts: Qu'écouter aujourd'hui?" *L'Humanité: journal socialiste quotidien* (September 12, 1935): 4.
Robinson, Harlow. "Bolshoi Gold: Revised Shostakovich Ballet Comes to L.A." *The Los Angeles Times*, August 2, 1987.
Robinson, Harlow. "A Shostakovich Ballet Returns from Limbo." *The New York Times*, January 30, 1983.
Ross, Janice. *Like a Bomb Going Off: Leonid Yakobson and Ballet as Resistance in Soviet Russia*. New Haven, CT: Yale University Press, 2015.
Rouge et noir. "Ballets de Monte-Carlo" [souvenir program]. Paris: Nicolas-Éditions Artistiques, [1939].
Rouge et noir. Choreography by Leonid Massine. Performed by Ballet Russe de Monte Carlo. 1948. Victor Jessen Video Archive, Jerome Robbins Dance Division, New York Public Library.
Rubin, Vl[adimir]. "Vybory v strane sporta." *Smena*, no. 13 (July 1929): 11.
Russell, Robert, and Andrew Barratt, eds. *Russian Theatre in the Age of Modernism*. Basingstoke, UK: Macmillan, 1990.
Sapozhnikov, Sergei. *Moi Shostakovich*. Moscow: Artisticheskoye ob-vo "Assamblei iskusstv," 2006.
Savenko, Svetlana. "Stravinsky: The View from Russia." Translated by Philipp Penka. In *Stravinsky and His World*, edited by Tamara Levitz, 255–72. Princeton, NJ: Princeton University Press, 2013.
Sayers, Lesley-Anne. "Rediscovering Diaghilev's 'Pas d'Acier.'" *Dance Research* 18, no. 2 (Winter 2000): 163–85.
Sayers, Lesley-Anne, and Simon Morrison. "Prokofiev's *Le Pas d'Acier*: How the Steel Was Tempered." In *Soviet Music and Society under Lenin and Stalin: The Baton and Sickle*, edited by Neil Edmunds, 81–104. New York: Routledge, 2009.
Scheijen, Sjeng. *Diaghilev: A Life*. Oxford: Oxford University Press, 2010.
Scherr, Apollinaire. "Ratmansky: From Petipa to Now." In *The Oxford Handbook of Contemporary Ballet*, edited by Kathrina Farrugia-Kriel and Jill Nunes Jensen, 651–68. New York: Oxford University Press, 2021.

Scholl, Tim. *From Petipa to Balanchine: Classical Revival and the Modernization of Ballet*. New York: Routledge, 1994.
Scholl, Tim. *"Sleeping Beauty": A Legend in Progress*. New Haven, CT: Yale University Press, 2004.
Searcy, Anne. "Alexei Ratmansky's Abstract-Narrative Ballet." In *The Oxford Handbook of Contemporary Ballet*, edited by Kathrina Farrugia-Kriel and Jill Nunes Jensen, 490–502. New York: Oxford University Press, 2021.
Searcy, Anne. *Ballet in the Cold War: A Soviet-American Exchange*. New York: Oxford University Press, 2020.
Serdyuk, Natalya. "Balet Mikhailovskogo teatra – MALEGOTa." PhD dissertation (submitted), Institute of Art History of the Russian Academy of Sciences (St. Petersburg). Personal copy shared by the author.
Sheremet'yevskaya, Natalya. *Dlinnyye teni: o vremeni, o tantse, o sebye*. Moscow: Balet, 2007.
Sheremet'yevskaya, Natalya. *Tanets na estrade*. Moscow: Iskusstvo, 1985.
Shostakovich, Dmitrii. "Balet i muzyka." *Vechernyaya Moskva*, April 5, 1935.
Shostakovich, Dmitrii. "Deklaratsiya obyazannostei kompozitora." *Rabochii i teatr*, no. 31 (November 20, 1931): 6.
Shostakovich, Dmitrii. *New Collected Works*. Edited by Manashir Yakubov. Vols. 60–65. Moscow: DSCH, 2006–18.
Shostakovich, Dmitrii. *Pis'ma I.I. Sollertinskomu*. St. Petersburg: Kompozitor, 2006.
Siegel, Marcia B., and Millicent Hodson. "Restaging Works from the Ballets Russes: A Conversation Between." *Experiment: A Journal of Russian Culture* 17, no. 1 (January 2011): 345–74.
Sirotkina, Irina. *Chestoye chuvstvo avangarda: Tanets, dvizheniye, kinesteziya, v zhizni poetov i khudozhnikov*. St. Peterburg: Evropeiskii universitet v Sankt-Peterburge, 2014.
Sirotkina, Irina. "Dance-*Plyaska* in Russia of the Silver Age." *Dance Research* 28, no. 2 (October 25, 2010): 135–52.
Sitsky, Larry. *Music of the Repressed Russian Avant-Garde: 1900–1929*. Westport, CT: Greenwood, 1994.
Slonimskii, Yuri. *Chudesnoye bylo ryadom s nami: zametki o petrogradskom balete 20-x godov*. Leningrad: Sov. kompozitor, 1984.
Slonimskii, Yuri. *Sovetskii balet: Materialy k istorii sovetskogo baletnogo teatra*. Moscow: Iskusstvo, 1950.
Smith, Marian. *Ballet and Opera in the Age of Giselle*. Princeton, NJ: Princeton University Press, 2000.
Smith, Marian. "Borrowings and Original Music: A Dilemma for the Ballet-Pantomime Composer." *Dance Research: The Journal of the Society for Dance Research* 6, no. 2 (Autumn 1988): 3–29.
Smith, Marian. "*La sylphide* and *Les sylphides*." In *Music, Theater, and Cultural Transfer: Paris, 1830–1914*, edited by Annegret Fauser and Mark Everist, 256–75. Chicago: University of Chicago Press, 2009.
Sollertinskii, I. I. *Istoriya sovetskogo teatra*. Vol. 1. Leningrad: Khudozhestvennaya literatura, 1933.
Sollertinskii, I. I. "Kakoi zhe balet nam v sushchnosti nuzhen?" *Zhizn' iskusstva*, no. 40 (1929): 5.
Sollertinskii, I. I. "Novyi balet *Dinamiada*." *Zhizn' iskusstva*, no. 38 (1929): 14.
Sollertinskii, I. I. *Stat'i o balete*. Edited by M. S. Druskin. Leningrad: Muzyka, 1973.
Sollertinskii, I. I. "*Svetlyi ruchei*: Baletnaya prem'yera v Bol'shom teatre." *Sovetskoye iskusstvo*, December 5, 1935.
Sollertinskii, I. I. "*Svetlyi ruchei* v Gos. Malom opernom teatre." *Rabochiy i teatr*, no. 12 (1935): 14.
Sollertinskii, I. I. "Tvorcheskiye profili muzykal'nykh teatrov Leningrada." *Sovetskaya muzyka* 28, no. 11 (1935): 78–87.

Sollertinskii, I. I., et al. "Za novyi khoreograficheskii teatr," *Zhizn' iskusstva*, no. 25 (1928): 3–6.
Sotheby's (London). "Autograph Manuscripts and Letters of Dmitri Shostakovich (1906–1975)." In *Fine Printed and Manuscript Music including the Mannheim Collection*, 146–56. Published in conjunction with an auction at Sotheby's (London) on December 6, 1991. Sale catalogue.
Souritz, Elizabeth. "Constructivism in Dance." In *Theatre in Revolution: Russian Avant-Garde Stage Design*, edited by Nancy Van Norman Baer and John E. Bowlt, 129–43. New York: Thames & Hudson, 1991.
Souritz, Elizabeth. *Soviet Choreographers in the 1920s*. Translated by Lynn Visson. Edited, with additional translation, by Sally Banes. Durham, NC: Duke University Press, 1990.
Spence, Daniel Owen. *A History of the Royal Navy: Empire and Imperialism*. London: Tauris, 2015.
Spurling, Hilary. *Matisse the Master: A Life of Henri Matisse, the Conquest of Colour, 1909–1954*. New York: Knopf, 2005.
Starr, S. Frederick. *Red and Hot: The Fate of Jazz in the Soviet Union*. Rev. ed. New York: Limelight, 1994; 1st ed. Oxford University Press, 1983.
Steichen, James. *Balanchine and Kirstein's American Enterprise*. New York: Oxford University Press, 2018.
Stepanov, Ivan. *Zhan-Pol' Marat i ego bor'ba s kontr-revolyutsiei 1743–1793 g*. Moscow: Krasnaya nov', 1924.
Stern, Elizabeth. "Politics in Pointe Shoes: The Genesis and Afterlives of Stalinist *drambalet*." PhD dissertation, Princeton University, 2019. Personal copy provided by the author.
Stites, Richard. *Russian Popular Culture: Entertainment and Society since 1900*. Cambridge: Cambridge University Press, 1992.
Sulcas, Roslyn. "In Nod to History, Two Ballet Rivals Spring to Life." *The New York Times*, January 6, 2014.
Svetlyi ruchei: Komediinyi balet v 3 deistviyakh i 4 kartinakh. Libretto by F. Lopukhov and A. Piotrovskii, with articles by F. Lopukhov and A. Piotrovskii, D. Shostakovich, Yu. Slonimskii, and M. Druskin. Leningrad: Gos. Akademicheskii Malyi Opernyi teatr [Ivan Fedorov], 1935.
Svetlyi ruchei: balet v trekh deistviyakh i chetyrekh kartinakh. Le ruisseau limpide: ballet en trois actes et quatre tableaux. Libretto. Moscow: Izdaniye Gos. akademicheskogo Bol'shogo teatra Soyuza SSR, 1935.
"Svetlyi ruchei." *Vechernaya Moskva*, September 15, 1935.
"Svetlyi ruchei v Bol'shom teatre." *Vechernaya Moskva*, December 1, 1935.
Swift, Mary Grace. *The Art of Dance in the U.S.S.R*. Notre Dame, IN: University of Notre Dame Press, 1968.
Symons, James M. *Meyerhold's Theatre of the Grotesque: The Post-Revolutionary Productions, 1920–1932*. Coral Gables: University of Miami Press, 1971.
Talnikov, D. "Opyt sovetskogo baleta: *Svetlyi ruchei* v GABT." *Literaturnaya gazeta*, January 10, 1936.
Taruskin, Richard. *Defining Russia Musically: Historical and Hermeneutical Essays*. Princeton, NJ: Princeton University Press, 1997.
Taruskin, Richard. *Russian Music at Home and Abroad: New Essays*. Oakland: University of California Press, 2016.
Teatralnaya dekada. "Balet *Svetlyi ruchei* v Bolshom teatre SSSR." November 11–20, 1935.
Titus, Joan. *The Early Film Music of Dmitri Shostakovich*. New York: Oxford University Press, 2016.
Titus, Joan M. "Modernism, Socialist Realism, and Identity in the Early Film Music of Dmitry Shostakovich, 1929–1932." PhD dissertation, Ohio State University, 2006.
Thompson, Howard. "Screen: Soviet Heroism; 'Leningrad Symphony' Keynotes Restraint." *The New York Times*, June 23, 1958.
Tyerman, Edward. "Resignifying *The Red Poppy*: Internationalism and Symbolic Power in the

Sino-Soviet Encounter." *Slavic and East European Journal* 61, no. 3 (2017): 445–66.

"Usloviya konkursa libretto sovetskogo baleta," *Zhizn' iskusstva*, no. 2 (January 6, 1929): 2. Also printed in *Rabochii i teatr*, no. 2 (January 6, 1929): 17.

"The USSR and Disarmament." U.S. Department of State. Division of International Security Affairs. Regulation of Armaments Branch. August 1946. https://www.cia.gov/readingroom/docs/CIA-RDP80B01676R000600010011-5.pdf.

"V leningradskom Malom opernom teatre." *Vechernaya Moskva*, May 5, 1935.

Van Vechten, Carl. "Alicia Markova in 'Rouge et noir.'" Carl Van Vechten Slides, Jerome Robbins Dance Division, New York Public Library, 1948. https://digitalcollections.nypl.org/search/index?utf8=%E2%9C%93&keywords=rouge+et+noir#.

Vestnik Akademii Russkogo baleta im. A.Y. Vaganovoi, no. 7 (1999): 64–69.

Vlasova, Ekaterina. "Stalin smotrit 'Svetlyi ruchei.'" In *Naslediye: Russkaya muzyka-mirovaya kul'tura*, vol. 1, edited by Ekaterina Vlasova and Elena Sorokina, 155–66. Moscow: Moskovskaya gosudarstvennaya konservatoriya imeni P.I. Chaikovskogo, 2009.

Vol'fson, S. M., ed. *Leonid Yakobson. Tvorcheskii put' baletmeistera, ego balety, miniatyury, ispolniteli*. Leningrad: Iskusstvo, 1965.

Wells, Elizabeth. "'The New Woman': *Lady Macbeth* and Sexual Politics in the Stalinist Era." *Cambridge Opera Journal* 13, no. 2 (July 2001): 163–89.

Wiley, Roland John. *The Life and Ballets of Lev Ivanov: Choreographer of* The Nutcracker *and* Swan Lake. Oxford: Clarendon Press, 1997.

Wiley, Roland John. *Tchaikovsky's Ballets*. Oxford: Clarendon Press, 1985.

Wilson, Elizabeth. *Shostakovich: A Life Remembered*. Princeton, NJ: Princeton University Press, 1994.

Yakubov, Manashir. "*The Golden Age*: The True Story of the Premiere." In *Shostakovich Studies*, edited by David Fanning, 189–204. Cambridge: Cambridge University Press, 1995.

Yankovskii, M[oisei]. "Bolt." *Rabochii i teatr*, no. 11 (April 21, 1931): 11.

Yermolayev, Alexey. "*Svetlyi ruchei* v Bol'shom teatre." *Rabochaya Moskva*, October 14, 1935.

Yezhegodnik imperatorskikh teatrov, Sezon 1901–1902. St. Petersburg: Direktsii imperatorskikh teatrov, 1901.

Zakharov, Rostislav. "Pobyeda sovetskogo baleta." *Vechernaya krasnaya gazeta*, June 8, 1935.

Zeller, Jessica. *Shapes of American Ballet: Teachers and Training before Balanchine*. New York: Oxford University Press, 2016.

Zemlemerov, V. "Na muzyku Leningradskoi simfonii." *Sovetskaya kultura*, March 18, 1961.

Zolotoi vek. Balet v 3 deistviyakh. Libretto by A. V. Ivanovskii, with articles and explanatory text by Khud.-Polit. Sovet Baleta GATOBa, D. Shostakovich, A. Gauk, E. Kaplan, V. Vainonen, L. Yakobson, V. Chesnakov, V. Khodasevich, and N. Malkov. Leningrad: Gosudarstvennoye izdatel'stvo khudozhestvennoi literatury, 1931.

Index

For the benefit of digital users, indexed terms that span two pages (e.g., 52–53) may, on occasion, appear on only one of those pages.

amateur theatre
    aesthetics and audiences, 71–73
    in *The Bolt*, 65–66, 68, 70, 72–74, 77–78, 80, 84–85
    See also poster art; TRAM
Artistic Council. *See* Leningrad State Academic Theatre: Artistic Council
Artistic-Political Council for Ballet. *See* Leningrad State Academic Theatre: Artistic Council
Asafyev, Boris, 6–7, 24, 34

Balanchine, George, 13–14, 54–55, 119, 133, 137
Balanchivadze, Georgii. *See* Balanchine, George
ballet music (generally)
    in Soviet ballet and ballet criticism, 4, 6–8, 33–34
    "specialist" vs. "modernist" traditions, 6, 7–8, 33–34
    See also Shostakovich, Dmitri: ballet music
"ballet symphony," 133–34, 137–38
Ballets Russes, 2–3, 8, 114, 132, 133, 134
Belsky, Igor, 14–15, 129, 133–34, 135–38, 146–47
Blue Blouse, 65
Bobyshev, Mikhail, 99, 108–9, Plates 7–11
Bolshoi Theatre
    archival collections, 11
    and Grigorovich (*The Golden Age*), 9, 129, 138–40
    history of, 9–10
    and *The Limpid Stream*, 1, 99–100, 105, 106–7, 109, 124, 125, 132–33, 170n.13, 171n.27
    and Lopukhov, 1, 99–100, 127–28
    and Ratmansky (*The Bolt* and *The Bright Stream*), 9, 142–43
    repertoire and state of, 3–4, 25–27, 40–41, 53, 68–70
The Bolt (Ratmansky). *See The Bolt*: and Ratmansky

The Bolt (Shostakovich/Lopukhov)
    by act, 74–85
    archival collections, 11–12
    balletic models, 3–4, 5–6, 14, 32–33, 63
    creative context and commission, 1–2, 19–20, 62, 64–68
    and industry, 68–70
    music of, 34, 74–77, 78–79, 82–83 (*see also* Shostakovich: ballet music)
    and popular art, 70–74
    premiere and reception, 17–18, 64–65, 117, 119
    and Ratmansky, 9, 129, 142–43, 145–46
    and satire, 9–10, 19–20
    See also Lopukhov: and *The Bolt*
The Bright Stream (Ratmansky). *See The Limpid Stream: The Bright Stream* (Ratmansky)
Bruni, Tatiana, 64, 68–70, 77–78, 84

Chesnakov, Vladimir, 36, 37
classical ballet
    and *The Bolt*, 65, 73–74
    and *The Golden Age*, 38, 43–51, 57, 59–61
    and socialist realism, 118
    Soviet critiques of, 29, 37, 39
    and Soviet repertoire, 22, 25–27, 31–32
Crazy Sashka, 72–73
Cultural Revolution, 37–38, 67–68, 71, 100–1

dance symphonism, 6–7, 33–34, 134, 136–37
Dance Symphony: Magnificence of the Universe (Lopukhov), 6–7, 27–28, 33–34, 134, 137
Delibes, Léo, 6, 8, 112, 113, 120, 121–22
Deshevov, Vladimir, 68–69
Diaghilev, Sergei, 2–3, 6, 73–74, 114, 133, 146–47
"Dinamiada," 30, 39–40, 41, 53
Dmitriev, Vladimir, 105, 109, Plates 12–15
dramaticheskii balet. *See* drambalet

190 INDEX

drambalet
   dramaticheskii balet balet, 29
   genre of, 9–10, 15, 29, 100–1, 116–17, 134, 136–37
   khoreograficheskii balet, 29
   The Limpid Stream (Romantic comedy) versus, 100, 118–19, 123–24, 126, 127

Factory Storm, 72–73
fizkultura, 3–4, 30, 46, 52–54, 140–41
Fokine, Mikhail, 6, 25–26, 27, 31–32, 33–34, 113–14, 117, 137
Foregger, Nikolai, 3–4, 26, 33–34, 68
The Four Moscows (projected), 68–69
Futbolist (Moiseyev/Tasfasman), 53–54

Glazunov, Aleksandr, 6, 18, 38, 99
The Golden Age (Shostakovich/Yakobson/ Vainonen/Chesnakov)
   by act, 43–61
   archival collections, 11–12
   balletic models, 4–6, 14, 32–33
   and ballroom dance, 26, 38, 45–46, 57–61, 79
   and choreographers, 4, 36, 40–42 (*see also* Yakobson)
   and classical ballet, 47–51
   commission of, 4, 20–21, 24, 30, 35
   creative context and topics, 1–2, 4–6, 16–22, 33, 35, 36–38, 62–63
   and Grigorovich (*see* Grigorovich)
   music of, 7–8, 34–35, 45–46, 48–51, 55–56, 58–61
   production of 1930, 9–10, 38–43
   and sports, 30, 32–33, 38, 43–44, 45–46, 51–57 (*see also fizkultura*)
   See also "Dinamiada"; Khodasevich; Leningrad State Academic Theatre: libretto competition of 1929
Goleizovsky, Kasyan, 3–5, 26, 29–30, 33–34, 40, 41, 52
Grigorovich, Yuri, 9, 14–15, 129–30, 138–39, 140–43, 145, 146–47
Gvozdev, Alexei, 24

High Stalinism, 100–1

The Ice Maiden (Lopukhov), 27–28, 52, 110–11, 117, 118–19
Imperial
   Imperial period, 2–3, 22–23, 26–27, 38
   Imperial Theatre (or ballet), 6, 22, 25–26, 42, 112, 113–15, 132, 171n.29
Iron Foundry (*Zavod*) (Mosolov), 68–69
Ivanovsky, Aleksandr, 30, 39–40

Joseph the Beautiful (Goleizovsky), 26, 33–34, 40

Khodasevich, Valentina, 36, 44–45, 56–57, Plates 1–4
khoreograficheskii balet. *See drambalet*
Kirov Theatre (and ballet), 22, 54–55, 133–34, 137, 138
Korshikov, Georgy, 64

Lady Macbeth of Mtsensk District (Shostakovich)
   denunciation of, 1–2, 8–9, 99–100, 126, 127–28, 146
   revival of, 8–9
   in Shostakovich's early career, 8–9, 10, 21, 35, 78–79, 85–86
   success of, 85–86, 99–100, 120–21, 127, 132–33
Leningrad State Academic Theatre
   Artistic Council, 4–5, 13–14, 24, 32, 36, 41–42, 117 (*see also* Shostakovich: and Artistic Council; Sollertinsky: and Artistic Council)
   and *The Bolt*, 62, 64, 85–86
   and *The Golden Age*, 36, 37–43, 62
   as institution, 22–24, 27–28, 119–20
   libretto competition of 1929, 24, 30, 39, 69
   and Lopukhov, 22, 27–28, 85–86, 115, 119–20, 127 (*see also* Lopukhov)
   repertoire (ballet), 27, 68–70, 116–18, 119, 120, 123–24, 127
   repertoire crisis, 29–30, 33
   and Shostakovich's ballets, 20–21, 115, 120–21, 125, 127 (*see also* Leningrad State Academic Theatre: and *The Bolt*; Leningrad State Academic Theatre: and *The Golden Age*)
   and Sollertinsky (*see* Sollertinsky)
Leningrad Symphony (Belsky), 129, 133–38
The Limpid Stream (Shostakovich/Lopukhov)
   by act, 101–15
   archival collections, 11–12, 13
   balletic models, 4–6, 14, 32–33, 63
   at the Bolshoi Theatre. *See* Bolshoi Theatre
   The Bright Stream (Ratmansky,) 9, 129, 142–46, 147–48
   collaboration between Shostakovich and Lopukhov, 7–8, 115, 120–21, 126–28
   creative context and topics, 1–2, 4–6, 9–10, 99–101, 115–20, 123–24, 126–28
   denunciation of, 8–9, 99–100, 125–26, 133–34, 145–46
   and Lopukhov. *See* Lopukhov: and *The Limpid Stream*

at the Maly Theatre. *See* Maly Opera Theatre
music of, 7–8, 34–35, 104–5, 109–11, 113–15, 121–23 (*see also* Shostakovich: ballet music)
recycled music, 78–79, 85–86, 104–5, 122
and Romantic ballet
as model, 5–6, 14, 63, 100, 101–3, 121–22, 126–28
musical borrowing, 112–15
national components, 103–7
Romantic forest, 79, 107–11
See also Bobyshev; Dmitriev
Living Newspaper, 65
Lopukhov, Fyodor
and Belsky, 129, 133–34, 136–37, 146–47
and *The Bolt*
choreographer of, 3–4, 11–12, 62, 64, 69–70, 75, 84–85
debacle of, 64, 85–86, 114–15
choreography, 110–11, 146–47
approaches to, 26, 27–28, 29–30, 31, 52, 53–54
Shostakovich's encounters with, 4–5, 31–32
Dance Symphony, 6–7, 27–28, 33–34
and *The Golden Age*, 41
and Leningrad State Academic Theatre, 22–23, 24, 69 (Artistic Council), 117–18
and *The Limpid Stream*, 1, 11–12, 34–35, 118–19
choreographer, 1, 99, 114–15
and classical dance, 123–24
libretto, 99
in Lopukhov's (and Shostakovich's) careers, 99–100, 101, 114–15, 126–28
as Romantic ballet, 108, 110–11, 118–19, 126–27 (*see also The Limpid Stream*: and Romantic ballet)
and Maly Opera Theatre, 115, 119–20, 127
and *The Nutcracker*, 26, 27–28
and Shostakovich, 1–2, 13–14, 63, 147–48 (*see also* Shostakovich: collaborations with Lopukhov)
See also individual entries for Lopukhov's ballets
Lunacharsky, Anatoly, 2–3
Lyubinsky, Zakhar, 23, 40, 41–42

Maly Opera Theatre (Maly Theatre)
archives of, 11
ballets and repertoire (1920s–1030s), 27, 40, 115, 119–21
ballets to Shostakovich's music (1960s to present), 137–38, 142–43

and *The Bright Stream*, 142–43, 174n.57
and *The Limpid Stream*, 99, 105, 108–9, 113
and Lopukhov, 27–28, 115, 119–21, 127–28
and Shostakovich, 20–21, 85–86, 99, 125
Mariinsky Theatre (and Library), 3–4, 11, 18, 22, 25–26, 42, 136, 138 (*see also* Kirov Theatre; Leningrad State Academic Theatre)
Massine, Léonide, 14–15, 68, 73–74, 129, 137, 146–47
Meyerhold, Vsevolod
methods and works of, 3–4, 52, 57–58, 71
and Shostakovich, 4–5, 19–22, 71, 164n.11
Mikhailovsky Theatre, 11, 142–43, 174n.57, Plates 5–11. *See also* Maly Opera Theatre
mir iskusstniki, 6
Mosolov, Aleksandr, 68–69

NEP, 37–38, 67, 72, 139, 140–41
New Economic Policy. *See* NEP

Pas d'Acier (Prokofiev/Massine), 27, 68, 69–70
Petipa, Marius
apotheosis, 83–84
legacy in *The Golden Age*, 5–6, 14, 46, 47, 48, 50–51
and Massine, 132
nineteenth-century repertoire of, 22, 117, 125
Shostakovich's admiration for, 4–5, 31–32
in Soviet ballet repertoire, 22, 25–28, 108, 117–18
See also The Golden Age: and Petipa; *The Sleeping Beauty*
Petrov, Pavel, 4–5, 27, 31–32
Ponna, Mariya, 4–5, 13–14, 28, 30–31
poster art, 65, 73–74, 75, 77–78
Pravda, 1–2, 99–100, 106–7, 122, 125–26, 127–28
Prokofiev, Sergei, 6, 24, 27, 68, 132–33, 134, 146

Ratmansky, Alexei, 9, 14–15, 129–30, 142–48
The Red Poppy (music by Glière), 26–27, 29–30, 40–41, 117
The Red Whirlwind (Lopukhov), 27–28, 29–30, 31–32, 52
Romantic ballet
French Romantic ballet, 83–84, 106–7
Goleizovsky's satire of, 26
in Soviet repertoire, 116–19, 120
See also The Limpid Stream: and Romantic ballet
Rouge et Noir (L'Etrange farandole) (Massine), 129, 130–33

INDEX

Shostakovich, Dmitri
- and archival collections, 11–13
- and Artistic Council, 4–5, 13–14, 24, 32, 36, 41–42 (*see also* Leningrad State Academic Theatre: Artistic Council)
- attitudes toward ballet, 4–6, 13–14, 15, 16, 30–35
- ballet music (of Shostakovich)
  - approaches and conventions, 6–8, 33–35
  - *divertissement*, 46, 57–61, 65, 75–85, 103–5
  - reception of
    - in critical discourse, 8–10
    - by choreographers, 14–15, 129–30, 132–33, 135–36, 137–38, 139–42, 145–48 (*see also* individual entries for *The Bolt*, *The Golden Age* and *The Limpid Stream*: music of)
- ballets (as works)
  - context and significance of, 1–2, 5–8, 13–15, 30–35, 146–48
  - scholarly discourse on, 8–10
  - Shostakovich's attitudes to
    - *The Bolt*, 62, 64–65
    - *The Golden Age*, 45–46, 51, 56–57
    - his own ballets, 8–9, 138
    - *The Limpid Stream*, 120–22, 123–24
  - unrealized projects, 4–5, 16, 33–34, 40, 125, 127–28 (*see also* ballet music (of Shostakovich))
- *The Bedbug*, 4–5, 16–17, 19–20, 42, 57–58
- collaborations with Lopukhov, 7–8, 34–35, 62, 63, 64, 99, 101, 115, 120–21, 122, 126–28
- early career, 16–22
- *First Symphony*, 18–19, 35, 36, 129, 130, 132–33, 145–46
- *The Little Mermaid*, 4–5, 16
- *The Shot*, 71
- and Sollertinsky, 13–14, 32, 64–65, 124, 125 (*See also* Sollertinsky)
- *Symphony No. 7* ("Leningrad"), 133–35 (*see also Leningrad Symphony* (Belsky))
- *Symphony No. 11*, 137–38, 174n.43
- *Three Fantastic Dances*, 4–5, 30–31
- *The Young Lady and the Hooligan*, 79, 137–38
- **The Sleeping Beauty** (Tchaikovsky/Petipa)
  - and allusion to the "Rose Adagio," 49–50 (*see also The Golden Age*)
  - in ballet criticism, 6–7
  - conventions of, 59–60, 83–84, 110–11, 117
  - Lopukhov's revival of, 27–28
  - Shostakovich's appreciation of, 31–32
  - *See also* Tchaikovsky, Pyotor

Slonimsky, Yuri, 12, 16, 124, 127–28
Smirnov, Viktor, 64–65
socialist realism, 15, 100–1, 105–6, 115–16, 118
Sollertinsky, Ivan
- and Artistic Council, 13–14, 24, 32
- and Choreographic Institute, 32
- critiques of Shostakovich's ballets, 7–8, 11–12, 34, 49–50, 99, 122–23, 124–25, 139–40
- friendship with Shostakovich, 13–14, 32, 64–65, 125
- libretto competition of 1929, 30, 39
- writings on ballet, 6–7, 29–30, 32, 34, 37, 116

Stalin, Joseph, 1, 99–100, 125–26
State Academic Theatre. *See* Leningrad State Academic Theatre
Steel (Mosolov). *See* Mosolov
Stravinsky, Igor
- in ballet criticism, 6, 34, 133, 134
- performances of his music, 19, 27–28
- Shostakovich compared to, 7–8, 49–50, 139–40, 146
- *See also* ballet music: "specialist" vs. "modernist" traditions

Swan Lake (Vaganova), 117–19
Sylvia (Delibes), 112–15, 121–22
symphonic ballet, 6–7, 130, 133–34, 137
symphonism, 6–7, 34, 163n.7

Tchaikovsky, Pyotor
- in ballet criticism, 6, 34
- and Shostakovich
  - allusions in Shostakovich's ballet music, 8, 38, 45–46, 49–51, 62
  - Shostakovich compared with, 7–8, 139–40, 146
  - Shostakovich's admiration for, 4–5, 31–32
- *See also The Sleeping Beauty*

Theatre of Working Class Youth. *See* TRAM
TRAM, 19–20, 65, 72, 84–85

Vaganova, Agrippina, 24, 85–86, 117–19
Vainonen, Vasily, 36, 41, 42

Whirlwind, The (Goleizovsky), 26, 29–30, 33–34, 52

Yakobson, Leonid, 36, 41, 54–55, 56–57, 134, 137–38

Zavod (libretto competition), 69
Zavod (from *Steel*). *See Iron Foundry*

www.ingramcontent.com/pod-product-compliance
Lightning Source LLC
Chambersburg PA
CBHW020257240725
30029CB00010B/15